"Have I Got a Tip For You..."

And Other Tales Of Dirty Secrets, Political Payoffs And Corporate Scams

---

A Guide to Investigative Reporting

By
STANLEY PENN

Published by Dow Jones & Company, Inc.
World Financial Center
200 Liberty Street
New York, N.Y. 10281

ISBN 1-881944-01-8

Library of Congress Catalog Card No. 93-074914

Printed in the United States of America

CONTENTS

ACKNOWLEDGMENTS

My thanks to:

Paul Steiger and Barney Calame for thinking that some of my experiences might be interesting and even instructive to new members of The Wall Street Journal staff, and for asking me to write this book

Richard Martin for editing the manuscript

Greg Leeds and Randy Price for designing the cover and setting the type

Jim Pensiero and Barbara Haislip for careful scrutiny and expert copy editing

Bruce Levy and Dee Motic for researching and resurrecting even the most elusive of my old stories.

FOREWORD

STANLEY PENN was born in New York, went to public schools there and attended Brooklyn College for two years before graduating from the University of Missouri with a degree in journalism in 1949. Stan and his wife, Esther, still live in New York, as do their son, Michael, a psychotherapist and clinical social worker, and daughter, Laurel, a personal trainer.

Stan worked briefly for the City News Bureau in Chicago before he joined the Journal's Chicago bureau as a reporter March 31, 1952. It was a time when bylines rarely appeared anywhere in the Journal except on page one and the editorial page. Even on page one, bylined stories frequently were crowded out by a popular new type of feature story, The Wall Street Journal News Roundup. Stan's first leder ran May 29. His second appeared June 30. In July he was promoted and transferred to the Detroit bureau.

That first page one piece was headlined "Sweat Savers: Power Garden Tools Carve Out a Widening Place in Public Favor; Yearly Business Vaults from $8 Million to $120 Million In Decade, Is Still Rising; Lawn Mowing Time Is Halved." The second was "Candy Comeback: Supermarket Success Of Packaged Product Outweighs Bar's Decline; Transparent Bags and the Windows-Front Box Aid a 22% Sales Rise; Bars, Meanwhile, Drop 6%."

Yes, it was a different era and the Journal then was different too. But in some ways, not so much. Stan covered cars and labor in Detroit. He was brought to New York in 1957 and given a beat that was huge by today's standards. It encompassed most of the entertainment industry, movies, music and theater; the electronics and electrical equipment manufacturers; office equipment makers and real estate. Some of the hottest companies in business journalism then were on Stan's beat, including IBM, Xerox, General Electric and ITT. Gradually, he widened his beat to include gambling, tax-dodging, scams of all kinds, and the mob.

In the news-room Stan was recognized as a tireless reporter; his desk usually was heaped with court documents, SEC reports and company prospectuses. Outside, among promoters, corporate gatekeepers and lax regulators he was a scourge. By 1965, Stan had become one of the Journal's, and journalism's, top investigative reporters. But he never became a prima donna. Stan recognized the advantages of combining his own investigative skills with the sourcing and depth of knowledge of beat reporters; many of his best page-one stories were joint efforts, often ones he had invited other reporters to join him in digging out.

Stan won the Pulitzer Prize for national reporting in 1967 with a Journal reporter in Washington, Monroe "Bud" Karmin, for exposing U.S. organized crime links to gambling in the Bahamas. Their stories brought down the government of the Bahamas; Stan tells about it in Chapter 3.

Stan also won a Loeb Award in 1967, also shared with other Journal reporters, but this was for a different story, part of a page-one series on competition among big companies. Stan's piece told how the "other" computer makers were trying to fight back against IBM's dominance; you can read it on page 114.

Stan retired from the Journal at the end of 1990 and then wrote this book. It isn't what I was expecting when we asked him to put together a guidebook on investigative reporting for the staff; this is much better. And it typifies Stan's whole approach to journalism: Come up with a better story than anyone expects and write it with style, wit and depth. We hope you find the results here both helpful and enjoyable.

—PAUL E. STEIGER
Managing Editor
The Wall Street Journal

INTRODUCTION

WHEN SOMEBODY would ask, "What do you do as an investigative reporter?" I found it too pretentious to say that I try to expose wrongdoing. Instead, my glib reply would be, "I take expense-paid trips to the Bahamas."

There was some truth to that. During more than 20 years as an investigative reporter, I made probably a dozen trips to the sunny Bahamas, doing pieces on bank fraud, political corruption and drug trafficking. The British Colonial Hotel, in Nassau, where I stayed, had its own private beach, and a lovely swimming pool with a bar nearby. The kitchen did an excellent job in preparing fish, particularly grouper, which is a favorite of mine.

The trips didn't go unnoticed among my colleagues in New York. When winter came, and a cold wind rattled through the downtown canyons, John O'Riley, a senior editor, would drop by. "Isn't it time for one of those Bahamas trips?" he'd ask dryly.

I enjoyed the job, but every story was a struggle. Could I prove that the subject of my story was engaged in skulduggery? Usually, everything hinged on whether I could get an elusive document, or if I could overcome a key individual's reluctance to give me information.

I was often tense when I submitted the piece to the editors. In my view, this was a superb story—one of my best ever. But maybe it had a hole in it, which I'd carelessly overlooked. My editors, who inhabited a Kafkaesque world I could never comprehend, might reject it.

Even if the piece was deemed fit for publication, an editor usually felt it could be improved. Parts of it needed to be clarified, I'd be told, or the story cried out for more color, which, to my displeasure, meant I must do additional reporting.

After the piece was published, I had a letdown. What would I do now? Where would my next lead come from? Sure, I had pretty good sources. But I couldn't always count on them to deliver. Often, a tip didn't pan out. At times, it seemed, everyone in the office was busy on a story, except me.

In digging for information, I used no special tricks. Unlike a former colleague, who posed as a wealthy Greek shipowner for a story on gambling junkets, I never impersonated anyone. Nor did I ever wear a disguise. True, one time, in Detroit, I hid in a hotel broom closet, which adjoined a ballroom, where delegates of the United Auto Workers were meeting in secret. I eavesdropped on them, scribbling notes in the dark, when suddenly a cleaning woman pulled open the door. Startled at the sight of me, she turned and fled. I felt foolish. It was the last time I hid in a broom closet.

Anybody who wants to be an investigative reporter should ponder this: Bylines are infrequent. It may take two to three months to finish a single story. That translates into six bylines a year, at most. Be prepared for long, tedious hours in courthouse archives. Don't fly into a tantrum if an affidavit, for some inexplicable reason, is missing from the case file. And get accustomed to the idea that the subject of your story, who fears he is going to be roasted by you, may refuse to be interviewed.

The good part is that you dig up information your readers would not otherwise know about. Better yet, your story, exposing the criminal or ethical wrongdoing of a sleazy character, may trigger an official investigation. The villain—a corrupt public official perhaps, or a corporate officer—could be ousted from office as a result of your piece. When that happens, admittedly a rare event, the investigative reporter has achieved nirvana.

What follows are examples of how investigative articles are done. I take you with me, step by step, from the time I begin the story, until I file it. I show where the tip for the story comes from, and how to get the facts to prove that the tip's allegations are accurate. Each example makes a point, illustrating a different problem that must be overcome in order to do the story. For example:

- Is it too risky to use as a source a person who has an ax to grind?
- Is it proper to base a story on information from someone insisting on anonymity?
- Is it safe to rely on what a source says, or must the reporter see a document for corroboration?
- Can a lie be justified, to induce a key figure to grant an interview?
- If a reporter gets damaging information about a company president, who is also a news source, should he write the story, even if it means alienating a good source?

Sometimes, a tip leads nowhere. I recount two painful experiences involving leads I pursued that I thought might turn into red-hot stories. If they had become articles, they would have given the Bush White House heartburn.

Each time, I thought I was getting close to pay dirt, only to reach a dead end. Even now, I ask myself: Did I prove beyond any doubt that the tip was false, or didn't I dig deep enough? I'm not sure what the answer is.

—STANLEY PENN
New York City, July 1993

CHAPTER 1

SUSAN'S HUSBAND, THE WHISKEY MAGNATE

I

T'S NOT EVERY DAY somebody's wife asks a reporter to do an expose about her husband. So, naturally, I was taken aback by Susan Rosenstiel's phone call. She said she was married to Lewis Rosenstiel, the head of Schenley Industries, a big-time liquor company, the shares of which were traded on the New York Stock Exchange. Hubby, she said, was a tax cheat, had defrauded shareholders, and was a pal of gangster Meyer Lansky.

She'd been told by her lawyer to call me. I'd never heard of her before. Lew Rosenstiel, it seems, was demanding a divorce. It didn't take a genius to see this was a woman scorned, hoping to use me to blacken Lew Rosenstiel's reputation.

My first impulse was to say, "Tell it to somebody else." The idea of using a stranger as a news source made me uncomfortable. My sources were mostly lawmen, lawyers in private practice, company executives. I trusted them. I knew they wouldn't deliberately mislead me

But Susan Rosenstiel? I knew nothing about her. What little she said about herself didn't exactly inspire confidence. She'd been a model in Manhattan's garment district. Her first marriage to a wealthy Romanian lasted two months. Rosenstiel kicked her out after they'd lived together five years.

When strangers asked to talk to a Wall Street Journal reporter, the switchboard often gave them to me. Typically, the phone callers claimed to be victims, begging me to expose their persecutors. Some sounded wacky. One man, in a frantic voice, said:

"The government wants to kill my mother, my father and my brother. I'm dying. My girlfriend is an informer. Oh, what a game they're playing. Why do they want to hurt me and my family? This shouldn't happen to any American family. They torture you. They put out a contract on me. I called (author) Sy Hersh. He doesn't know what to do. I called (Newsday's) Bob Greene. He hung up on me. You got to help me."

Many callers said they'd been cheated out of their life's savings by unscrupulous promoters. Maybe so. But what could I do? I had no subpoena power to obtain incriminating documents. For all I knew, these individuals

1

were victims of their own greed. When I tried to kiss them off by suggesting they call the FBI, they grumbled that nobody wanted to help them.

Looking into Susan Rosenstiel's allegations could be a big mistake, I said to myself. People with an ax to grind give a one-sided version of events. I had visions of a libel suit by Lew Rosenstiel, accusing the Journal of recklessly disregarding the facts.

Tough Roy Cohn was Lew Rosenstiel's lawyer. Cohn was the one-time chief counsel to the late U.S. Sen. Joseph McCarthy, the anti-communist witch hunter. Cohn had a reputation for making hostile witnesses squirm. For sure, Cohn would find skeletons in Susan Rosenstiel's closet. He'd paint me as the dupe of a vengeful wife.

Doing a story about Lew Rosenstiel wouldn't be hard, provided he were under criminal investigation. The investigation could be used as the news peg, which would justify publishing the story. This would undercut any claim by Rosenstiel the piece had been inspired by malice.

But, as far as I could tell, no law enforcement agency was investigating him. He'd never been convicted of a crime—not even indicted. The burden would fall on me to show he was disreputable, no easy task.

Despite misgivings, I agreed to interview her. It wasn't every day I got the opportunity to listen to a society dame who lived on Park Avenue in the posh Regency Hotel denounce her husband. We met in her lawyer's office.

She wore a black silk dress and an ankle-length sable coat. A diamond brooch on her chest lit up the room. Accompanying her was her white Pekingese. It had a pink ribbon around its scrawny little neck.

Right off the bat, she said nobody must know she was my news source, fearing it could hurt in her court fight against her fiery 74-year-old husband. I was noncommittal.

Susan, 43, was a small, slender, attractive blonde. She had a demure look. When she spoke of her husband, bile poured out. She scornfully referred to him as "the supreme commander."

As she told it, her marriage had begun on a happy note. The old geezer had even written love poems to her. She showed them to me. Said one:
"Susie is the light of my life
All must see her, my wonderful wife."
Another said:
"I am the rooster that rules the roost
And you are the hen that sits on the nest
So, here's 'Happy Anniversary' and all the rest."
They honeymooned in Havana, then a gambling paradise ruled by Cuban dictator Fulgencio Batista. A vase with flowers on the dresser greeted the newlyweds when they checked into their hotel suite overlooking the Caribbean. A note in longhand, wishing happiness to the Rosenstiels, was signed, "Jake Lansky"—Meyer Lansky's brother.

"Who's Jake Lansky?" Susan asked.

"'Oh, just somebody I know'" Lew Rosenstiel replied, according to Susan.

2

"When I got back to New York I found out all about Meyer and Jake Lansky. I was shocked."

The whiskey magnate's wife lived in Byzantine luxury. Susan's allowance was $200,000 a year. She divided her time among Lew Rosenstiel's 28-room Manhattan townhouse; a Greenwich, Conn., 1,800-acre estate, and a Miami hideaway. There were parties on Lew Rosenstiel's yacht, plus frequent buying sprees in Paris and Rome. Afterward, she relaxed on the French Riviera.

Susan insisted she'd been a loyal, faithful wife, joining him at tedious black-tie industry dinners, where—Susan said—corporate moguls swapped dirty jokes and illegally shared inside information.

"He was very difficult to live with," Susan said. "He was suspicious of everybody."

According to her, Lew Rosenstiel once staged a hoax to test the loyalty of top Schenley executives. They received a telegram saying Rosenstiel had died of a heart attack, and they should report to Rosenstiel's Manhattan townhouse. The executives assembled in a downstairs living room. The old curmudgeon's death, some of them said, would improve Schenley's prospects. Unknown to them, said Susan, the room was bugged. In their upstairs bedroom, the Rosenstiels heard every word.

In bathrobe and slippers, gripping a cigar between clenched teeth, Rosenstiel stormed out of the bedroom. He stood silently at the top of the staircase.

"They looked up and saw who it was, and eyes popped out," Susan said. "It was hilarious. He pointed to everyone who had bad-mouthed him and said, 'You're fired.'"

Susan told me that Rosenstiel viewed Samuel Bronfman, head of Distillers Corp.-Seagrams Ltd., the world's biggest liquor company, as his arch enemy. He believed—without any evidence, as far as anyone knows—that Bronfman was plotting to kill him. Susan described this incident: The pair were in their chauffeur-driven limo, heading for Conyers Farm, Rosenstiel's Greenwich estate, after returning from their honeymoon. Rosenstiel kept twisting in his seat, looking out the back window, then yelling at the driver to increase his speed.

"I said, 'You'll kill us if we don't slow down,'" said Susan.

"He said, 'They're after me, they want to kill me.'

'Who?' I asked.

'Bronfman's people!'"

According to Susan, her husband repaid her devotion by demanding a divorce. She wouldn't give it to him. The only grounds for divorce in New York then was adultery. Ever resourceful, Lew Rosenstiel hired snoopers, in efforts to prove she was an adulteress. Despite round-the-clock surveillance, they couldn't get any evidence.

His name would be mud when she got finished with him, she promised. Through me, Susan said, the world would learn that he'd allegedly enriched

3

himself at Schenley shareholders' expense, improperly billed Schenley for his personal expenses, and bribed Mexican government officials in an attempt to get his marriage to her dissolved.

Had she reported any of this to the FBI?

Nope, said Susan.

Why not?

Because, Susan said, FBI chief J. Edgar Hoover and Lew Rosenstiel were friends. Hoover would never investigate his buddy Lew. Roy Cohn, Rosenstiel's attorney, was another Hoover pal. Susan said one time she'd seen Hoover and Cohn in drag at a party for gays in Manhattan's ritzy Plaza Hotel.

All this I listened to in amazement. Could any of it be substantiated? For example, did she have Jake Lansky's "happy honeymoon" note? No, she said. It hadn't occurred to her to save it.

I looked up Lew Rosenstiel's press clippings in the public library. A photo showed a tall, husky man with thinning hair. The tinted glasses and the long thin cigar sticking out of the side of his mouth gave Rosenstiel a mildly sinister look. He was depicted in articles as brilliant, domineering, hot-headed and a loner. Competitors disliked him for his refusing to cooperate on matters of mutual interest.

He'd never gone to college. Instead, he got a job sweeping floors in his uncle's Kentucky distillery. When Prohibition became law, he lost his job, finding work as a shoe salesman. Then he took a gamble that paid off big.

With a group of investors (where he got his stake is unclear), Rosenstiel bought up supplies of aged whiskey from distillers, who mistakenly believed Prohibition never would be repealed. In 1933, when the ban on the sale of liquor was lifted, Rosenstiel was sitting pretty, with nearly 20% of the U.S. whiskey inventory. For a time, Schenley Industries was No. 1 in sales.

Nothing in the clips showed he ever broke a law. There was nothing to back up Susan's contention he was Meyer Lansky's friend. Not even a hint he might be mentally unstable.

His friends were a Who's Who of famous people: Winston Churchill; Francis Cardinal Spellman of New York; President Roosevelt's former financial adviser Bernard Baruch; Thomas Dewey, the famed ex-Manhattan prosecutor, who became governor of New York, and twice was the Republican presidential candidate. Dewey had been Schenley's chief counsel for a time. It was hard to believe such people would be friends with a crook.

I was in a quandary. Part of me said I shouldn't get involved, that her story was too fantastic to be believed.

But I liked her spirit. Nobody seemed to intimidate her. Oh, maybe she exaggerated here and there. But if I could show that Rosenstiel was misusing Schenley funds I had a helluva story. I decided to test her credibility by investigating her claim about bribes paid to Mexican officials by Rosenstiel.

4

According to her, the whole sordid affair was described in Rosenstiel vs. Rosenstiel, in state court in Manhattan.

Susan had once been married to a Felix E. Kaufmann. They got a divorce in Juarez, Mexico, and Susan married Lew Rosenstiel. According to court documents, Rosenstiel later hired Ben Javits—brother of U.S. Sen. Jacob Javits of New York. Ben Javits's task: Find a way to dissolve Lew Rosenstiel's marriage to Susan.

Ben Javits went to work. A motion filed by a "Samuel Goldsmith" in the Juarez court charged that Susan's divorce from Kaufmann had been illegally granted. This led the Juarez court to nullify Susan's divorce. Rosenstiel, citing the Mexican court's ruling, got a Manhattan court to cancel his marriage to Susan on the ground she was still Kaufmann's wife.

Susan struck back. Selling diamond jewelry to raise funds, she hired prominent New York attorney Louis Nizer. Nizer investigated Ben Javits's actions in Mexico. On the strength of Nizer's evidence, the Mexican government found that the Juarez court had engaged in "crimes of falsification, fraud and threats." The government ruled Susan's divorce from Kaufmann was indeed valid.

As a result, the New York court reinstated her marriage to Rosenstiel. The court said, "Through a maze of forged documents, a fraud was uncovered."

Rosenstiel had paid Ben Javits $445,000. Of that, Javits funneled $160,000—in bribes and fees, according to Nizer—to a member of the Mexican cabinet, a state attorney general, and others. In the wake of these alleged irregularities, a New York court forbade Ben Javits to practice law for three months.

This convinced me Susan knew what she was talking about. I got the front-page editor's okay to see if I could come up with a story about Lew Rosenstiel. Most of the information came out of three New York courts, where the war between the Rosenstiels had been largely fought. Trial testimony and affidavits yielded the juiciest information. For example, in an affidavit, Susan said Rosenstiel's East Side townhouse was a labyrinth of electronic bugs and wiretaps. She added, "Practically every telephone call and conversation with a visitor was recorded while (Rosenstiel) lived there."

The documents showed that an outside group of investors had made an unsuccessful offer to buy Rosenstiel's stock in a bid to gain control of Schenley. It hadn't been previously reported. This became the news peg, weakening any possible claim by Rosenstiel's attorneys that the Journal hadn't a legitimate reason to do the story and Rosenstiel had been singled out for persecution.

Documents showed how the millionaire Rosenstiel avoided income taxes. Lew Rosenstiel's accountant, in court testimony, said Rosenstiel had charged $355,000 of his household costs to the company as a business expense over a certain period. Moreover, Rosenstiel arranged for Schenley to pay $200,000 for the upkeep of his yacht—another alleged business expense. Oil and gas shelters reduced his taxes even more. Federal income taxes accounted for only 7% of Rosenstiel's compensation. This went into the story.

From Susan I learned that a civil complaint by a minority Schenley shareholder had been filed in a Wilmington, Del., court, accusing Rosenstiel of improprieties. In a settlement, Rosenstiel had accepted a 17% pay cut; returned $135,000 to Schenley he hadn't been entitled to, and gave back to Schenley an extra $3 a share he received in stock options. This too was included in the piece.

Because she was fighting Rosenstiel in court, I agreed not to identify her in the article as my source. I felt I owed it to her. After all, if she had not showed me what documents to look for, I wouldn't have had a story.

To my dismay, I couldn't independently verify Susan's anecdotes about Sam Bronfman and Meyer Lansky, or that Rosenstiel had faked his death. So they didn't go into the article.

Schenley officials, Rosenstiel included, weren't willing to be interviewed. Carl Byoir & Associates, the whiskey company's PR firm, sent me a Rosenstiel bio, depicting him as a "philanthropist, a patriot and an innovator." It said he was known to employees as "The Chairman."

The headline is shown below; the story is on page 116.

The Schenley Saga

How the Personal Life Of Chairman Entwines With Corporate Affairs

———

Firm Figures Prominently
In Rosenstiel Legal Tiffs;
1965 Profit Moved Upward

———

Raiders Waiting in the Wings?

———

I never heard a peep of criticism from Rosenstiel or Roy Cohn. Eight months later, Rosenstiel retired as chief executive.

As a result of all this, I became a lot more ready to listen to people with an ax to grind. Unfortunately, it had its drawbacks. I began chasing too many leads that led nowhere. I worried that my byline count would drop.

Even so, my willingness to listen to strangers paid off. A page one piece, "Fighting Back," showed how Norman Oppenheimer, a New Yorker, who was suckered out of $250,000 in a stock scheme, sacrificed his family and career in his obsession to recover his money. His days were spent in court, where he acted as his own lawyer in pleadings against his adversaries. At night, he eked out a living as a hotel clerk. (See page 121.)

6

Another front pager, "Of Love and Money," focused on overweight, embittered Judith Scofield, who lost $600,000, all her savings, in the stock market, while having an affair with a Hayden, Stone & Co. stockbroker, who dropped her after she went broke. The story suggested the broker may have exploited her by churning her stock in unauthorized, unnecessary transactions, generating fat commissions for himself. (See page 124.)

Meantime, Susan was phoning me every morning. I complained to her I couldn't get any work done. Stop calling so much, I said. She hung up on me and wrote me a letter saying I had offended her.

One day, Susan's name came up in a public hearing held by a New York state legislative committee investigating Lew Rosenstiel's possible links to the criminal underworld. In testimony, Louis Nichols, a former aide to J. Edgar Hoover, and later a top Schenley executive, accused the committee of staging the hearings at Susan's behest. According to Nichols, "poison-tongued" Susan threatened Rosenstiel on the phone that "he would never live long enough to clear his name after she got through with him." The hearings failed to prove Rosenstiel had Mob ties.

Years passed. Then, in the late 1980s, she phoned me. "Stanley," said the familiar voice with the New York accent, "it's Susan Rosenstiel." She said she'd moved to the French Riviera to escape New York's winters. She was in New York on business. She suggested we have lunch, recommending a luncheonette in Manhattan's Murray Hill district.

At about age 67, she'd retained her good looks. Her blonde hair was brown now. If she wore diamonds, I didn't notice them.

We discussed Rosenstiel, Roy Cohn, and J. Edgar Hoover. They were all dead. Cohn—who'd once told a reporter, "Rosenstiel is a hero to me; he is one of the few rugged individuals left in America"—had visited the 84-year-old Rosenstiel at his deathbed in a Miami hospital, where Rosenstiel signed a document making Cohn an executor of Rosenstiel's $75 million estate. Cohn was later removed as executor after a Florida judge ruled that the senile Rosenstiel had been tricked by Cohen into believing the document he signed concerned his litigation against former wife Susan.

Over lunch, Susan told me she had information about an American stock swindler who was living on the Riviera and was wanted by U.S. authorities. He'd make a great story, Susan said. She'd be happy to help me on it.

I said I'd get in touch with her. But I never did.

7

CHAPTER 2

THE DRUG LORD

BROWN JUMPSUITS are the dress code for male prisoners in the Metropolitan Correctional Center, in lower Manhattan. Women inmates wear blue tops and bottoms. The only exceptions are major offenders. Segregated on a separate floor and kept under extra-tight surveillance, long-term prisoners are clad in orange.

Chinese drug lord Johnny Kon looks like a gymnast in his orange jumpsuit. He is muscular, of medium height, with sleek black hair and alert eyes. He speaks broken English. Kon's Hong Kong-based gang was one of the biggest and most violent of the Chinese criminal organizations that have grabbed control of the illicit U. S. heroin trade. Kon's gang, in just four years, smuggled nearly a ton of Southeast Asia heroin into the U.S., enough to supply 1,000 addicts with a daily fix for 30 years.

Kon greets me courteously, with a smile, which can't conceal his bitterness. He's 46, and has just received a 27-year prison sentence, with no chance for parole. He complains his punishment is too harsh, he's been made an example of, there is no justice.

Feeding his bitterness is the knowledge that a man he trusted betrayed him to U.S. drug agents. He had saved this ingrate's life not once but twice, he says. As if puzzled by the ways of man, Kon asks, How could a person show such ingratitude?

We spend an hour together, his attorney Ivan Fisher, in attendance. Kon answers some questions; ducks others. As I leave the jail cell, Kon shakes my hand, a host bidding his guest goodbye. He will be 73 when he is freed, his best years behind him, if he survives prison life.

If I were the one who snitched on Kon, I'd sleep with a gun by my side.

The path that led me to Johnny Kon began with a statistic in an obscure federal report. You ask: Is this where I get my stories—from government handouts? Aren't great investigative reporters such as Bob Woodward and Seymour Hersh blessed with confidential sources? Well, of course I had sources, but I couldn't always depend on them for leads. All around me, reporters were earning their paychecks by banging out stories. I simply couldn't sit at my desk picking my nose waiting for some source to phone in a tip.

Searching for story ideas, I put myself on mailing lists of government agencies, including the Justice Department and Federal Bureau of Investigation. Admittedly, scanning dry government reports is a tedious way to dig for a story. How much more exciting if a tipster phoned me, promising a hot scoop if I met him at Grand Central Station, Gate 11, in 30 minutes, saying I'd recognize him by the tic in his left eye, and the red scarf around his neck, and when he whispered "Bosnia," I should reply, "Herzegovina," so he'd know it was me.

The government reports, available to anyone for the asking, contained mostly old stuff, or information of no great consequence, surely nothing to provide a lead for a front-page story. Leafing through the reports seemed a waste of time until a tiny item leaped out at me in a publication called "International Narcotics Control Strategy Report," published by the Bureau of International Narcotics Matters, which is a unit of the U.S. State Department.

The State Department gives foreign countries money to fight drug traffickers, and the Bureau of International Narcotics is supposed to make sure the funds aren't wasted. The narcotics bureau issues an annual report, which makes gloomy reading. Despite repeated claims of drug-producing countries that they were cracking down against the drug lords, narcotics production kept increasing. The table of statistics on page 16 of the bureau's report showed world-wide cocaine production rose 41% in five years. Marijuana was up 16%. This came as no surprise to me. What grabbed my attention was heroin. Production, world-wide, more than doubled in the same period.

I found that hard to believe. As the Journal's expert on narcotics matters, I thought that heroin use—after an upsurge in the late 1970s—had tapered off, and that heroin junkies were switching to other drugs, so as to avoid AIDS caused by infected hypodermic needles.

It was no secret that the drugs of choice these days were cocaine, which is snorted, and cocaine crack, which is smoked with a pipe. Unlike cocaine, favored by Wall Streeters and the Hollywood crowd, heroin had an unsavory reputation. Deadbeats, losers and society's dregs used heroin. Heroin overdoses caused deaths.

But, if the statistic were correct, the monster drug heroin, contrary to public perception, was quietly enjoying a comeback. If true, I had a meaty story.

Since nearly half the nation's 500,000 heroin addicts lived in New York, I asked John J. Hill, head of the city's police narcotics division, if heroin addiction was on the increase.

"Definitely," Hill said. He looked up the numbers. "Just in the past year, heroin arrests in New York have jumped 80%."

How did he explain it?

"There's more available," Hill said. "It's all over the street. And it's better stuff."

Better? What did that mean?

"It's a purer heroin," Hill said.

According to an official in New York State's substance abuse division,

9

high-purity heroin didn't require injection with a needle. "You just spread the heroin on a napkin," he said, "and inhale it with a straw. It gives the same jolt as if you injected it. No needle, no AIDS."

Another reason for the heroin revival was its new-found popularity with crack users, who were mostly young people. Crack, a stimulant, produced a powerful high. Crack users found that heroin, a depressant, eased the crash that followed the high.

That young people were mixing crack with heroin was ominous. "It could give us a younger generation addicted to heroin," the state official said.

OK. Now I knew why heroin consumption was on the upswing. Certainly, it was newsworthy. But it wasn't enough for a front pager. For one thing, I needed to find out why heroin suddenly was available in such huge amounts in the U.S. In New York, the supply was so great, street dealers had increased the purity to 40% from 5%, without hiking prices. Lower East Side clothing discounters didn't offer such bargains.

A Drug Enforcement Administration agent said heroin was flooding the U.S. because of bumper opium crops being produced in Southeast Asia. The "Golden Triangle," a mountainous region at the juncture of Laos, Thailand and Burma, had overtaken Mexico and Southwest Asia (Pakistan and Afghanistan) as America's chief source of heroin. The "Golden Triangle" heroin, known to junkies as "China White," jumped fourfold in output in five years.

"You know what the really interesting part of the heroin story is?" the agent said. "It's the Chinese gangs. They're pushing the Mafia out of the New York market."

The Mafia. Immediately my ears perked up. This could be the key to the story. America's most feared criminal organization was losing out to the Chinese. I hadn't read that anywhere.

I talked to a New York FBI agent, whose specialty was the Mafia. He said:

"For many years, the U.S. heroin trade was controlled by the Sicilian and U.S. Mafia. New York was the heroin wholesale distribution capital. The mob would import heroin to New York and resell it to dealers on the East Coast and Midwest."

But federal prosecutions of mob bosses in the "Pizza Connection" and "Commission" cases had loosened the Mafia grip on New York, said the FBI man. The Chinese heroin networks, headquartered in Southeast Asia, had seized 75% of the New York market. The unthinkable had happened: The lordly Mafia, hat in hand, had to ask the Chinese gangsters would they please sell them heroin?

The outline of the story was starting to take shape. The Mafia had been ousted from its dominant role in the heroin trade by upstart Chinese entre-preneurs. Furthermore, high-purity "China White," in record amounts, was pouring into the U.S., enabling addicts to smoke it, so they could avoid using needles and getting AIDS.

Even so, I didn't have enough for a story. To dramatize the theme, I needed to focus on some big-time Chinese heroin trafficker. Through him, I could highlight the Mafia's diminished role, the rise of Southeast Asia heroin gangs, plus give a glimpse into the Chinese underworld. Wanted: a Chinese drug lord.

The Manhattan district attorney's office came up with a candidate: Ryan Tai, a heroin distributor, associated with the Ghost Shadows, a criminal gang in Manhattan's Chinatown.

What made Tai attractive was that he'd recently been convicted of drug trafficking. Lawmen are readier to talk freely about convicted or indicted criminals than those not yet formally charged. Moreover, Tai offered a great deal of colorful detail. For example, when he talked to associates on the phone, he spoke only in code. He used a whorehouse in Manhattan as a cover for his drug deals. The suspicious Tai, making sure customers weren't government informants, would pat down their bodies with an electronic device, looking for a concealed wire recorder.

Trouble was, Tai, who was a Manhattan heroin distributor, didn't quite fit the bill. As I saw it, the central figure in my story must be a Chinese smuggler, so I could highlight the growing role of Southeast Asian heroin in the U.S.

I told a PR man for the DEA in New York what my problem was. A short time later, a DEA agent, formerly based in Thailand, phoned me.

"I got just the guy for you," the agent said. "Johnny Kon. He's just been sentenced."

I asked if Kon had been big time.

"He was one of the biggest."

How did the agent hear about him?

Said the agent, "I was part of a task force that hunted him down. He led us a merry chase till we finally got him."

Did the DEA have a lot of good stuff on Kon?

"Plenty."

Kon would do. I told the DEA agent I wanted to sit down with him for a long interview.

Just one problem, the agent said. He would not be allowed to be interviewed unless Catherine Palmer, an assistant U.S. attorney in Brooklyn, who prosecuted Kon, agreed to see me. In short, Palmer called the shots. Palmer, who was willing to be interviewed, was in the middle of a trial. Two weeks went by before she was available.

Palmer, a small, energetic woman, was an expert on the Chinese heroin networks. Her conviction rate of narcotics smugglers was among the highest in New York. To the Chinese underworld, Palmer was "The Little Dragon Lady," if a New York tabloid was correct.

From Palmer and the DEA agent, who didn't want to be identified, I learned that Johnny Kon peddled fur coats to U.S. soldiers through PXs during the Vietnam War. Later, he arranged R&R tours of Hong Kong for

GIs. After the war, he turned to smuggling fur coats and stolen jewelry. His gang, "The Flaming Eagles" robbed Hong Kong jewelry shops. New recruits were required to take an oath of silence. "If I betray the oath," a recruit pledged, "let the organization deal with me. I will even accept death without complaint."

Kon soon had enough status in the underworld to join a major criminal organization, the Wo Shing Wo triad. Hong Kong had some 50 triads, with a combined membership of over 100,000. The triads, which began as secret societies in opposition to the ruling Manchu dynasty in the 17th century, had raked in a fortune from crimes ranging from extortion to heroin manufacturing and trafficking.

As my sources told it, Kon found the allure of heroin irresistible. Using his triad connections, he hooked up with Bangkok brokers, who were directly linked to the Shan United Army and the Third Chinese Irregular Force, outlaw bands that controlled the "Golden Triangle." Kon benefited from the connection by purchasing heroin for a rock-bottom $7,000 a kilo, then reselling it to New York distributors for $90,000—an 1,186% gross profit. He smuggled the heroin by commercial airline, concealing it in ice buckets, vases and metal picture frames.

How did the DEA become aware of Kon? Ed Madonna, a DEA agent in Seattle, said Kon came to the DEA's attention in 1984, when the Royal Hong Kong Narcotics Police seized a load of heroin on a trawler that Kon shipped from Thailand. But, not till 1985, when two of Kon's couriers were captured at Seattle airport, did the DEA realize Kon was a heroin smuggler. The couriers were seized with 216 pounds of heroin. "The amount blew our minds," Madonna said. "Kon was the first one who woke us up to the fact that Southeast heroin had become a major factor in the U.S."

Thus began "Operation Seahorse," aimed at plugging the heroin pipeline. The investigation reached a climax with Kon's arrest in 1988. In return for lesser sentences, some of Kon's former accomplices, overcoming their fear that he would exact retribution against them, gave damaging testimony.

It would enliven the story if I could interview the ex-gang members who testified against Kon. But they refused to talk to me.

What a dope I was. I'd completely forgotten to examine the case file on Kon in Brooklyn's federal court. Court files can be a treasure-trove of first-hand information. In the Kon file were copies of letters to friends and associates that Kon had written in prison, as well as sworn affidavits from Kon's ex-associates showing how his heroin network operated.

Disclosed in the affidavits was the vital role in the gang's affairs performed by Kon's wife, 47-year-old Catherine Kon. While hubby supervised heroin shipments from Asia, Catherine Kon handled matters in New York. It was she who scrutinized airline security procedures at Kennedy Airport, instructing money couriers to fly China Airlines. "She said the China Airlines examination is not very intensive," said Eric Luk, an ex-Kon aide, in his affidavit.

Under fictitious names, Catherine Kon rented safehouses in New Jersey to store the heroin smuggled into New York by her husband. In the basement of a safehouse, the heroin was removed from the product it was concealed in, and dumped onto a plastic sheet spread on the floor. The heroin powder was spooned into plastic bags, weighed on a scale, and sealed, to await delivery to Chinatown distributors.

In an affidavit, Antonio Vacas, an ex-associate of Kon's, said the odor from the heroin as it lay on a heap on the floor was overpowering. He had to cover his mouth and nose with a wet rag to keep from inhaling it, Vacas said.

Kon was a will-o'-the-wisp. Using phony passports and capitalizing on connections with corrupt public officials, he traveled in and out of the U.S., Japan, Taiwan, the Philippines and South America. The only way the DEA could grab him was by getting inside information about the gang's operations. And that's how the DEA nailed Kon—by infiltrating the gang.

Kon, in jail-house letters, charged that "Foreign Boy" had betrayed him. Kon wrote to a friend: "I am just so mad that it was Foreign Boy who hurt me...so many of us have fallen into this trap today."

Elsewhere in his letter he said: "...In case Foreign Boy calls. Tell him that there should be a limit to trying to hurt me. In order for his Big Brother to stay alive, it depends on one word of his. All he has to do is to deny all the testimonies that he has given in court. Then I will be saved. You have to tell him that. I have not ever hurt him. Why did he do it this way? He can save me."

But Kon doubted that "Foreign Boy" would help him. "His heart is so vicious," Kon wrote. "He is not so soft-hearted like me, leaving people a chance to live."

It would be a good touch for the story if I could identify "Foreign Boy." I examined the case file. It was my guess that "Foreign Boy" was one of the three ex-gang members who testified against Kon. The three: Lau Shu Ming, Eric Luk, and Antonio Vacas.

It didn't take a genius to realize that Antonio Vacas wasn't Chinese. He must be "Foreign Boy," I decided. Palmer, the prosecutor, could confirm it for me. But she might be unwilling to do so, on the ground "Foreign Boy" could be at risk if his identity was revealed in my article.

I reread Kon's letters, looking for "Foreign Boy's" real name. It wasn't mentioned. However, Kon did say in a letter that "Foreign Boy's" name had been made public during court proceedings in Hong Kong.

When I pointed this out to Palmer, she readily confirmed that Antonio Vacas had been the mole. From Palmer and two DEA agents, I found out how Vacas was "turned," and how the trap was set to grab Kon.

Vacas was a Eurasian. In late 1986, while pretending to be a Hong Kong businessman, he was detained at the Seattle airport on suspicion his passport had counterfeit departure stamps. If found guilty, he'd probably be deported. A DEA computer showed that Vacas had links to Kon. If Vacas talked, he could help bring down Kon.

Ed Madonna, DEA agent in Seattle, found a way to get Vacas to open up. He handcuffed Vacas and said he was under arrest. If Vacas didn't spill what he knew, he'd rot in jail the rest of his life, Madonna bluffed. Vacas knew plenty. He had smuggled heroin for Kon into the U.S., and carried back millions of dollars in $10s and $20s stuffed in suitcases to Hong Kong. Vacas helped Kon obtain phony passports for himself and his wife when Kon fled Hong Kong after being implicated by a crew member on a heroin trawler that the Hong Kong police seized.

Vacas, fearing a long prison stretch, became an informant. In return, federal agents agreed to drop any charges against him. He would get expense money, plus a handsome cash reward if his aid resulted in Kon's conviction. Vacas was a big help, supplying names of gang members, Kon's aliases, as well as photos of the gang, including Kon and Helen Chow, his 27-year-old mistress, a former Hong Kong actress.

Vacas was fully aware he might be murdered if Kon discovered he was a snitch. Vacas recalled the fate of Ng Chieu-Ming, the crew member on the heroin trawler who implicated Kon. Kon had sworn to get revenge. Before Ng could testify, he was shot and killed, and the case against Kon in Hong Kong collapsed. The identity of Ng's killer was never determined.

Luring Kon to the U.S., so he could be arrested, seemed a remote hope. But then the Thai police seized a 301-pound heroin shipment that would have grossed $13 million for Kon in the New York market. This was a major blow. Most of Kon's wealth was invested in commercial real estate. Moreover, he'd recently sustained large losses at the gaming tables in Macao. Kon was in a cash bind. His Bangkok heroin brokers had tightened credit, demanding most of the payment upfront, instead of the usual 15% down payment.

To raise cash, Kon would have to liquidate some of his U.S. holdings. A trap was set. Vacas flew to New York. Then he notified Kon he'd found a buyer for the properties Kon had put up for sale. He asked Kon to come to Manhattan to sign the papers.

Kon took the bait. Under a phony name and Costa Rican passport, he flew to the U.S., meeting with Vacas on a Sunday night in the New York Hilton coffee shop. Emerging from the shop, Kon was confronted by 12 armed federal agents.

Kon fumed. After his arraignment in Brooklyn's federal court, Kon warned two DEA agents: "Others will die, (then) you," according to Palmer.

Many prosecutors are uncomfortable in press interviews, giving information grudgingly. Palmer was different. She provided terrific detail, including this anecdote: After Catherine Kon's arrest, she was locked up in the same prison as her husband, but on a different floor. Shortly after, Kon was informed that his mistress, Helen Chow, who'd been arrested in Tokyo, was being extradited to New York. She would be put in the same prison and on the same floor as Catherine.

14

Catherine Kon didn't know Helen Chow was her husband's mistress. Kon decided this was the time to break the news to Catherine. She became distraught, wept, and attempted to hit him with a chair. Bitter Catherine was transferred to a different prison.

In seeking to interview Kon, I expected no startling disclosures. He would probably deny his guilt—or claim that his role in the heroin network was minor. But, by quoting Kon, no matter what he said, I could bring him to life. The readers would get a "feel" of the man.

That Kon agreed to be interviewed didn't surprise me. As a convicted felon, he hadn't any reputation to protect, so he had nothing to lose. Maybe the thought crossed his mind that if he portrayed himself as a victim, he'd appear in the article as a sympathetic figure.

Shortly before I visited Kon, a package was sent to Palmer at her downtown Brooklyn office. It contained a loaded .22 caliber rifle, set to go off when the package was opened. But the gun failed to fire when the package was unwrapped. "I think it was more luck than anything else that it didn't go off," U.S. Attorney Andrew Maloney said later.

Did Kon try to kill Palmer? I asked.

No, said Kon, sounding shocked I'd even think such a thing. He bore Palmer no ill will, he insisted.

Why did Kon become a drug trafficker?

He said he was a businessman, who happened to get involved in drugs as a favor to friends. "They asked me to help them so I helped," Kon said blandly.

Kon showed emotion only when I brought up Vacas. "I saved his life twice," Kon said heatedly. "He was in the drug business, and he asked me for help."

In a letter to Helen Chow, Kon wrote, "I have telexed Hong Kong...We are looking for Foreign Boy, and will continually do so." Wherever you are, Mr. Vacas, be on the alert.

The headline is below; the story is reprinted on page 128.

Asian Connection

Chinese Gangsters Fill
A Narcotics Gap Left
By U.S. Drive on Mafia

———

Johnny Kon and His 'Eagles'
Hit Paydirt as the Market
For Quality Heroin Surges

———

But a Canary Puts him in Jail

———

CHAPTER 3

GREASING SIR STAFFORD

WHEN BILL LAMBERT was a reporter for the Portland Oregonian, he won a Pulitzer Prize for exposing political corruption involving the Teamsters union. Later, Lambert did a Life Magazine expose that led to the ouster of Abe Fortas as a U.S. Supreme Court Justice. Lambert had the kind of sources that made your mouth water.

So I wasn't happy to hear that Lambert was working on the same expose as I was—how big-time gambling came to the Bahamas. No matter how long I worked at the Journal, I knew I'd never get a story this juicy again. If Lambert scooped me, I'd dig a hole and bury myself.

As an investigative reporter, I produced half-a-dozen front-page pieces yearly, which meant I had very few bylines. Acquaintances, noting they hadn't seen a byline of mine in months, sometimes asked if I were still at the Journal. That irritated me. With a touch of self-pity, I tried to explain how hard, how time-consuming, this type of reporting was.

To justify my meager output, I tried to dig up stories that would have an impact, draw attention, cause a stir. The Bahamas story, no question, could be explosive, if I could nail it down. But if Lambert came in first, my efforts would be wasted. My editors, upset at being beaten, might not even run my piece. Even if it got published, it would look like a rehash of Lambert's.

Two individuals, both in a position to know what they were talking about, claimed to have knowledge of payoffs to Bahamian government officials concerning the award of a casino license in Freeport, the Bahamas. Monroe Karmin, a reporter in the Washington bureau, was assigned to work with me.

Our task: Prove payoffs were made.

One key source, a federal lawman, I knew slightly. The other was an insider—a former official of a Bahamian company that made the alleged payoffs. Not for a moment did I doubt that what they told me was true. Even so, I told myself, it wasn't enough. I wanted to see documents—preferably corporate documents naming the recipients and the amount of the payoffs.

Assuming the documents existed, they'd be tough to get hold of. Which raised a question: Must the story be substantiated with documents? Was I being too demanding? After all, the information about the payoffs came from highly trustworthy sources. That should be enough. How much corroboration did we need before being certain the story was nailed down?

The piece had all the ingredients of a movie thriller. Among the cast of characters:

Wallace Groves, a crooked Wall Street operator, who'd received a two-year prison sentence for using the mails to defraud stockholders in a company he controlled. When he got out, Groves exiled himself to the Bahamas, a British Crown Colony, settling in Grand Bahama Island, a flat stretch of sand, scrubby pine and limestone, largely deserted, except for blacks who lived in shanties along the coast. From the government, Groves bought 211 square miles—half the island—for as little as $2.80 an acre. He called his enclave Freeport. In it, he had sole power to license businesses as he saw fit, and could evict almost anyone who displeased him—perhaps the sweetest deal since King Charles II gave Hudson's Bay Co. sole trading rights for most of Canada in 1670. As part of the bargain, Groves agreed to turn Freeport from a sleepy backwater into a resort-commercial center.

Lou Chesler. He was a 300-pound promoter, a super salesman, a pioneer in the sale of land on the installment plan. Groves turned to Chesler, who said a glitzy, Las Vegas-type gambling casino would attract tourists. Chesler would later say he sought the "advice" of crime syndicate boss Meyer Lansky in organizing the casino and hiring employees.

Lastly, Sir Stafford Sands. He was the colony's Minister of Finance and Tourism, the most powerful figure in the Bahamas. Groves needed the OK of the ruling Executive Council to obtain a casino license.

The stage was set. Sir Stafford, hired by Groves, petitioned the council—of which Sir Stafford was a member—for a license. It was granted. Not long after, Monte Carlo Casino flung open its doors for business.

For his efforts, according to our two sources, Sir Stafford received secret payments from a Groves company exceeding $1 million in fees, plus $500,000 in a 10-year consulting agreement. Others who benefited with consulting agreements included Premier Sir Roland Symonette and "Bobby" Symonette, the premier's son and House of Assembly speaker.

If the consulting agreements became public, the scandal might scare off foreign investors. Moreover, the weak, disorganized, black political opposition would be handed a weapon with which to attempt to unseat the ruling whites.

Groves and Sir Stafford, of course, would never publicly admit the existence of the consulting agreements. To do so would be to destroy their reputations in the Bahamas.

How then to verify the payoff allegations? One way: attribute the charges to our sources. They were highly trustworthy, and the information, given to each of us independently of the other, matched. But there was a problem. The sources demanded anonymity.

I could understand why they didn't want to be identified in the article. The former company official feared he could be murdered if his name were made known. The lawman was barred by government policy from leaking confidential information to the press. Lawmen, of course, fed confidential information all the time to reporters they trusted. But it was done on condition they not be identified.

We couldn't identify our sources. Did this mean we couldn't get the story in print? I knew in my bones the payoff allegations were true. It seemed absurd that we might not find a way to publish it.

Maybe we could get the story in the paper by saying our information came from sources that didn't wish to be identified. In effect, the key paragraph would say that Sir Stafford Sands and other top Bahamian officials had accepted secret payoffs from promoter Wallace Groves after awarding Groves an exclusive casino license in Freeport, "according to informed sources."

But promising confidentiality to the sources could put Karmin and me in hot water. If a grand jury investigated the facts and we were subpoenaed, we might be forced to testify.[1] If we refused to identify our source, we might go to jail. If we were sued for libel and we refused to identify our sources, a jury might decide we had made up that part of the story and the Journal could be on the hook.

There was another reason against basing a piece on anonymous sources. Destroying reputations by quoting nameless people wouldn't be right. Not to sound sanctimonious about it, but it seemed to me an abuse of a newsman's power.

Plainly, we needed firsthand documents to substantiate the allegations. This way, we wouldn't have to worry that our sources had been inaccurate, their memories faulty. This was a major story. It could produce waves. If it was inaccurate in any significant way, Karmin and I wouldn't have any future in journalism.

And, yet, I kept thinking, are documents essential? Am I being overcautious? Am I imagining problems where none exist? I'm 99% sure the sources are correct. You can't get much more certain than that. If this story gets away from me, I won't be able to hold my head up. It'll show I'm not mentally tough enough for hard-nosed reporting.

How would my editors react if we failed to come up with the story? They might say, "Stan, don't let it get you down. You did the right thing. Basing a story on anonymous sources—especially a story this explosive—just isn't acceptable. Don't blame yourself. Better we don't do the story than succumb to bad journalistic practices."

But would they mean it? They'd never forget that when it counted I failed to come through. They might think Penn isn't cut out for investigative reporting. He's too soft. Maybe Penn should go into sales promotion.

Meantime, Karmin and I pushed ahead on another front. We collected background information about Groves, Sir Stafford, the Lansky crowd, and

---

[1]In the U.S., the law varies from state to state and between federal courts, so if there is an issue, it is worth consulting one of the Journal's lawyers.

the Bahamas.

Through interviews, we found that the merchant-politicians who dominated the Bahamas were known as "the Bay Street Boys," and Sir Stafford was their leader. They'd enriched themselves by awarding government contracts to companies they controlled. Although the Bahamian whites were in the minority, they'd gerrymandered the voting districts, helping them to maintain political control over the majority blacks.

Ministers in the self-governing colony were unpaid; so doubling as merchant and public official was legal. There was no conflict-of-interest law in the Bahamas barring self-dealing. Technically, Sir Stafford didn't do anything illegal in representing Groves before the same council of which he was a member. Nonetheless, Sir Stafford used his political clout for private gain, which was why he wanted his actions kept a secret.

Portly, balding, the 52-year-old Sir Stafford was an intriguing figure. He had a glass eye, a taste for young women, a penchant for expensive lounge jackets. He was knighted by Queen Elizabeth in 1962. As the Bahamas's most prominent lawyer, he represented many U.S. companies with Bahamian subsidiaries. He was a liquor merchant, and headed a grocery chain. He entertained lavishly at "Waterloo," his 17-acre Nassau estate.

Helping us was "Tex" McCrary, a New York PR man, at one time the host of a radio talk show, together with wife Jinx Falkenburg, a one-time tennis star. McCrary had done PR for the Groves-Chesler interests, touting Freeport as a tourist mecca, using his persuasive skills in efforts to discourage the U.S. press from taking too close a look at what was going on. Increasing evidence that the Freeport casino had been penetrated by the gangster Lansky left McCrary uncomfortable. He switched sides, offering his expertise to Lynden Oscar Pindling, the black opposition leader.

Pindling, 36, stocky, was a London-trained lawyer. Shortly before we met him, Pindling, in a fiery speech at the United Nations, said: "We are concerned because precious little of the wealth of our little country flows down to the man in the street. We are worried because each day, more and more, there is accumulating evidence that the whole of the destiny of the Bahama Islands is being taken out of Bahamian hands and grasped by foreign gangster gambling interests."

His audience yawned, as did his Bahamian followers. Pindling had said it all before. What he lacked was hard evidence to back up his corruption charges.

We dined with Pindling in a Third Avenue bistro. He had a grave manner, with no time for small talk. His deep voice had a British inflection mixed with the lilting cadence of the Bahamas. If his Progressive Liberal Party won power, he'd be the Bahamas's first black premier.

Pindling had been told by McCrary that Karmin and I were trying to break a story on corruption in the Bahamas. This made me nervous. I worried that Pindling might announce in the Bahamas that The Wall Street Journal was on the verge of publishing an expose on the Bay Street Boys.

Lambert, alerted, might feel pressure to rush his piece out, leaving Karmin and me at the starting gate.

As we discovered, the white Bahamian businessmen, who stood to benefit from the influx of tourists drawn to the Freeport casino, applauded its coming. The black churchmen, for the most part, sharply criticized the casino, warning it could attract dope peddlers and prostitutes. Sir Etienne Dupuch, editor-publisher of the Nassau Tribune, the islands' leading paper, and a member of the Bahamian Senate, wrote angry anti-gambling editorials.

This stopped after Sir Stafford arranged for Sir Etienne to be a secret consultant to a Groves company. Sir Etienne, in a letter to Sir Stafford, a copy of which we obtained, insisted he didn't sell out.

"This arrangement," Sir Etienne wrote, "must not in any way be considered as influencing my decision in the Senate, or the policy of the Tribune." His consulting fees would go to needy children, Sir Etienne promised.

Allan Witwer, a former PR man for Sir Stafford's Ministry of Tourism, wrote an unpublished manuscript, "The Ugly Bahamians," that could have greatly embarrassed the Bay Street Boys. But a curious thing happened. Hill & Knowlton, the big New York PR firm, which did PR for the Ministry of Tourism, arranged for a friendly group to purchase the manuscript for $53,000. The manuscript was never published.

McCrary put us in touch with a former Groves company official. In a 20-page, double-spaced memo, this insider gave a behind-the-scenes account of the Groves-Chesler operation. Included were intimate details of the casino activity, with a description of the roles of Dino Cellini and George Sadlo, both of them later deported from the Bahamas as undesirables.

Said the insider:

"Cellini and Sadlo were Lansky's men. At the closing of the casino each night, all of the (money) boxes were taken from the tables and brought into the counting room. There were three sets of keys to the boxes, but it was important that either Cellini or Sadlo be present before a box was opened."

Documentation for Lansky's links to Sadlo came from the Kefauver Senate Committee hearings in 1950. Testimony before the committee showed that Lansky and his brother Jake, along with Sadlo, operated illegally the Club Boheme gambling casino in Florida. An accountant for Boheme testified that at the end of the night, after they closed each table, the money was removed to the cashier's cage, where it was counted.

"Who counts it?" a committee investigator asked.

"Mr. Lansky," the witness replied.

"Personally?"

"Yes; or Mr. Sadlo, or whoever is there with (Lansky)."

The consulting fees to the Bay Street Boys were paid by Grand Bahama Development Co., a Groves affiliate, according to the insider. Sir Stafford's fee was the largest. The checks were sent out monthly. Dr. Raymond Sawyer, one of the recipients, bitched mightily if the checks were late.

"I can recall at least four letters of complaint when the check was no more than two or three days after the first of the month," said the insider.

I asked the insider if the names and payoffs were listed in Grand Bahama Development documents.

Yes.

Did he have them?

No, he didn't.

Could he get them?

No. They were under lock and key in Freeport.

But a lawman, investigating Lansky's involvement in Freeport, had copies of the corporate documents, said the insider.

The lawman said, yes, Sir Stafford and others had been on the Groves payroll as secret consultants. But he was reluctant to show me the corporate records.

Why? Because Grand Bahama Development, as a privately owned company, wasn't required to publicly disclose most of its activities. The documents I was so eager to get my hands on were nonpublic information. It could be awkward for the lawman if it became known he had leaked documents. Lawyers for Groves and Chesler could argue that their clients had been wrongfully denied due process.

The lawman, of course, could leave the documents on a desk in an unoccupied office, and I, by chance, could happen to wander in, examine them, take notes, and leave. But this was subterfuge, and I knew the lawman would not agree to it.

In effect, I said to the lawman, take pity on Karmin and me. I explained we had just about completed our reporting, and were ready to write the story. What a pity if, at this late date, the story couldn't get done because we'd not been able to get our hands on the company documents.

I said that we already knew who got the payoffs, and how much. The ex-Groves company official had told us. The only thing we needed was verification.

He let me see the documents. What a relief. The end was in sight. The time had come to confront the suspects.

The sunny Bahamas featured fishing, sailing and golfing. Nassau, the capital, with its pink colonial houses and lush gardens, had a picture book look. Horse-drawn surreys showed tourists the sights, steering clear of the "Over the Hill" section, the black slum that lacked sewers and sidewalks. In colorful Rawson Square, at the harbor's edge, women hawked straw goods. Bay Street, the main thoroughfare that snakes along the harbor, was jammed with liquor, perfume and jewelry shops. Policemen, in white pith helmets and bright red belts, directed traffic. Lyford Cay, a 20-minute car ride from the noisy downtown, was where the rich and famous spent their winters.

The Bahamas had a sinister side. The islands had been a haven for shady operators since the 1600s, when pirates seized ships bound for the

New World and used the Bahamas as a hideout. During the American Civil War, Bahamians profited by smuggling arms made in Europe into the Southern Confederacy, thereby foiling the Union blockade. In the Prohibition Era of the 1920s, Bahamian merchants disregarded the liquor ban in the U.S. by supplying American bootleggers with European booze.

Now, the Bahamas were a haven for foreign tax evaders. Undeclared income from the U.S. was routed to Nassau, where money managers concealed it in secret accounts. Some of it was gangster-owned, laundered behind the veil of bank secrecy laws, so that it couldn't be traced when the mobsters reclaimed it.

Dentist Raymond Sawyer, in a downtown Nassau office, was peering into a patient's mouth when Karmin and I barged in. Sawyer, a member of the council that awarded Groves his casino license, had signed on for a five-year consulting agreement, according to the corporate documents I'd seen.

Dr. Sawyer, who also operated a Nassau racetrack, said he knew nothing about consulting agreements, and to please not pester him during office hours.

Documents showed that Premier Symonette—who had extensive interests in shipping, liquor and real estate—had a five-year agreement. Not so, said the premier.

Sir Stafford, answering questions in writing, said he knew nothing about a consulting agreement. He denied receiving payments of the magnitude shown in the corporate records, although conceding he did legal work for Groves and his Bahamian companies.

Only "Bobby" Symonette confirmed to us that he'd been under contract as a consultant. "Bobby," an expert sailor, claimed to have ended his agreement a few months previous.

The presence of the Freeport casino distressed some of Nassau's upper crust, including Shirley Butler, wife of a Nassau banker. Mrs. Butler's father, Sir Harry Oakes, a wealthy former Canadian mining magnate, had been murdered in his Nassau home in 1943, amid allegations—never proved—that the U.S. mob got rid of him because he'd opposed plans for a casino in Freeport.

Over dinner on the veranda of "Jacaranda," the Butlers' home near downtown Nassau, Mrs. Butler deplored Groves' casino as an error in judgment and taste.

"An offshore Las Vegas in the Bahamas horrifies me," she said.

Freeport, where Groves held sway, was 15 minutes by plane from Nassau. In the Bahamas Handbook, a booster publication, Groves was depicted as both genius and perfect family man.

"Secure in the tenure of a prodigious business success," the handbook chirped, "he is made happier still by the possession of a dream house on the beach, a charming wife and five healthy exuberant children."

The monarch refused to be interviewed. But Groves's PR man was available. He stood by my side as I soaked up color in the casino, situated in the posh Lucayan Beach Hotel.

The casino had thick carpets, and a huge crystal chandelier that looked down on the crap shooters, blackjack dealers and spinning roulette wheels. The customers—some in black tie and evening gown—spoke in hushed tones, as if in a cathedral.

Surveying the action was the casino manager, 61-year-old Frank Ritter (alias Red Reed). Ritter was an expert on instant credit. He knew who to give it to, how much, and who the deadbeats were.

Ritter and his aides—Max Courtney (real name Morris Schmertzler), and Charlie Brud (real name Charles Brudner)—were wanted for trial in the U.S. on tax evasion-racketeering charges. Before fleeing to the Bahamas, they'd allegedly operated a nationwide bookmaking business.

I played roulette and lost $80.

After losing my first $20, the PR man removed $20 from his money clip and stuck it in my pocket.

"Don't, please," said I, returning his money.

He insisted he wasn't trying to bribe me; simply a goodwill gesture. He hoped I wasn't offended.

Such shennanigans didn't surprise me. In New York, a former Chesler aide had said:

"One of the first things the mob did (after infiltrating the casino) was to insist on putting certain newspaper people on the payroll. Others were given carte blanche privileges at the hotel and casino, even to the point that some of them were allowed to win money at the casino."

According to this insider, a Florida newspaper columnist was secretly on the casino payroll at $200 a week, and a "top reporter" for another Florida paper received $300 weekly from the casino interests. (We never got around to verifying it.)

Later that night, the PR man mentioned that two female friends of his were giving a party in their hotel room and I was invited. He assured me they weren't bimbos.

I said I was too tired to go.

Just one drink, he urged.

I said I'd take a rain check.

They were intelligent, attractive women, he persisted. Just one for the road, c'mon. He'd told them about me. They'd never in their whole life met a Wall Street Journal reporter.

Was it a setup? Lure me into the room, spike my drink with a knockout pill, photograph me in bed with a prostitute, then warn me against publishing the corruption story or the damaging photo would be publicly released? I never found out.

The first of the Bahamian pieces was titled:

Las Vegas East

U.S. Gamblers Prosper
In Bahamas With Help
From Island Officials

Top Local Political Leaders
Grant Casino License, Also
Receive Consultants' Fees

Is There Link to U.S. Crime?

The second was headlined:

Kingdom in the Sun

Tough-WilledAmerican
Turns a Bahamas Island
Into Thriving Enterprise

Wallace Groves Lures Firms
And Tourists to Freeport,
Enforces Rigid Controls

A Clash with Louis Chesler

Published in October 1966, the articles were reprinted in the Bahamas, which had a population of 140,000 then. If the Bay Street Boys feared a political backlash, they didn't show it. They scheduled an election for January 1967, warning that a Pindling victory would destroy the Bahamas economically. (The stories are reprinted on pages 132 and 137.)

Pindling's Progressive Liberals scored a narrow, upset victory; Pindling became premier, and Sir Stafford exiled himself to a castle in Spain.

In Nassau, a Royal Commission of Inquiry, after public hearings, verified the Journal's findings. Sir Stafford, the commission report found, received at least $1.8 million from the Groves's companies, using his influence on the Executive Council to benefit Groves with a casino license. Sir Stafford, in testimony, denied doing anything wrong.

Life Magazine's piece on the Bahamas appeared in February 1967. It was a lovely piece, 15 pages that dealt with every kind of corruption in the

Bahamas, with lots of pictures. Lambert shared the byline with Richard Oulahan.

It would be nice to report that the Bahamas under Pindling were scandal-free. But that would be wrong.

The Bahamas became a haven for big-time drug traffickers. "Mother" ships from Colombia dropped anchor in Bahamian waters, transferring cocaine and marijuana to small speedy boats, which smuggled the dope into Florida. Allegations of payoffs to high Bahamian officials by the traffickers were widespread.

NBC-TV, in a 1984 investigative report, accused Premier Pindling of accepting $100,000 monthly from Colombian drug lord Carlos Lehder. Pindling denied it. An official commission of inquiry, which looked into it, couldn't prove it.

But the commission raised the possibility that Pindling was enriched with some highly questionable fees. A Bahamian law firm had collected a $600,000 finders' fee, of which $333,979 ended up in a bank account for Pindling's benefit. A different Bahamian law firm received a $120,000 fee, $91,000 of which was diverted to a Nassau contractor, in part payment for a house he built for Pindling. In both cases, Pindling denied any wrongdoing.

In August 1992, Pindling's 25-year reign ended. His party was defeated in parliamentary elections by the center-right Free National Movement.

Ironically, he was brought down by charges of corruption—the same issue that in 1967 had carried him to power.

CHAPTER 4

ON QUAYLE'S TRAIL

I'M IN THE OFFICE, working on a Mafia story, and hoping to get through the day without interruptions.

My boss, Barney Calame, shows up. Suddenly, the air is charged. Barney looks tense—tenser than usual.

He hands me a memo, which I read. It's unsigned. When I ask who wrote it, Barney says he doesn't know.

Barney left out of the loop? It must be highly secret if Barney doesn't know.

Maybe I'm wrong, but my devious mind tells me that Boss Norm Pearlstine, or Peter Kann, Boss of All Bosses, wrote the memo; that it was given to Paul Steiger, Pearlstine's righthand man, who instructed Barney, Steiger's aide-de-camp, to put a reporter on it pronto.

It's no ordinary memo. The allegations, if true, can shake the nation. If I nail it down, I look like a hero. It can earn me a pay increase, tight budget or no tight budget.

According to the memo, Vice President Dan Quayle may have used cocaine. What's more, Quayle, when he was a U.S. Senator, reportedly pulled strings to get a preferential prison transfer for his alleged cocaine dealer. In return, the felon agreed not to blab that Quayle snorted cocaine. If the memo is correct, "60 Minutes," the TV news magazine, hopes to break the story.

It takes my breath away. Quayle a cokehead? Quayle being blackmailed by an imprisoned dope dealer? This could destroy the career of the rosy-cheeked, 44-year-old vice president—the Hoosier with the Boy Scout face. Knowing daddy was a lawbreaker would be a terrible blow to Quayle's kids.

Calame says I should check out the memo. I promise to get right on it.

But I grumble to myself. Am I expected to beat "60 Minutes" to a story that Mike Wallace probably has been chasing for months?

Also, assuming Quayle was a user, and assuming he's being blackmailed by a drug trafficker, where do I start? I don't have a single lead.

I tell Barney I'd like to interview the person who wrote the memo. Maybe the memo writer can find out the identity of the cocaine dealer. In addition, I'd like to interview the memo writer's tipster.

Barney will see what he can do. He returns with bad news. The memo writer wants to remain anonymous—meaning he or she won't speak to me. The memo writer doesn't know who the cocaine dealer is, nor does the memo writer wish to reveal how he or she obtained the information.

What's going on? Why won't the memo writer help me? I'm pissed. It's as if I must investigate a story blindfolded.

And why has this hot potato been dumped in my lap? I'm not the paper's only investigative reporter. Ed Pound, in Washington, and Bill Carley, who sits right in back of me, both are top-notch. Does Barney have it in for me? What did I ever do bad to Barney?

If I ask Barney, "Why me?", he'll answer, "Stan, you're our expert on drug trafficking. You've got the sources. Why not you?"

Thanks, Barney.

I study the two-page memo. It's unsigned, isn't addressed to anyone, and has no date. I wonder: How does the mysterious memo writer know that "60 Minutes" is investigating? Can it be that Peter Kann was at a fancy dinner party for media magnates, that CBS's Larry Tisch drank too much, disclosing the secret about Quayle, and that Kann, a hotshot reporter once, dashed into the bathroom, where, without being seen, he scribbled notes about Quayle on his shirt cuff?

My guess is, "60 Minutes" paid the cocaine dealer a fat fee to inform on Quayle, and has the story wrapped up.

You have to admire "60 Minutes." According to the memo, the "60 Minutes" people obtained copies "of two letters written by Quayle to get the drug dealer/prison inmate a preferential prison transfer."

Furthermore, "60 Minutes" has "documentation" of two "violent" nosebleeds suffered by Quayle.

Nosebleeds? How could "60 Minutes" find that out? Quayle's loyal wife, Marilyn, would never tell. Did Quayle dine with Mike Wallace and, when blood suddenly spurted from Quayle's nose onto the London sole, did Wallace ask, "What's wrong, Dan?," and Quayle replied: "I snort cocaine, Mike, but I'd appreciate if you kept it to yourself."

I know it's no joking matter. This is potentially a big story. Trouble is, if I get beat on it I look bad. Nobody's going to remember "60 Minutes" had a huge jump on me. On my tombstone will be inscribed: "Penn let the Quayle story get away."

I phone the federal Bureau of Prisons, in Washington. The bureau is empowered to give inmates transfers. All requests for transfers must be in writing. If Quayle interceded for the coke dealer, Quayle's letter is on file— assuming, of course, Quayle didn't hire G. Gordon Liddy of Watergate fame to break in and swipe the letter.

I ask the prison bureau's PR man: "Am I entitled to see letters from public officials seeking favors for prisoners?"

You sure are, the PR man says. I should file a request under the Freedom of Information Act. If my request is approved, I'll be shown whatever letters they have.

That sounds easy, until the PR man asks for the inmate's name.

I say I don't know who the inmate is. But I can furnish the name of the public official (Quayle) who allegedly requested the transfer.

Not good enough. I must have the inmate's name.

Damn. I knew it wouldn't be easy. It never is.

Who might know the cocaine dealer's name? A Democrat might.

I phone a Democratic staffer on a congressional committee that deals with narcotics matters. The aide recalls that, during the 1988 presidential election campaign, V.P. candidate Quayle was rumored to have smoked marijuana.

Those rumors have been investigated and can't be verified, I tell the staffer.

"Did you hear anything about cocaine?" I ask.

"Not a word," the staffer says. "But it sounds like something he'd try."

The staffer suggests I get in touch with the Democratic state committee in Indiana.

A state committee spokesman says the cocaine story is strictly rumor. Would I be interested in the marijuana rumor? "A guy in prison says he was Quayle's (marijuana) dealer."

"It's been completely discounted," say I. "I'm interested in cocaine."

"I wish I could help," he says.

According to the memo, the information about Quayle reportedly is stored in a Drug Enforcement Administration computer. The memo notes that Robert Stutman, ex-boss of the DEA's New York office, is now a CBS consultant on narcotics matters.

I know Stutman. Once, when he headed the DEA's Boston office, I interviewed one of his agents. Stutman sat in. This discouraged the agent from telling me too much. However, as DEA's boss in New York, Stutman was quite helpful to me. After Bush was elected president in 1988, Stutman was rumored to be a candidate for federal drug czar. William Bennett got the job instead.

That Stutman is a CBS consultant doesn't seem terribly significant. Whether a DEA computer has classified information about Quayle is strictly conjecture. Feeding classified government material to the media is illegal. Stutman wouldn't do that.

But, I say to myself, he might've helped "60 Minutes" legally. It's quite possible an affidavit linking Quayle to a cocaine dealer is on file in a U.S. courthouse somewhere. If so, the affidavit is in the public record. But the media are unaware of its existence.

Without breaking any law, Stutman could conceivably inform "60 Minutes" where the public affidavit is. Government officials provide such leaks all the time. "60 Minutes" then could go to the courthouse, pull the file case and get the affidavit.

But this is all conjecture.

Where does it leave me? I can, of course, ask Stutman what he knows about Quayle, if anything. I'd be wasting my time. Stutman is with CBS. There is no reason for him to help me.

According to the all-knowing memo, "60 Minutes" planned to do a segment on Michael Levine, a former crackerjack DEA agent, based in New York. Levine, no fan of Stutman's, has just published a book, "Deep Cover." In it, Levine accuses the "suits"—his contemptuous term for DEA officials— of bungling major drug investigations through incompetence.

If the memo is correct, "60 Minutes" assigned a producer and a correspondent to the Levine project, with Levine agreeing to go to Panama and California to tape portions of his story. Abruptly, the segment was canceled. "We have been told," says the memo, "that '60 Minutes' executive producer Don Hewitt canceled (the segment) because he didn't want to offend Stutman and risk losing the Quayle 'drug' story."

If true, Levine must be furious with CBS. An appearance on "60 Minutes," one of TV's most popular shows, would help boost sales of Levine's book. Perhaps Michael Levine, eager for vengeance, is The Wall Street Journal's tipster.

I reach Levine on the phone. He is still teed off at CBS.

"They filmed me, and then they dropped me—no reason given," Levine fumes. "The producer who told me I'm being dropped was really upset. She was beside herself."

"Did she say why they dropped you?"

"No," Levine answers. "I just assumed that with Stutman named drug adviser, I became persona non grata."

"Did you hear reports about '60 Minutes' planning a piece on Quayle using cocaine, and getting a prison transfer for his cocaine dealer?"

Levine says he hasn't heard a word. Can I believe him? I think so. Why should he lie to me? If he was sandbagged by "60 Minutes," he hasn't any reason to protect them by deceiving me. Surely, Levine would know if Quayle interceded for a cocaine dealer. This would be common gossip at DEA, where Levine has many friends. If Levine is unaware of allegations about Quayle's purported cocaine use, they could be baseless.

I seek help from someone close to "60 Minutes." My source reports back that "60 Minutes" lists all the segments that are in the planning stage on an office blackboard. The source says "Quayle" isn't on the blackboard.

I see three possibilities: "60 Minutes" isn't investigating Quayle, in which case I'm wasting my time. Or, "60 Minutes" dropped the Quayle project after determining the allegations couldn't be proven. Or, the investigation is so hush-hush, Don Hewitt doesn't dare list it on the blackboard fearing it will leak out.

I'm having strong doubts about getting to the bottom of this story. But I can't just walk away from it. I've only been on it a few days. I can't honestly tell Barney I'm convinced the allegations in the memo are false.

Press clips say Quayle attended DePauw University, a small, liberal arts school in Greencastle, Ind. In 1969, Quayle, then a 22-year-old senior, ducked service in the Vietnam War, using a family connection to get into the Indiana National Guard.

He was a two-term congressman, and then was twice elected to the U.S. Senate. He was Bush's 1988 running mate. That year, shortly before Election Day, a convicted drug smuggler, Brett C. Kimberlin, phoned news organizations from prison, claiming he and Quayle smoked marijuana at a fraternity party in Indiana in 1971. Kimberlin contended he sold marijuana to Quayle "15 or 20" times in 1971-73. Quayle was then a student in the Indiana University Law School, in Indianapolis.

Is Kimberlin believable? He's a convicted perjurer. Currently, he's doing a 50-year prison sentence for marijuana smuggling and planting bombs in Speedway, Ind., in 1978, causing severe injury to one individual. I conclude he's not believable.

Kimberlin's claim of having sold marijuana to Quayle has never been corroborated. Quayle denied using it, or that he ever met Kimberlin.

Even so, I'm desperate for a lead. Kimberlin may know who Quayle's purported cocaine dealer is. I find the name of Kimberlin's attorney in the clips, and phone him.

The attorney says he will check for me.

He calls back. "The guy's name is Jordan," the attorney says.

I'm elated. Finally, I'm getting somewhere.

"When Quayle was a senator," the attorney adds, "he intervened to get Jordan transferred to a 'Level 1' facility in Lexington, Ky."

"Level 1 is a 'soft' prison?" I ask.

"Right. Basically, it's a camp. White collars go there. They give furloughs at Level 1."

What a brilliant stroke to call Kimberlin's attorney. I have a solid lead.

I give Jordan's name to the Bureau of Prisons. The PR man looks in the computer to verify that Jordan is a federal inmate.

The computer draws a blank. No Jordan. The system hasn't any convicted cocaine dealer by that name.

I tell Kimberlin's attorney he gave me the wrong name.

"That's what my source told me," he says defensively. I'm guessing his source is Kimberlin.

I ask Kimberlin's attorney if he knows where Jordan, or whatever his name is, was convicted.

"Indiana."

"Any idea when?"

"Sometime in the early 80s, is what I hear."

That's a lead. The U.S. attorney in Indianapolis ought to know if Quayle interceded for a convicted cocaine dealer.

Trouble is, the U.S. attorney is a Republican appointee. He won't be eager to help me. For all I know, he and Quayle may have been law school classmates.

An assistant U.S. attorney gets on the phone. I ask for the names of cocaine traffickers convicted in Indiana in the 1980-85 period, plus the attorneys who represented them.

Am I kidding? It would take days of research. He can't spare anyone for that.

"Does this have anything to do with Quayle?" he asks.

"Yeah."

"You're wasting your time. The marijuana story has been checked and rechecked. Believe me, there's nothing to it."

His cocksure manner bothers me.

"I'm asking about cocaine."

"I haven't heard anything about it. I would've heard, if there was anything to it."

The Indiana Bar Association gives me names and phone numbers of the state's top criminal defense attorneys. Maybe one of them has a lead. I don't know where else to turn.

An attorney claims that Quayle, when he was a U.S. senator, interceded with prison authorities on behalf of a convicted sex molester. But the alleged molester wasn't a cocaine dealer.

"I wish I could help," the attorney says. "I guess you know '60 Minutes' has been working on the same story."

I get a sinking feeling.

"I heard," I said. "When did they call you?"

"Oh, it must be at least six months ago."

"Did you get the impression they were getting anywhere?"

"Hard to tell," he says. "They didn't say too much."

Another Indianapolis lawyer says he hears that a free-lance writer in Washington, D.C., got wind of Quayle's involvement with a cocaine dealer, but felt the story was too big for him to handle alone, so he arranged to share it with "60 Minutes."

He doesn't recall the free-lancer's name. It wouldn't do me any good if he did. If I called the free-lancer, he'd alert "60 Minutes" that The Wall Street Journal was hot on the trail.

The feeling grows on me that I'm running out of time. It's almost a week I've been on the story, and I still have no idea who the mystery cocaine dealer is.

Saturday night, I sleep fitfully. Early Sunday morning, I scan the New York Times' TV listings. The listings often tell the three "60 Minutes" segments scheduled for that night. The Quayle expose isn't one of them.

Thank God. I'm like a condemned man who received a stay of execution.

Monday morning, a message awaits me at the office. A former DEA agent, (not Michael Levine), who has been putting out feelers on my behalf, needs to talk to me.

The ex-DEA man says: "The word I get is, in the spring of 1989, a newspaper reporter—don't know who—came up with the stuff about Quayle using cocaine. This reporter went to a DEA agent in the Miami office and said he wants confirmation. The agent went into the computer and confirmed it."

"Just like that?"

"That's what I hear."

"I thought the information is classified."

"I would think so."

"Why would he give it to a reporter?"

"I'm telling you what I hear," the ex-DEA man says impatiently. "It comes from a very good source."

"Who's the DEA agent who told the reporter? I'll call him. Maybe he'll tell me."

"My source doesn't have a name. But he shouldn't be hard to track down."

I'm puzzled. If the reporter got confirmation about Quayle, why didn't the piece run? It would easily be the biggest story of the year.

I call the PR man for DEA in Miami. I tell him what I heard.

"Nobody from this office gave out any information to any reporter about Quayle," he insists.

"How can you be so sure?"

"If it happened, I'd know."

"Maybe the agent did it behind your back," I suggest.

"Then how come a story never appeared?" the PR man shoots back.

Good question. I have no answer.

Meantime, my colleague Bill Carley is curious about what I'm working on. Amused, he says he never saw me work so hard. Am I on to something big?

I say matter-of-factly that I'm looking into whether Dan Quayle used cocaine and if he's being blackmailed by the dealer who sold it to him.

Carley is impressed. How did I get on to it?

I tell him somebody at the Journal—I don't know who—heard about it, and I've been asked to check it out.

My guess is Carley is thinking that the story could be a prize winner, and why didn't Barney assign him the story instead of Penn?

I don't want Carley to feel bad, so I tell him I don't have a single lead, that "60 Minutes" has a big jump on me, and I wish I hadn't gotten involved.

Carley listens sympathetically, probably saying to himself that it sounds like a can of worms.

I get a break at last. An Indiana attorney, who I'd been unable to reach last week, calls back. He says a John C. Calhoun is the guy I'm looking for.

"He sold Quayle the cocaine?"

"Whoa, I didn't say that. You asked who did Quayle intercede for. Calhoun is your man. Quayle got him a transfer from Sandstone prison, in Minnesota, to Lexington, Ky. Calhoun was the head of a fairly substantial cocaine ring in Indiana.

"Did you hear anything else?"

"(Calhoun) is supposed to have said he believes his product went to

32

Quayle," the attorney says. "But it's hearsay."

"When did Quayle intercede?"

"Rumor is, he wrote the letter when he was a senator. Calhoun is out now."

"I appreciate your help."

"Give me a share of the byline," he kids.

"One more thing," I say. "Was Calhoun convicted in Indianapolis?"

"I assume so."

The indictment and conviction papers are a matter of public record. The U.S. attorney in Indianapolis would have them. If I ask for them, I'll likely be told that nobody is available to make copies for me.

I phone the federal court in Indianapolis instead. Lola May, a clerk in the public reference room, looks for Calhoun's name in the file. She finds it. Calhoun was convicted in 1982. She'll send me the pertinent documents by Federal Express.

What a lovely person Lola May is.

There's still a long way to go. Assuming Quayle got Calhoun a transfer, I must prove Quayle is being blackmailed. To do that, I must show Quayle used cocaine.

While waiting for the documents from Ms. May, I start the ball rolling at the Bureau of Prisons.

I give Calhoun's name to the PR man.

Yep, inmate Calhoun shows up on the computer screen.

I say it's important I get, as quickly as possible, any letters that Quayle wrote on Calhoun's behalf.

The PR man brings me back to reality. He can't do anything for me till my Freedom-of-Information Act request is approved, he says.

I know from past experience that an FOIA request can take weeks, if not months, to process.

"I'm really under great pressure," say I. "Can't you expedite things?"

A reporter's wailing is nothing new to the PR man. He says the agency will act expeditiously. I send in my FOIA request.

Meantime, I receive the documents from clerk Lola May. They look promising. The indictment shows that Calhoun, leader of a 17-member drug ring, was involved in the manufacturing and sale of cocaine. The group was indicted in August 1982, including Janet Firman, Calhoun's girlfriend.

Calhoun never went to trial. Instead he pleaded guilty in a plea bargain, receiving a prison sentence of 11 1/2 years. No mention in the documents of Quayle.

I track down Calhoun's prosecutor, now a U.S. magistrate in Indiana.

"Why didn't Calhoun go on trial?" I ask.

"He agreed to a guilty plea," the ex-prosecutor says. "He was the first defendant to settle. He cooperated in the investigation, and I made known to people the extent of his cooperation."

"What people are you talking about?"

"The Bureau of Prisons and the parole board."

Was Calhoun ever transferred to a minimum security prison? I ask.

He doesn't know. He says he lost touch after Calhoun was sentenced.

Now for the big question: "I hear Quayle interceded for Calhoun."

"I wouldn't know about that," the former prosecutor says.

"Was there anything in the court record to show Calhoun sold cocaine to Quayle?"

"Nothing."

"What do you think?"

"If Quayle used cocaine?"

"Yeah."

"There's nothing in the court record to show it," he says carefully.

Can he shed light on Calhoun's background?

"He came from an upper middle class family," the ex-prosecutor says. "His father was a lawyer. The son attended prep school and later became a professional artist."

Calhoun and Quayle would appear to come from the same social milieu. I wonder if I should call up DePauw to see if Calhoun went there. No, not yet. Quayle's friends at the school might alert him about the Journal investigation. Any letters Quayle wrote on behalf of the coke dealer might disappear from the Bureau of Prisons' files.

Do I sound paranoid? I don't think so. I may be closing in on the biggest story of the year. I can't take chances of slip-ups.

After waiting a few days, I inquire of the Bureau of Prisons if my FOIA request is being processed.

The FOIA officer is out of town. She'll get to it when she returns. I don't like the sound of that.

"Isn't there anybody else who can handle it?"

"She'll be back soon," the PR man assures me.

I'm irritated. Here I am, in a race with "60 Minutes," and the lousy federal bureaucracy won't get off its behind.

He assures me the matter will be handled expeditiously.

I must keep my temper in check. If I antagonize the U.S. Bureau of Prisons, my FOIA request may not get processed till 2001.

Another Sunday arrives. My luck is holding up. "60 Minutes" still hasn't scheduled "Quayle."

I'm not sure what to make of it. Is "60 Minutes" still working on the story? Was CBS pressured by the Bush administration to kill it? That can't be. In all likelihood, "60 Minutes" hasn't been able to substantiate the allegations.

I respect "60 Minutes." Yet they're not as gung-ho as they once were. Many of their investigative pieces these days often are a rehash of what the press ran.

If "60 Minutes" gave up, I may be the only reporter in the U.S. who is still dogging Quayle. What a coup if I could nail the story down.

I get a call from the FOIA officer at the Bureau of Prisons. She can't locate my FOIA request. Did I send it?

I can't believe what I'm hearing.

I say I faxed it, giving the date it was sent.

Ever so politely, the FOIA officer raises the possibility that I sent the request to the wrong fax number.

I tell her the number. She says it's the right one. She says the agency's fax machine may have been unplugged when I submitted my request. Would I be good enough to send it again?

I find this intolerable. I could lodge a complaint with the attorney general. But he belongs to the Republicans. President Bush has no interest in helping me dig up evidence that ends Quayle's career.

Meekly, I resubmit my FOIA request.

How is my "Quayle" project progressing? my wife asks. I say I'm not getting anywhere. This disappoints her. She wants to see an expose on Quayle—by me, or by anyone. She believes the U.S. will fall into the Dark Ages if Quayle ever becomes president.

The FOIA woman is on the ball. A package from her has arrived.

It's true! Quayle interceded for Calhoun.

The documents show that on Aug. 8, 1983, Calhoun, then an inmate at the federal prison, Sandstone, Minn., wrote to "the Hon. Dan Quayle," asking Quayle's help in getting a transfer, noting that he'd been turned down by the warden.

Sandstone is a "Level 2" prison. It means it has tighter restrictions than a "Level 1" jail. "Level 3," the least desirable, has the most dangerous criminals.

In his folksy letter, the 37-year-old Calhoun says he's never met Quayle. Calhoun says he's a Hoosier, same as Quayle; a property owner, and, "curiously, like yourself," a graduate of DePauw.

He'd be grateful if Quayle could get him transferred to Lexington, Ky., so he could be in the same prison as his wife.

"She and I met on a drug-related occasion," Calhoun writes. "Drugs persisted as part of our lives. It is a rational and reasonable request that we should have time to get to know each other free from chemical dependency, as this is how we intend to proceed upon our re-entry into society."

Calhoun adds: "There are numerous husband-and-wife 'teams' at Lexington who are benefiting from this 'unit' rehabilitation."

Whereupon, Quayle urges the Bureau of Prisons to transfer Calhoun. This triggers a reply from G.A. Ralston Jr., a regional director. Ralston says Calhoun's request was rejected by the warden because of the "severity of his offense," and "the short time" he'd been at Sandstone.

Quayle makes a second request a few months later. This time Ralston is conciliatory. Calhoun is scheduled for a "program review," Ralston writes, and, if things work out, "I am sure that the unit team will consider him for transfer to a lower security institution."

Calhoun gets his wish. He is switched to Lexington on April 26, 1984, after 14 months at Sandstone. He remains at Lexington till Jan. 30, 1986, when he is sent to a Cincinnati halfway house. Six months later, he is paroled. Sentenced to 11 1/2 years, Calhoun is in prison for less than three years.

Why should Quayle help a jailed cocaine dealer? Likely, Quayle would say public officials routinely help constituents. He might point out that Indiana Sen. Richard Lugar also interceded for Calhoun. Quayle might say the letter for Calhoun was written without his knowledge.

But the worst he can be accused of is bad judgment. It doesn't prove he used cocaine, or was blackmailed by Calhoun.

It's time to phone Calhoun.

I talk to Calhoun's attorney. "Can you give me his phone number?" I ask.

"(Calhoun) isn't giving interviews," the attorney says.

"Why not?"

"He just wants to live a quiet life. He's been through enough."

"I guess you know why I'm calling," I say.

"I can guess."

"Did Quayle and Calhoun know each other?"

"They were at DePauw University at the same time." The attorney adds, "One played golf, and the other hung out. There was no personal relationship between them."

"How do you know that?"

"Calhoun told me."

I ask: "What about reports Calhoun was Quayle's cocaine supplier?"

"I talked to Calhoun about this. Calhoun says he never met, sold, or had any dealings directly with Quayle."

"'Directly?' What does that mean?"

"Calhoun says there were rumors some of his cocaine reached Quayle. But he had no evidence of it."

I have no evidence Calhoun is lying. So, having exhausted every angle, I give Barney a memo. There's no story, I say.

This leaves me with an empty feeling. No article. I knocked myself out, with nothing to show for it.

But by showing the cocaine rumors can't be proved, maybe I accomplished something.

CHAPTER 5

CASE HISTORY OF A LEAK

PHIL LEVIN HAD EVERYTHING: A net worth of $100 million, a rock-solid marriage and a job he liked as president of Madison Square Garden Corp.

Levin spent weekends at his 100-acre estate in Warren, N.J. Weeknights, he slept at the elegant Hotel Pierre on Manhattan's East Side, in a pied-a-terre that his wife, an art collector, decorated with paintings by great French impressionists, including Monet, Renoir and Degas.

I was invited up once. It looked like a museum. In a mock-serious voice, I said to Levin, "Phil, are these real?"

"I paid enough, they better be," the short, stocky, gruff-voiced Levin said.

Madison Square Garden owned the Garden sports arena and two professional teams, basketball's New York Knicks and ice hockey's New York Rangers. Levin was the Garden's second biggest shareholder. The largest holder was Gulf & Western Industries (these days known as Paramount Communications Inc.), then headed by Charlie Bluhdorn, a manic personality with an explosive temper.

Levin was the Garden's chief operating officer, but Bluhdorn was always sticking his nose in, and they clashed frequently. There were rumors—whether true or not, I didn't know—that Bluhdorn was seeking a tactful way to ease Levin out as Garden president.

Levin was no namby-pamby. Getting rid of him would be difficult.

One day, a Bluhdorn aide asked me to drop by. I went to his office, where the aide proceeded to leak derogatory information about Levin. It was highly confidential information, and mustn't be attributed to Gulf & Western, I was instructed.

Surely, the aide didn't drop the goodies in my lap on his own. Bluhdorn, I assumed, was the source. I didn't bother to ask the aide if my assumption was correct, knowing he wouldn't tell me.

I also didn't ask why damaging evidence against Levin was being leaked. What did it matter? Investigative reporters were fed leaks all the time. It wasn't my job to look for motive.

Was the leak accurate? That was all that mattered.

Well, not quite. This time, the situation was different, more complicated, raising sticky questions.

Fact is, I didn't want to hurt Levin. It didn't mean we were friends.

Levin and I lived in different worlds. He could afford to lose more money at roulette in Monte Carlo in a single night than I made in a year.

Reporters, of course, shouldn't let their feelings interfere with their judgment. Even so, I couldn't help liking Levin. He was decent; down-to-earth and, most important of all, a good news source, who never lied. If I attacked him in a story, he wouldn't talk to me again.

The leak involved two Chicago-area racetracks that Levin operated. The Illinois governor then was a Republican, and Republicans controlled the state racing board. Levin happened to be a liberal Democrat from New Jersey.

The racing board had been informed by state investigators that the outsider Levin had had dealings with unsavory individuals. A meeting was held by the board to determine if Levin's license should be revoked. Levin was allowed to retain his license, after being warned by the board he'd be kicked out if he ever tarnished Illinois racing's squeaky clean image.

After the hearing, Levin secretly gave $100,000 to some Illinois Republican bigwigs. The gift—"campaign contributions," it was called— came from Chicago Thoroughbred Enterprises, a company Levin headed.

I saw the canceled checks.

It looked as if Levin had been blackmailed by the Republicans. But why was Gulf & Western leaking the information to me?

I didn't believe for a moment that Gulf & Western was attempting to embarrass the Republican Party. No corporation wants to get into a fight with a major political party.

I could only conclude that Gulf & Western was seeking to tarnish Levin's reputation.

Levin, of course, would deny he had made payoffs. He could point out— correctly—that Illinois law permitted corporate donations to state and local political campaigns .

Levin could protest all he liked. A sleazy deal had been cooked: Illinois Republicans allowed Levin to keep his racing license in return for payoffs. That's how it looked to me, and the public would see it the same way.

Gulf & Western had fed me an exclusive story, and I should be grateful. Yet, I didn't want to lose Levin as a source. So I searched for reasons why I shouldn't do the story.

I said to myself: The political contributions weren't illegal, despite how it looked. Levin had no choice. If he didn't give the money, he'd have lost his license. It would've caused a scandal, and his career could've been destroyed. A person who wasn't reputable enough to operate racetracks in Illinois wouldn't be allowed to be president of Madison Square Garden, a high profile, publicly held company. Levin had shown poor judgment in his choice of acquaintances, but he didn't deserve to be punished for that.

As far as I knew, Levin had never broken any criminal laws. He'd made his pile by building shopping centers—more than 100 of them—from Maine to Florida, not to mention apartment buildings in New Jersey and

Pennsylvania. The fact that he was from New Jersey and in real estate didn't mean he was associated with the Mob.

Levin had been a news source ever since he got involved with movie maker Metro-Goldwyn-Mayer. He had purchased a 4% stock interest in MGM and been appointed to the board. He became dissatisfied with MGM management, and started a proxy fight. Pretty soon, I was talking to Levin regularly. I'd meet him in a bar near the Pierre, and he'd fill me in on the proxy fight, including his battle strategy, what his adversaries were up to, and who said what to whom.

As I well knew, Levin was using me, hoping to be portrayed as an aggrieved MGM shareholder, fighting a stodgy management. That was all right with me. His information was accurate, and he was giving me exclusives. He treated me like a confidant. I liked that feeling.

Show biz excited Levin. When he got control of MGM, he promised, he'd restore the company to its former pre-eminence as the biggest, most successful film factory in Hollywood, when its stable of stars included Clark Gable, Greta Garbo, Mickey Rooney and Judy Garland.

Levin and his wife became familiar figures at MGM's New York movie premieres. Their chauffeur-driven Rolls Royce would deposit them right in front of the theater. One time, the Levin car couldn't get close enough to the curb because of congestion. He fired off a letter to MGM management. Henceforth, he demanded, the way should be open for him to park directly at the curb and not in the second or third lanes.

Levin lost the proxy fight. But he got over it, selling his MGM stock for a $22 million profit, and buying 4% of Gulf & Western's outstanding shares. Bluhdorn, wary of Levin, named him to the board, where he could keep an eye on him.

Levin viewed Bluhdorn as a phenomenon—the hardest driving executive he'd ever met.

"Morning, noon, night, he never lets up," Levin said in grudging admiration.

"Do you get along with him?" I asked.

Levin shrugged. "Charlie Bluhdorn says to me, 'Phil, you were never meant to be corporate.'"

The abrasive Bluhdorn would fly into a rage at the slightest provocation. Screaming at his victim, his hands flailing the air, his voice grating on you like an electric drill, Bluhdorn often seemed to lose control of himself.

He gave the impression he had no anxieties, no self doubts. He treated his aides like errant children; he humiliated them whenever it suited him. They must be highly paid, I assumed, or they would not put up with such abuse.

Once, I was in his office when he let loose a tirade on the phone at a young British director. The director, at a party in a Manhattan hotel the preceding night, had celebrated completion of his first Paramount movie. He had too much to drink, overslept, and failed to show up for a Life maga-

zine interview. Bluhdorn was in a frenzy. He called the director a drunk, an idiot, a fool; commanded him to apologize to Life, and to beg Life to reschedule the interview. If he failed, Bluhdorn threatened, he would never make a movie for Paramount again.

Bluhdorn could be friendly. One time, he smiled and chatted with my wife and me at a party for a movie starring Peter O'Toole, who attended the New York premiere in black tie and white sneakers. Bluhdorn, a year older than I, told my wife what a smart young husband she had, as if I were a precocious schoolboy.

In his black horn-rimmed glasses and black hair combed straight back, Bluhdorn had an intimidating appearance. He rarely took vacations, and hated sports. He tried to learn to ski once, broke a bone in his foot, and never put skis on again. Deal-making was his obsession. Born in Vienna, he came to New York at 16. At 23, he owned a commodities import business. At 32, he started Gulf & Western. Under Bluhdorn, known on Wall Street as the "Mad Austrian," G&W feverishly gobbled up companies, growing from a tiny auto parts supplier to a monster conglomerate, including movie making, sugar refining and consumer finance. In a 1976 Mel Brooks movie, G&W is ridiculed as "Engulf & Devour."

Need I mention I didn't care for Bluhdorn?

A story attacking Levin would benefit Bluhdorn.

Just how Bluhdorn would benefit, I couldn't be certain. The article might be used by Bluhdorn to convince Madison Square Garden's board of directors that Levin was too controversial to stay as president. Or, in the event Levin began a proxy fight for control of Gulf & Western, Bluhdorn could cite the article in newspaper ads, warning G&W shareholders not to support a man linked in The Wall Street Journal to unsavory individuals.

I pictured a triumphant Bluhdorn crowing to aides about his wise decision in leaking the Levin story to me.

"Was I right, or wasn't I?" I could hear him saying. "From here on, Stanley gets all our leaks. I like Stanley. Maybe we should hire Stanley, and dump all those PR jerks we have. We're not getting our story out. As Gulf & Western grows, so grows the country. The public doesn't know that. Stanley could tell that story. Stanley has credibility. The assholes in the press would listen to Stanley."

What should I do? I had no choice: To keep my self-respect, I must chase down the story. The Journal paid my salary, not Levin. Levin was a big boy. Levin could take care of himself. That Bluhdorn might benefit from the piece wasn't my concern. I just had to be sure I had an airtight story.

Levin allegedly gave $50,000 to the Cook County (Chicago) Republican Campaign Fund; $25,000 to the Illinois Republican Victory Dinner Fund, and $25,000 to the campaign fund of Edmund J. Kucharski, chairman of the Republican Cook County Central Committee. Kucharski was also the Illinois assistant secretary of state, appointed by the Republican governor.

The task was to prove that the checks shown to me were authentic.

Should I phone the Republicans first, or Levin? This called for some thought.

Calling Levin first could be a mistake. Levin was shrewd. He might deny he wrote the checks, or refuse to comment, then quickly warn the Illinois Republicans not to answer my questions when I called up.

If Levin and the Republicans refused to comment, I'd be in a bind. I had no story unless I could prove that Levin gave $100,000 to the Republicans.

I phoned Edmund Kucharski. Probably he was a hack politician with a low IQ. Hopefully, I could catch him off guard before he realized he should keep his mouth shut.

Kucharski wouldn't take my phone calls. I sent him a registered letter. Ten days later I got an answer in the mail.

"I cannot confirm" the $25,000 contribution, Kucharski wrote. As for Levin, "suffice to reiterate that I do not know P. Levin, have never met him and do not know any of his associates, nor have I ever met one."

Kucharski had outfoxed me. It would be pointless phoning the other Republican recipients. I would just get a runaround.

I called Levin, and said: "Phil, I know all about the $100,000 you gave the Illinois Republicans. I've got the documents in front of me: $25,000 to the esteemed Edmund Kucharski, $50,000 to the Cook County Fund, $25,000 to the Illinois Victory Dinner Fund."

I said I'd read a transcript of the racing board's hearings; that it looked to me that he'd been pressured into giving the money; that I was writing a story about it, and felt I should call him so he could say whatever was on his mind.

Levin asked how I heard about the political contributions. I said my lips were sealed.

There was silence, then Levin said he'd be willing to answer my questions. Thing was, he had to go to Chicago on business. He had an idea: I should fly out with him. This way, he could give me his undivided attention, without the phone interrupting.

I said it sounded fine to me.

I agreed to meet him at his apartment in the Pierre, and his limo would take us to the airport.

His wife, Janice, let me in. Levin was on the phone, making last-minute calls. With Mrs. Levin's OK, I inspected their paintings. Mrs. Levin was a gracious hostess, serving me Nova Scotia salmon on thin slices of black bread, and a white burgundy to wash it down.

The situation I was in seemed unreal. Here I was embarking on a story that could ruin Levin's reputation. He knew it, and his wife probably did too. Yet, I was being treated as an honored guest.

I began the interview after the plane took off for Chicago. Levin readily admitted giving $100,000 to the Republicans.

"Why?" I asked.

"For background?"

"It means I can use it but not quote you, right?"

"Right."

"I agree."

Levin said his racing license would've been revoked if he didn't dish out the money. Compounding his problem, he said, was that he was a Democrat in Republican country.

Why didn't he report it to the FBI? I asked.

Levin shrugged.

I could guess why. The FBI would want him to wear a concealed wire to show there was a shakedown. Levin would consider it demeaning to be wired.

"You were being blackmailed, right?"

He didn't answer.

"Was it blackmail?" I repeated.

"For background?"

"Yeah."

"What do you think?" he said.

In the story, I said Levin acknowledged giving $100,000, but refused to say why. Then I wrote:

"Sources familiar with his thinking say Mr. Levin believed he had been unfairly attacked by the racing board and was fearful that the racing license might be in jeopardy as a result. He is said to have held the belief that he, a liberal Democrat from New Jersey, had to improve his standing in Illinois Republican circles."

At the hearings, Levin's nemesis was racing chairman Alexander MacArthur, a cousin of the late Gen. Douglas MacArthur. The racing official showed up in a cowboy hat, cowboy boots and a cowboy belt with a holster to keep his sunglasses in.

"We like our racing clean," MacArthur lectured Levin.

At another point, MacArthur said sternly: "A man running a race track in Illinois should be like Caesar's wife—he should be above reproach."

Hot-headed Levin had made enemies in Illinois by firing the socially prominent Marjorie Everett as president of Chicago Thoroughbred Enterprises, taking the job himself. Mrs. Everett had received a longtime contract to head the racetrack company after selling her majority interest in it to Transnation Development, which Levin and Gulf & Western controlled. Transnation was later merged into Madison Square Garden.

At the hearings, Bluhdorn took pains to distance himself from Levin, saying he had urged Levin not to fire Mrs. Everett.

"I told him, 'Phil, don't do it.' We had a great moral obligation to her. What it got down to, I pleaded with Mr. Levin without any success at all. I wasn't the only one that did it. But I particularly did it. And he said, 'I like her, but I can't live with her.'"

The racing board's investigation of Levin stemmed from Mrs. Everett's ouster. His business dealings in the U.S., Mexico and Canada were scrutinized. One investigator even posed as a real-estate specialist, to conceal his identity from Levin's acquaintances.

Investigators found that Levin had dealings with one Moe Morton, depicted at the hearings as an associate of organized crime figures. Levin, it seems, was part of a group that bought a 50% interest in Acapulco Towers, a luxury apartment-hotel in the Mexico resort town, from a Morton associate. Morton, who managed the building, owned the remaining 50%.

Gangster Meyer Lansky had hidden in Acapulco Towers to escape police surveillance, and Chicago Mafia chief Sam Giancana paid a visit to Moe Morton's yacht in Acapulco, state investigators reported. Levin told the board he'd been completely unaware of Moe Morton's alleged underworld ties.

Levin hadn't done anything illegal. Still, why didn't he investigate Morton's background before investing in Acapulco Towers? It raised questions about Levin's judgment.

Levin took a verbal beating from the racing board for his 9% stock ownership of Parvin-Dohrmann Co., which operated a Las Vegas gambling casino and had been accused by the Securities and Exchange Commission of stock rigging and falsifying reports to shareholders.

Levin had tried to get Bluhdorn to buy Parvin-Dohrmann for Gulf & Western, but Bluhdorn, wanting no part of gambling casinos, said no. Levin then dumped the stock, clearing the way for his appointment as president of Madison Square Garden.

We'd be landing in Chicago in a few minutes. The interview had gone nicely. If my questions got under Levin's skin, he didn't show it. His attitude seemed to be: Write what you want to, I'll survive it.

But then I brought up Angelo (Gyp) DeCarlo, a thug in the Sam DeCavalcante New Jersey crime family, and Levin's mood darkened. DeCarlo was then doing time in prison for extortion.

At the racing hearings, evidence was produced that 36 phone calls were made from DeCarlo's New Jersey home to Levin's home in New Jersey in 1967. In 1969, Levin's home made two phone calls to DeCarlo's home.

Levin testified that DeCarlo's son, Lee, and Levin's son, Adam, made all the calls. The boys, he testified, played in the same dance band, and attended the same private school in Plainfield, N.J.

I asked Levin, Was he ever involved with DeCarlo?

Levin said never.

He reminded me he had testified that DeCarlo belonged to a New Jersey country club that Levin bought. Levin converted it into an all-Jewish club, and DeCarlo, who wasn't Jewish, was forced out.

I took all this down.

"Are you going to use the DeCarlo stuff?" Levin asked casually.

"Oh, I may," I said, knowing full well I would.

"Why?" Levin said. "The phone calls didn't involve me. They were between the kids."

43

"Well, it's still part of the public record," I said.

"I don't see where it helps your story any."

I didn't reply, hoping he'd drop the matter.

Levin said insistently, "I'm asking a favor. I don't care if you mention me in connection with Moe Morton, or anyone else. But leave DeCarlo out of it. I don't want my son mixed up in it."

"It's in the public record, Phil."

"Fuck the public record! Nobody is gonna remember my kid was mentioned in the hearings, but the whole country will know about it if you print it in The Wall Street Journal."

"I can't see why you're so upset. I'll quote your testimony that the kids made the calls."

Levin gave me an icy stare.

"I don't want my kid in it."

If I left out DeCarlo, I'd be shading the piece to suit Levin. I'd be his accomplice.

"What about it?" Levin demanded.

"You're not being fair."

"Which means you're gonna use it."

"I want to think about it," I said.

"Yeah, you do that," Levin said with sarcasm.

I wrote the story, including the phone calls between Levin's and DeCarlo's kids, and gave it to the editor. I had not yet phoned Illinois Gov. Richard Ogilvie or racing chairman MacArthur for their comments. I would wait till the last minute before springing the story on them, hoping it wouldn't leave them enough time to weaken the impact of the piece by denouncing it at a press conference before it was published.

When I called MacArthur, he stoutly maintained he hadn't any knowledge of political contributions, and hadn't been pressured by Gov. Ogilvie or anyone to revoke Levin's license. "The governor is as square as a box," said MacArthur. "Everything is black and white to him. He is a non-meddler. The only instructions I ever received were, 'Sail the ship, captain.'... There has never been any politics that have come into it."

Gov. Ogilvie said MacArthur had his complete trust. "I had no conversations whatsoever with MacArthur about the Levin matter... I have no knowledge of any contributions Levin may have made to anyone."

The story's headline:

Politics & Business

Contributions by Firm
To Illinois GOP Follow
Helpful Racing Ruling

———

Company Run by Phil Levin,
Allowed to Operate Tracks,
Gives the Party $100,000

———

Officials Deny a Connection

———

I never heard from Levin. Seven weeks later, in August 1971, He died of a heart attack in his suite at the Pierre. He was 62. Bluhdorn was 56 when he died of a heart attack in 1983. He was on a G & W jet, returning from a business trip to the Dominican Republic. (The story is on page 142.)

CHAPTER 6

"THE CHOSEN ONE"

I N A **1989** NEW YORKER magazine essay that produced a stir in the journalism world, writer Janet Malcolm accused reporters and book writers of resorting to deception to get interviews. "Every journalist who is not too stupid or too full of himself to notice what is going on knows that what he does is morally indefensible," Malcolm charged.

As Malcolm told it, the wily reporter dupes the subject of the article into believing he'll be treated with sympathy and fairness, only to depict him as a scoundrel or fool. Malcolm depicted journalists as "confidence" men, preying on the "vanity, ignorance or loneliness" of their subjects, "gaining their trust and betraying them without remorse."

What Malcolm says has a certain plausibility. Sometimes, I'd be turned down for interviews, with the explanation that, while the subject of the story had nothing against me personally, he or she felt a general distrust of reporters.

Investigative reporters probably get rebuffed more than any other group of reporters. A person who's accused or suspected of a crime often believes his problem will only be made worse if he agrees to an interview that leads to an article discussing his controversial actions. The individual tells himself he doesn't want to be the victim of a hatchet job. To him, the reporter is the enemy.

Yet, persons suspected of wrongdoing frequently give press interviews. Why? Is it because they're dumb? If Malcolm is correct, the subject has been tricked into it by the reporter and the article, or book, turns out to be far different from the sympathetic account promised by the journalist when he begged for the interview.

Without a doubt, pressure on the reporter to get an interview is enormous. An editor may refuse to publish the piece unless the central figure is interviewed. Who can blame the editor? An interview with the subject enlivens the story, turning the figure into flesh-and-blood. Moreover, without the subject's version of events, the piece may end up looking one-sided.

This brings me to Keith Gordon. Unless I could interview him, I'd have no front-page story.

Gordon—known to his followers as "Brother Gordon," and "The Chosen One"—was a charismatic figure, who headed the Ethiopian Zion Coptic Church, a branch of the Rastafarian cult, based in Jamaica. The church operated a commune in the hills overlooking the Caribbean at the southeast end of the island. This church was different from your basic, everyday place of worship.

To Jamaican Coptics, ganja (Jamaican for marijuana) was a religious sacrament. It was smoked at church services by parents and children alike. The child was permitted by the parent to draw on a marijuana cigarette as a reward for good behavior. Coptic women, during their menstrual period, were segregated in separate quarters, forbidden by the elders to prepare food or smoke marijuana. The church had 100 priests and 2,000 followers, mostly poor black Jamaicans.

According to my information, the Jamaican Coptic church was a front for a large marijuana smuggling ring, headed by Keith Gordon. The gang had smuggled nearly one million pounds of marijuana into the U.S. in a six-year period. It owned a fleet of ships. It was one of Jamaica's largest landowners. It also had property in Florida, Georgia, Iowa, Maine and Massachusetts, as well as 7,000 acres of prime agricultural land in Colombia. Brother Gordon's chief aides were white American hippies. The gang seemed to live a charmed life. Jamaican authorities were unable to shut them down.

Proving the church was a cover for drug smugglers would be no problem. I had a document from the U.S. Drug Enforcement Administration saying that Gordon derived his income from marijuana growing and smuggling, plus some legitimate enterprises. Most of his wealth, according to the DEA, was invested in banks in the Cayman Islands, where his firm, Coptic Enterprises, was registered.

Nor would I have any problem proving to my editor this could be a significant story.

Jamaica had become a major marijuana supplier to the U.S., in part because of Gordon's organization. Illicit marijuana was Jamaica's fastest growing export, helping keep the failing economy afloat. Marijuana was destabilizing the Jamaican government, according to the DEA. The island was laced with secret, illegal air strips. Local police were paid off, and armed drug traffickers came and went with impunity. The government hadn't any radar to spot traffickers' planes, and only two police helicopters were in working order at a given time. The Jamaican government was so broke, it didn't even have a truck to take confiscated marijuana to court as evidence.

My problem would be to induce the Ethiopian Zion Coptic Church to let me interview "The Chosen One."

Think about it: Why should Keith Gordon—an accused big-time marijuana smuggler—grant me an audience? A piece in The Wall Street Journal would do him no good. It might conceivably put pressure on the Jamaican government to crack down on his drug-smuggling gang. Giving me an interview would seem to be against Gordon's own best interests. And from all I heard, this slippery ex-convict was nobody's fool.

My editor had given me the green light to go ahead, after assurances from me that I could obtain an interview with the gang leader, and that I'd provide an on-the-spot look at the marijuana-smoking commune. I knew what the consequences would be if I failed to deliver. The editor might kill the piece. Or, if it lacked an interview with Gordon, the piece might be slashed and buried inside the paper. That mustn't happen! I was paid to do page one stories.

I also knew if I failed to deliver what I promised, I could get a reputation on the paper as untrustworthy.

When I did an out-of-town story, my procedure was to line up key interviews before leaving New York. This was to avoid the risk of being turned down after I reached my destination. This time, I couldn't line up the interview. As hard as I tried, I couldn't get through to Coptic officials in Jamaica. A Jamaican lawman, reached by phone in Kingston, the capital, told me Gordon was an elusive figure, who hated the press. A DEA agent in Kingston said on the phone that a reporter for an American newsmagazine had tried to sneak into the mountain commune, only to be discovered by guards and kicked out.

At the time, nine Ethiopian Zion Coptic members were on trial in federal court in Miami on marijuana-conspiracy charges. Gordon, one of those indicted, had failed to show up. The defendants' lawyers probably wouldn't permit me to interview the defendants. But maybe they'd be good enough to tell me how to get in touch with Brother Gordon. I flew to Miami.

A Miami-based Coptic group had caused a big hullabaloo. Its headquarters was a $400,000 mansion on Star Island—a posh residential section in Miami Beach. Residents in the neighborhood were demanding that city authorities shut the church down, claiming it was a bad influence. Local TV had shown Coptic kids smoking ganja at prayer meetings.

Observing the courtroom proceedings was Brother Louv (pronounced love) head of the Miami Beach branch. Louv, formerly Thomas F. Reilly, a six-foot, seven-inch, college-educated Bostonian, wore a floor-length green robe, signifying he was an elder in Gordon's church.

I went up to him, identified myself, and asked how could I find Keith Gordon.

He gave me a sour look. "Why don't you leave us alone?" Brother Louv said. "We don't bother anybody."

I said blandly that I just wanted to interview him.

"You're interested in marijuana," Brother Louv accused. "We're not in the business of selling marijuana. The Justice Department and DEA are liars. They should be investigated, not us."

Did he have Mr. Gordon's phone number? I persisted.

"Talk to him," Brother Louv snapped, pointing to a defense lawyer nearby.

The lawyer said Gordon didn't want to have anything to do with the press.

"I'm not taking sides," I said. "I want to do an objective story."

The lawyer replied with sarcasm, "I'm sure Gordon has heard that before." Then: "Why don't you write about what the Coptic church is doing to feed the poor? If not for the church, a lot of them there would starve."

"I might put that in," I said reasonably, "if I can get an interview."

"Since when is the Journal interested in poor people in Jamaica?"

"If it fits into my story, I'm interested."

Grudgingly, the lawyer said, "You might give Peggy Cooke a call in Kingston. But I don't promise anything."

"Who's she?"

"She's a Jamaican Coptic—Gordon's personal assistant." The lawyer gave me her phone number.

I flew to Kingston. Heat, humidity and blinding sunlight hit me when I got off the plane. Kingston is supposed to be a scenic town. A travel brochure said I mustn't miss the Prime Minister's official residence, depicted as a lovely old building in a courtyard overflowing with colorful bougainvillea.

The Kingston I saw in the taxi ride to the hotel was a slum: shabby, cinder block houses with corrugated tin roofs; narrow, broken sidewalks; abandoned shops, mangy dogs roaming the streets. The reggae music was deafening.

Except for employees, the hotel lobby was empty. This didn't surprise me. Repeated articles in the U.S. press about muggings had cut sharply into the tourist business. During a national election only eight months previous, street violence left 750 Jamaicans dead from shootings and knifings.

The bellhop who showed me to my room warned me not to go out at night by myself. I shouldn't open my room door unless I knew who it was. I should store my valuables in the hotel safe.

"Maybe I should get a bodyguard," I kidded.

I couldn't get Peggy Cooke on the phone, so I went to the bar. It had one customer. I sat down next to him at the counter.

"Am I glad to see another face," the man said.

He was from Chicago—an industrial equipment salesman. He hadn't written a single order. "It was dumb to come," he said. "This place is going down the tubes."

He asked what I did. When I told him, he leaned toward me, making sure he couldn't be overheard, and said he had a scoop for me.

"Businessmen and professionals are leaving in droves," he confided. "They take whatever they can, load up their pleasure boats, and it's Miami, here we come."

I said I didn't realize things were that bad.

The salesman said: "The only ones left will be the poor and the dope dealers."

I had dinner with him. It was a mistake. He didn't stop bad-mouthing Jamaica. First thing tomorrow, he promised, he was leaving the island, and never coming back. I shouldn't hang around too long either, he warned.

Later that evening, I got Peggy Cooke on the phone. She sounded breathless. She'd been running around all day, she said, and just got home. Yes, she'd been expecting my call. Her "Miami people," as she put it, had told her all about me.

"How can I help you, Mr. Penn?"

Now came the hard part.

If Janet Malcolm was correct—that reporters employ deceit to get interviews—my pitch would be:

"Miss Cooke, I want to write about your church. I think it would make a terrific story. I hadn't any idea till I talked to your Miami people about the wonderful things you folks are doing for the poor. You not only feed them, but employ them. People say if not for your church, the Jamaican economy would fall on its face. I want to tell my readers that. That's why I'd love to interview Mr. Gordon. I hear he's an incredible person. The Ethiopian Zion Coptic Church is doing one heck of a job, and deserves recognition. I don't have to tell you that The Wall Street Journal has a lot of wealthy readers. I'm not promising anything, Miss Cooke, but I wouldn't be surprised that when my story appears, your church will be flooded with cash contributions from America."

Public relations was Peggy Cooke's business. She wouldn't swallow such crap. Only a numskull would believe I came from New York to write a puff piece.

Instead, this is what I said:

"I'm not going to try to fool you. Lawmen I talked to—here and in Washington—all say the church is involved in marijuana smuggling. I know what your answer is, that it's a bunch of lies. Here's your chance to give the church's side. I want to do a fair, objective story, which I know you want also. If you tell me that every time the Jamaican press does a story on the church, it comes out twisted, I can only say, the Journal will treat you fairly. We don't sensationalize. We're even accused of being a little dull. I've never been accused of slanting a story. It's up to you. I've heard one version about the church from the law. I'm going to print it. But, to be fair to you, I want your side. If you ask Mr. Gordon, I'm sure he can spare a few minutes. And I want to see the commune, which I've heard so much about. Can we get together tomorrow morning?"

Cooke said she didn't doubt I'd be fair-minded. Though she didn't read The Wall Street Journal—her busy schedule simply didn't allow for it— she'd heard good things about the paper from her Miami people.

But certain facts had to be faced, she said. Elements in the press, according to Cooke, were bent on destroying the Jamaican Coptic church. Vicious lies had been spread. It was absolutely untrue that the church was smuggling marijuana. The press—not The Wall Street Journal, mind you—could be very devious. Was I aware that a female reporter from an American magazine tried to sneak into the commune to spy? The reporter could have been arrested for trespassing. Instead, she was removed—with a warning never to try such a stunt again.

Is this how the U.S. press gets its stories? Miss Cooke asked indignantly.

"I would never try to sneak in," I assured her.

"I know, I know," Cooke said. "I can tell from your voice you're not that kind of person, Mr. Penn. I don't deny there are decent journalists. But it's so hard to tell the good from the bad."

Cooke agreed to take a chance on me. Despite her tight schedule, she would fit me in. I should be ready at 10 a.m. tomorrow.

Next morning, Cooke pulled up in a white Honda. She was attractive, smartly dressed, with an exuberant manner.

First stop was the commune. We left Kingston, heading east on the coastal road. The Caribbean, with a black freighter on the horizon, was on my right. On my left were small factories, run-down dwellings, empty fields and burning garbage dumps. Junked cars rusted on the roadside. Bauxite dust from the nearby mines spread a yellow haze across the highway.

Cooke asked, "How old do I look to you?"

She looked to me to be in her mid-30s.

"Twenty-nine," I said.

She laughed. "I'm 42."

"I don't believe it," I said.

"It's because we take such good care of ourselves."

"What do you do?"

"We eat no artificial seasoning," Cooke said. "No ketchup, and no canned foods."

I asked what she did before she worked for Gordon.

She'd been in real-estate sales, but found it unrewarding. Cooke said her life took on new meaning when she joined the church.

Had she been able to line up an interview for me with Mr. Gordon?

She said she was doing everything in her power to set it up. Problem was, Brother Gordon was so busy. He went nonstop, hardly getting any sleep.

Cooke told me about the church's legitimate businesses. There was an auto parts company, a furniture store and a supermarket. The DEA had told me the church operated a fleet of ships. Cooke didn't mention that.

The car had a private radio hookup. From time to time, Cooke barked orders to aides into a transmitter. Her code name was "Pentagon."

Apologizing for this distraction, she explained the church was introducing a new kind of cookie, and that she had to see that everything went off without a hitch. The cookie was made from coconuts that grew in the commune. Thus far, the new cookies had been very favorably received. If I wished, Cooke said, I could mention the cookies in my article. She offered me another scoop: The Coptic church was attempting to find a commercial use for coconut husks, possibly as fiber for stuffing mattresses and upholstery in car seats.

I wrote all this down.

We passed the villages of Wickie Wackie, Grants Pen and Poor Mans

Corner. At Four Villages, we made a left at an intersection, driving up into the hills. There was a stillness in the air. Soon we came to a fenced-in enclosure. A sign on a high metal gate declared: "Righteousness endureth forever." We'd reached the commune.

A guard unlocked the gate, and silently motioned us in. We drove a short distance on a bumpy dirt road to a large clearing, where there were farmhouses, a meeting hall, a generator for electricity and a water tank. Dominating the landscape was a cone-shaped tabernacle. Beyond the clearing were vegetable fields and orchards.

I wondered if this was where the marijuana was grown.

On the front porch of a farmhouse sat four church members with beards and long scraggly hair. They inhaled ganja from a long-stemmed pipe that was passed from mouth to mouth. They watched impassively as I got out of the car and stretched my arms to get the kinks out.

I headed for the porch, intending to interview them.

"Come back!" Cooke ordered.

She said I mustn't disturb them. She would take me to the "elder," who would answer all my questions.

Foolishly, I'd neglected to inform the U.S. Embassy, or the DEA office in Kingston, of my whereabouts. Aside from Cooke, nobody knew I was here.

The "elder" was an unsmiling, bearded white man, who looked to be in his 30s. He asked where I lived.

"Manhattan," I said.

"Where?"

"The Upper West Side."

"I used to live there," the elder said. He had hated it. Making money was all anybody in New York cared about. He had quit his publishing job, come to Jamaica and never regretted it.

I said I found it a little too quiet for my taste.

"I would never leave," the elder said, as if I'd questioned his loyalty to the Coptics.

He showed me around. Cooke trailed behind.

"The commune has 3,000 acres," the elder said. "There was just wilderness when we came here. Now we grow pumpkins, peanuts, ginger and coconuts.

I said I was impressed.

"Besides our own people, we employ up to 1,200 workers who come from surrounding villages," the elder added.

He pointed to a cluster of banana trees and a scallion patch and said: "We don't hurt anyone. We don't beg. We practice self-reliance and self-control. Everything we eat is fresh."

Then he pointed to the deep blue Caribbean, which could be seen in the distance. "If we want fish," he intoned, "we drop a line and get fish."

I asked if the church grew marijuana here.

He replied blandly, "Anywhere you drop a seed, it grows. Ganja is a tree that comes out of the earth. Ganja is no crime. We don't break any of God's laws. Ganja is a herb, not a drug."

"Is it grown here?" I repeated.

"The church does not traffic in marijuana."

"Do you grow it?" I persisted.

He didn't answer. Instead, he said he had a lot of work ahead of him. To Cooke, he nodded goodbye, and strode off.

"He didn't answer my question," I said.

Cooke asked if I was hungry. I said no.

Two young white women in granny dresses and scarves on their heads were chatting in front of the tabernacle. One woman held the hand of a small girl, who also wore a granny dress and scarf. They looked as though they belonged in the 17th century.

I walked up to them. The women smiled demurely at me.

"You live here?" I asked.

They glanced at Cooke, who said it was OK to answer.

"Yes, we do," the taller one said.

"Do you like it here?"

"We love it," she said.

The smaller woman said emphatically, "We would never leave. We have everything we need."

"You don't miss the U.S.?"

They shook their heads no.

"Do the children get any schooling?" I asked.

"Everything they need is right here," the tall one said.

"Tell me, is marijuana grown here?"

Cooke broke in, "Mr. Penn, that's not fair. If you're finished we should go."

On the way back, I asked how the church justified giving ganja to children.

Cooke sighed. "Outsiders always ask that," she said. "Don't you know, ganja is a herb, a natural thing. We see it as something holy. Did you know we use it as preventive medicine? It's good for fever and chest colds. A child with an arthritic condition—ganja gets rid of it."

She said Coptics boil ganja in milk. "They use it in honey. "They make tea with it. Ganja is a way of life,"

"The government says ganja is illegal," I noted.

"The government," she said disdainfully. "Ganja was created by God. God is not wrong. It's blasphemous to tell God he is wrong."

We reached Kingston. She drove me to her house, which was in an upper-income section. She had an outdoor swimming pool and a two-car garage. The house was spacious, with high ceilings. I wanted to ask what her salary was, but worried it would antagonize her.

Cooke disappeared into her bedroom. She reappeared in a navy evening gown, with a scarf on her head. Dinner would be served soon. Her cook—a former chef at a luxury Kingston hotel, she said—was preparing steak.

While we waited in the dining room, she switched on the TV set. I sat through a 20-minute film showing Coptics at a prayer service in the tabernacle at the commune. When it was over, she went into the kitchen, returning with the steaks.

I picked at it, wondering if it was seasoned with marijuana.

Why wasn't I eating? she asked.

"My stomach's been upset the past few days," I lied.

"I'll get you tea." She sounded concerned.

Thinking the tea might have marijuana in it, I said, "I'd rather not take anything, thanks."

She looked offended, but didn't say anything.

Dusk was setting. I asked if my interview with Gordon was set.

Not quite, she said. She was waiting for a phone call. He'd been in meetings all day.

"He must work very hard," I said.

"Heads of huge corporations don't work as hard," Cooke insisted.

"Why doesn't he try to slow down?"

"People keep telling him that," Cooke said. "But he has so much to do. We worry about him."

The phone rang. Cooke was beaming when she put down the receiver. Brother Gordon would see me.

Unfortunately, Cooke said, she couldn't join me. A problem involving the coconut cookies had come up that had to be handled tonight.

I didn't like that. It could mean Gordon ordered her not to join me. If so, why? I wanted her with me. To me, she served as a kind of security blanket. A Jamaican police officer had told me that Gordon was a heavy ganja user, that he flew into tantrums when he got riled up. Early in his career, Gordon did a six-month jail sentence at hard labor for marijuana possession.

A car pulled up at Cooke's house. I got in and said goodbye. Cooke said she hoped I would get a good interview, and that she looked forward to reading my article.

It was dark when we reached Gordon's large, hilltop house on a quiet street overlooking Kingston. A woman met me at the front door. She led me silently to a dimly lit outdoor patio in the back.

Gordon and two aides were seated at a long, rectangular table. They smoked ganja from a pipe they shared. It was a hot sticky night.

The 49-year-old Gordon was a short, slight figure with a fierce expression. He motioned to me to sit down. His aides watched warily as I put my notebook on the table.

"You came to ask about marijuana?" Gordon said.

"I did."

"The U.S. government can never rid the world of marijuana," he said in a gravelly voice. "God makes ganja. Before the U.S., there was ganja. After the U.S., there will be ganja."

He fell silent. "Anything else?" he asked.

"How many Jamaican Coptics are there?"

The question seemed to upset him. I wondered if he thought I'd been sent by the CIA to spy on him.

His eyes blazing, he said, "Would you attempt to count all the sand in the sea?"

I asked what he thought of the U.S. government's contention that his church smuggled marijuana into the U.S.

"The government is a liar!"

He inhaled deeply on his ganja pipe. His face was contorted with anger. Was I getting on his nerves?

One of his aides said contemptuously, "This is the same government that gave us Richard Nixon, Agnew and Watergate. Can you believe anything it says?"

Gordon had closed his eyes. He seemed far away.

I asked him how he got started in his career.

No answer.

"He came from the people," his aide said. "He began by selling peanuts in the street. Then he sold food in a restaurant."

More silence.

The aide said Brother Gordon was very tired, that Brother Gordon hoped he'd been able to answer all my questions, and that Brother Gordon wished me a safe journey back to New York. A Coptic driver took me to my hotel.

The article was titled:

Smoke Screen?

To Jamaican Coptics Marijuana Use Is a Rite; To Police, It's a Wrong

---

U. S. Agency Says the Church
Is a Cover for Smuggling;
Its Leader Denies Charge

Much Ganja but No Ketchup

Peggy Cooke's coconut cookies—and the church's efforts to develop a commercial use for coconut husks—were in the piece, reprinted on page 145.

CHAPTER 7

SAY IT AIN'T SO, MR. BUCKLEY

IF NOT FOR **"DEEP THROAT,"** Washington Post reporters Bob Woodward and Carl Bernstein might not have broken the story on the Watergate cover-up—the scandal that forced Richard Nixon out of the White House.

Just like in a John Le Carre spy novel, Woodward met secretly with "Deep Throat" in underground garages. They employed code words. Woodward's flowerpot, with a red flag in it, was used to arrange meetings. When the pot was placed in a particular spot on Woodward's balcony, that meant there should be a meeting that night at 2 a.m. On his way to the meeting, Woodward has said he switched taxis at least twice to shake off Nixon's gumshoes. It was all very cloak and dagger.

"Deep Throat" drank scotch. He was a heavy smoker. That much we know. But who was he? Henry Kissinger maybe? Nixon's barber? Woodward has never said.

I had a "Deep Throat" once. We didn't meet in the dead of night, and I never used a flowerpot. We never resorted to code names or disguises. And I don't know what he looks like, since we never met face to face.

My "Deep Throat" was a Securities and Exchange Commission lawyer in Washington. He was in the section that investigates sleazy corporations suspected by the SEC of swindling the investing public. The SEC investigates as many as 200 companies a year. The SEC generally doesn't identify publicly companies it investigates unless it leads to a formal charge of wrongdoing.

From time to time, "Deep Throat" tipped me off about SEC investigations, which is how I learned about the shenanigans of William F. Buckley Jr., the snooty, right-wing intellectual.

Buckley is credited by many for reviving conservatism as a powerful force in America. But he had another side that was kept hidden until "Deep Throat" showed me where to look.

I came upon "Deep Throat" by chance. It began when I phoned the SEC public relations department for information. The PR man couldn't answer my question, but gave me to a lawyer in the enforcement section, who told me what I wanted to know.

I asked the lawyer did he mind if I called again if I ever needed an arcane SEC rule explained. He said sure. The upshot was that we became chummy over the phone.

He mentioned, for example, that the SEC was badly understaffed.

Congress gave the Federal Bureau of Investigation whatever it wanted, he complained, but starved the SEC. For every company the SEC investigated, he said, many companies were overlooked because of a lack of investigators.

I mentioned the SEC policy of not publicly disclosing investigations until charges were filed. However, I noted, companies targeted by the SEC often made such disclosures in their public filings. Problem was, reporters often didn't read the filings. Unless it was called to a reporter's attention, he wouldn't be aware that the company filing said it was being investigated by the SEC.

This was what I asked the SEC lawyer: If, when a juicy investigation turned up in a public filing, could he alert me?

This wasn't, I felt, an improper request. I was simply asking him to call my attention to information already made public by a company in its filing to the SEC.

He said he'd see what he could do.

Companies whose shares are publicly traded are required by the SEC to make full disclosure. The same applies to corporate insiders. Those found to have violated SEC law face civil injunctions, cash fines and suspensions. The worst cases are turned over to the U.S. Justice Department. Indictments, convictions and prison sentences against offenders may result.

The SEC has struck down some of the nation's most notorious manipulators. In 1972, Robert Vesco was accused by the SEC of looting IOS Ltd., a now defunct mutual fund company, of $224 million. He has been a fugitive ever since.

SEC investigations paved the way for criminal convictions, and jailings, of junk bond king Michael Milken, and Ivan (the Terrible) Boesky, former high priest of Wall Street manipulators.

The way the SEC works, it informs a company if it is under investigation for securities violations. The company decides if it considers the investigation important enough to inform shareholders. If it chooses not to make disclosure, the company can be vulnerable to damage suits by shareholders charging vital information was withheld from them.

So most companies make a public disclosure. But they don't call a press conference. Nor do they issue a press release. They bury it in their SEC filings. Why are they sneaky about it? They don't want to call attention to the fact they are suspected by the SEC of falsely inflating profits, deliberately underreporting losses, or other acts of wrongdoing. The share-price can nosedive from such publicity. No company official wants neighbors to read in the paper he is being accused by the SEC of conspiring to defraud the investing public.

Publicly held companies are required by law to file all pertinent information with the SEC. Reproduced on microfiche, the filings may be read by anyone in SEC public reference rooms. So a company that says in its public filing that it is under SEC investigation can insist—truthfully—that it hasn't withheld information.

But, alas, most investors—and many in the press, for that matter—rarely pore over company filings in SEC reference rooms. This means that SEC investigations mentioned in the filings may go unreported by the press.

A filing is packed with financial data. The tiny, single-spaced print can numb the eye. I know. I read dozens and dozens of them. They rarely feature a table of contents. Some filings may exceed a hundred pages. In reading them, I'd find it hard to keep awake. It was easy, therefore, to overlook a reference in the report to an SEC investigation.

"What's going on I should know about it?" I asked "Deep Throat" one time.

"Do you care for Beethoven?" the SEC lawyer asked.

"Was he a crook?"

"Seriously, do you like classical music?"

"Yeah."

"Do you ever listen to WNCN-FM in New York?"

"Occasionally."

He said Starr Broadcasting had owned it.

"Do I care?"

"You might find Starr interesting."

"Why?"

"Do you want me to write the story for you?"

I hustled over to the SEC office in downtown Manhattan. I pulled the file on Starr Broadcasting Group Inc., Westport, Conn.

After a half hour of peering into the microfiche machine, I found what I was looking for. Page 11, of a 10K report, dated December 1976, bottom paragraph, said:

"In August 1976, the SEC began a private investigation into possible violations of disclosure and other provisions of the federal securities laws."

Starr was a small, obscure company. A civil investigation of Starr wasn't exactly a hot story. It was worth eight paragraphs at most. I might not even get a byline for the story. Why am I wasting time with Starr Broadcasting?

It operated three pizza shops, 12 Texas outdoor movie theaters, and some radio-TV stations. Starr was in terrible financial shape. In the two preceding years, its combined loss totaled $7 million. The company was in default on part of its $25 million long-term debt. To raise cash, it had been forced to unload some broadcasting outlets, including WNCN-FM.

Yet Starr grabbed my attention. William Buckley—columnist, author, TV talk show host, publisher of the National Review magazine, lecturer, as well as one-time candidate for New York City mayor—was chairman of Starr and its biggest shareholder.

Buckley reminded me of a famous Picasso painting in Manhattan's Museum of Modern Art. The cubist picture showed a woman looking at herself in a mirror, but she bore no resemblance to her image.

Buckley was an eminent conservative theoretician, of high moral rectitude, deeply absorbed in the issues of the day. Yet Buckley was being investigated by the SEC for allegedly masterminding a fraud to benefit himself and a few close associates at the expense of Starr Broadcasting's public shareholders.

Buckley was an engaging figure. He had charm, wit, an aristocratic manner, a way with words. In 1965, as the unsuccessful Conservative Party candidate in the New York mayoralty race, he was asked by a reporter if he felt he had any chance of winning.

"No," said Buckley.

"Conservatively speaking," he was asked, how many votes did Buckley expect to get?

"Conservatively speaking, one."

What would Buckley do if elected?

"Demand a recount," Buckley said wryly.

A Wall Street Journal piece on Buckley, it seemed to me, would have considerable appeal. He was a celebrity. Yet few people knew he was being investigated for financial skulduggery. This was a Jekyll and Hyde story.

I didn't care for Buckley. His longtime hero was Joe McCarthy, the late Wisconsin Senator, who believed the federal government was infiltrated by Communist spies. Using the big lie, McCarthy destroyed people's careers. He'd been censured by the Senate for disreputable conduct in 1954. In my opinion, McCarthy was a political thug. I couldn't respect anyone who admired McCarthy.

In a 1954 book, "McCarthy and his Enemies," Buckley and co-author L. Brent Bozell, defended McCarthy as a bulwark against Communist subversion. "McCarthyism is a program of action...a movement around which men of goodwill and stern morality can close ranks," Buckley and Bozell wrote.

This raised a question: Given my dislike for Buckley, could I be fair? I felt I could. As a professional newsman, I wouldn't let my feelings color the article.

Moreover, all the key stuff would be drawn from Starr's filings with the SEC, as well as a shareholders' suit. I'd be darn sure not to overlook any relevant fact placing Buckley in a favorable light. And, of course, I would try to sit down with the guy to get his side.

The SEC investigation concerned Starr's purchase of a bunch of outdoor theaters in Texas. At one time, Buckley had been part owner of them.

I could picture the aristocratic, intellectual Buckley as publisher, say, of the Greek-Roman classics. I could see him as a manufacturer of harpsichords, or builder of sleek, ocean-going boats. But owner of drive-ins? It didn't fit his image.

Through a partnership, Buckley and three associates had purchased the drive-ins for $7.7 million, using mostly borrowed money. Buckley may have believed drive-ins were the wave of the future. Unfortunately for him, his investment proved to be a disaster.

A year after the purchase, the drive-ins were in the red. They were $8 million in debt. Interest payments on the debt were $100,000 a month. Buckley and his partners had personally guaranteed the loans. The massive debt must have weighed heavily on Buckley. It could mean financial ruin if a way couldn't be found to bail out him and his partners.

Publicly held Starr Broadcasting—the company Buckley headed—came to his rescue. Starr, justifying its action on the ground the ailing drive-ins were an attractive investment, bought them for $8.6 million. Thus, the personal debt that threatened to bring grief to Buckley had been dumped on Starr.

In reading Starr's filings, it looked to me like Starr paid far too much. When Starr agreed to buy them, the drive-ins had been appraised at $8.3 million. After the purchase, the same properties were valued—by a different appraiser—at $5 million, some $3.3 million below the original estimate. Eighteen months after the purchase, the Starr subsidiary that had acquired the drive-ins filed bankruptcy proceedings.

The SEC investigation appeared to have been triggered by a shareholders' suit. The complaint, filed in a New Orleans federal court by Paul and Jacqueline Solomon, two of Starr's 1,600 public shareholders, charged that Starr, by acquiring the drive-ins, misused its funds for Buckley's benefit and to the shareholders' detriment.

If I had been able to interview Buckley, I would have said, "Mr. Buckley, I've read Starr's filings with the SEC. It looks like the reason Starr bought the financially hard-up drive-ins was to save you from personal bankruptcy. Is that a fair reading, or is there something I don't understand?"

Through his secretary, Buckley said he was too busy to see me.

Here is the headline; story is on page 149.

Ill-Starred Venture

Holders' Suit Charges Buckley Misused Funds Of Starr Broadcasting.

It Says He, 3 Others Sold
To Firm Ailing Theaters
They Owned in Texas

A Friend Terms Him Naive

After the story appeared, Buckley rushed to defend himself. In a letter to the Journal, he said he didn't do anything wrong. He claimed to have been an onlooker in the purchase, having had "no role in structuring the details, or even the terms of the transfer." Buckley portrayed himself as being ignorant of corporate balance sheets. Furthermore, he didn't engage in a conflict of interest, because only "uninvolved directors" voted on the transaction, said Buckley.

In my article, a Buckley friend was quoted as saying that Buckley played only a "passive" role in the drive-in transaction. "The worst you can accuse him of," the friend said, "is naivete as to what was going on."

Was that true? In matters of high finance, was Buckley a mere babe in the woods? Buckley's chief interests were literature, politics, God and church. Perhaps, the intricacies of the balance sheet were beyond his grasp.

Later, a front-page piece by Wall Street Journal reporter June Kronholz shattered the impression fostered by Buckley and his friends that he hadn't any involvement whatsoever in Starr's purchase of the drive-ins. Kronholz, drawing on Buckley's business correspondence—and other documents that had become available since the appearance of my article 17 months earlier—made clear that Buckley took an active role in Starr's purchase of the drive-ins.

A Buckley memo indicated that, as an owner of the drive-ins, he carefully planned the sale of the drive-ins to Starr because he realized, according to his memo, "there was an imminent possibility I might be bankrupt."

Indeed, Buckley had the chutzpah to assure Starr's board of directors that the drive-ins were a good investment—"an attractive package," in his words—even though the theaters were losing $700,000 a year, and the Buckley partnership was behind on its interest payments, according to Kronholz's article.

Buckley, who had given Kronholz an interview, dashed off a letter to the Journal after her piece appeared. Written from Singapore, Buckley promised to rebut the charges at a future date.

In the letter, he said: "Meanwhile, if you care to have the local news, the headline on page 2 of this morning's Straits Times is: 'Woman raped twice/by monkey in Jakarta.' I know just how the woman feels."

The SEC came down hard on Buckley. In a 56-page civil complaint in 1979, Buckley, and others, were charged with violating the federal securities laws by fraudulently failing to make adequate public disclosure to Starr's shareholders about the purchase of the drive-ins. Starr failed to disclose that the "primary purpose of the transaction was to protect" Buckley and his partners "from personal bankruptcy," the complaint charged.

The fraud accusation stung. "Buckley had never been so upset in his life," wrote author John Judis, in "William F. Buckley Jr.," a 1988 biography.

In a consent decree, Buckley, while not admitting any wrongdoing, agreed to make a $1.4 million restitution payment. Also, he agreed not to join a public company as officer or director for five years. He resigned as chairman of Starr, vowing never again to serve on the board of a publicly held company—"given what I now know about the technical responsibilities of a director."

My source at the SEC later joined a private law firm. I lost touch with him. It would be ironic if his working days were being spent in protecting corporate clients against zealous SEC investigators.

CHAPTER 8

MAFIA LOCAL 560

JOEL JACOBSON, a former New Jersey AFL-CIO leader, seemed the right choice to be court-appointed trustee of Teamster Local 560, the notorious Mafia-dominated union in Union City, N.J. By all accounts, the 68-year-old Jacobson was incorruptible, intelligent, a hard worker and down to earth.

A one-time labor organizer of the International Ladies Garment Workers Union, he talked the rank and file's language. He grew up in Newark during the Great Depression and knew firsthand what poverty was. "I had little to eat and I saw people with fabulous money and I was just outraged," Jacobson told a reporter one time.

In short, Jacobson was Mr. Clean.

As I saw it, I would tell about Jacobson's efforts to turn a crooked Teamster local into a democratic union. His task was formidable: Purge the local of corruption, exorcise the ghost of its imprisoned boss, Anthony (Tony Pro) Provenzano, and create conditions for free elections, so when a reform candidate ran for union office, he needn't fear being encased in cement and dumped into the Hackensack River.

Admittedly, profiling good guy Jacobson wouldn't exactly test my skills as an investigative reporter. I could end up turning him into a saint if I'm not careful, I said to myself.

But the story took an unexpected twist. The digging I did undermined my premise. In the end, Jacobson hated my guts.

For five years, I'd waited to do this story. My interest began in 1982, when the Justice Department accused Local 560 in a civil complaint of being operated for the benefit of the Genovese Crime Family. I saved the news item.

In 1983, after 51 days of testimony at a non-jury trial, Judge Harold Ackerman upheld the government's charges that the Provenzano regime had conducted a reign of terror, during which union dissidents were murdered, union funds embezzled and employers extorted. "A shameful horror story," said Judge Ackerman, in ousting the old regime from power. I clipped this item as well.

Judge Ackerman's ruling was upheld on appeal in 1986. Joel Jacobson became court-appointed trustee, with the power to hire and fire union officers. That news item was added to my collection.

By late 1986, the time was ripe, it seemed to me, to see how Jacobson was doing.

The story about Jacobson looked easy. There'd be no digging in a courthouse for documents. For a change, I'd have nice things to say about the person I was writing about. People always like to talk about good guys, so I'd have no trouble in obtaining interviews.

What I would do, I'd accompany Jacobson on pep talks to the truck terminals to show him in action. Then I'd interview the rank and file to see what they thought of him. I'd weave in stuff about Local 560's bad old days. The story could be wrapped up with little sweat in a relatively short time.

Although I wasn't writing an expose, I felt I was earning my paycheck because it could be a significant story.

This was the first trusteeship clamped on a union under RICO—the Racketeer Influenced and Corrupt Organizations law. Under RICO, the courts could remove mob-dominated union officials from office. In the entire history of union labor, few locals matched Teamster 560 in violence and corruption.

How Jacobson did would be closely watched by government and labor officials. Nationwide, more than 400 individual local unions, including 36 Teamster locals, were mob-dominated. This was less than 1% of all the union locals in the country, but many of the Mafia locals were strategically placed, with the power to shut down industries through work stoppages. A trusteeship might be the only effective weapon to stamp out Mafia control of unions. On the other hand, Jacobson's failure to clean up Local 560 would cast big doubt on whether trusteeships could work.

I phoned Jacobson for an interview. He'd be delighted to see me, he said, leading me to assume he was making headway in gaining rank-and-file trust. If he weren't getting anywhere, I thought, he'd have turned me down. "It's just too early to comment, call back a year from now," he'd have said.

Jacobson could have gone into retirement, watching TV and playing patty-cake with his grandchildren. But he had too much nervous energy to take things easy. He was up at 5 in the morning, so he could go to the company terminals, where the Teamster drivers and freight loaders were.

I met him at 7 a.m., in front of Local 560 headquarters. We piled into his car and headed for Brinke Transportation, in Jersey City.

Was he worried about his personal safety in view of Local 560's reputation for violence? I asked.

Not a bit. "The government wanted to give me FBI protection," he said dismissively. "Ridiculous. How can I walk into a union meeting with three FBI guys?"

Jacobson had silver hair. He wore tinted glasses and an open-necked shirt. He figured, I suppose, he'd be viewed by the rank and file with scorn if he wore a tie. He came across as a combative, no-nonsense guy. And he had strong opinions. For example, he praised Judge Ackerman's decision to pick a union man for trustee, saying: "If he had put in, say, a former prosecutor or a former attorney general, that would have guaranteed defeat for

64

the trusteeship."

I found it ironic that he repeatedly referred to himself as a trade union man, despite the fact that, in recent years, he had been New Jersey's Public Utility Commissioner, and after that, the boss of the state's Energy Department.

Probably, Jacobson felt his effectiveness would be compromised if he were perceived by Teamster rank and filers as a government bureaucrat.

He was a cocky guy. When I asked how the rough, tough truck drivers were responding to him, he replied with an anecdote: His wife and he were invited to a recent Christmas party at a terminal by some rank-and-filers. "I didn't want to speak," Jacobson insisted. "But they dragged me to the mike. After I spoke, they gave me an ovation."

So what if he thought highly of himself? People accustomed to wielding power were often vain. I certainly didn't hold it against him.

Jacobson was received warmly at the Brinke terminal by his audience of 15 union members. In a jocular vein, he said, "I've been a laboring man all my life. You could've had someone worse than me. You could've had an FBI guy."

His audience laughed. Jacobson knew what they wanted to hear. To them, the government was the enemy.

Showing he hadn't any hidden motives, Jacobson said: "I'm not running for office, and I'm not sponsoring anybody. I look forward to the day when I can play with my two grandchildren."

His listeners chuckled.

He showed he was tough, telling about Dominick Romano, a Teamster who—Jacobson said—had been wrongfully dismissed from a trucking company on "trumped up charges" that Romano improperly got somebody to punch his time clock for him. When the company refused Jacobson's entreaties to rehire Romano, Jacobson played hardball. He hired Romano as a business agent, giving him jurisdiction over Local 560 members at the very same company that fired him.

"The company went wild," Jacobson said gleefully. "They recanted the allegation and reinstated Mr. Romano."

Jacobson's message was clear: He was no namby-pamby.

He recounted how he'd dumped a law firm employed by Local 560 when he discovered the firm charged "unauthorized fees" for legal services. He told how he won pay increases for members in new contracts, and how he was expanding the availability of dental and vision care.

Why didn't Jacobson take a poke at Mafia bigwig Tony Provenzano, the ex-boss of Local 560, who was in prison? Probably, Jacobson figured it was bad strategy to bring up the past. Be upbeat. Stress economic issues. Tell your listeners the good things you're doing for them.

Maybe Jacobson intended a subliminal message for his audience: See, you're far better off under me, a clean trade union man, than with a crook like Tony Pro.

When he finished, they gathered around him, wishing him well.

"I just want you to know, I think you're a fine gentleman," one said. Another said admiringly, "You talk just like a Teamster."

Jacobson was elated as he left Brinke.

"They consider me one of them," he said. "How do you think they would've reacted if I was a cop? Nobody would've showed up."

Taking the train back to Manhattan, I thought about Jacobson's impressive performance at the Brinke terminal. He had the rank and filers eating out of his hand. If they were representative of the union, Jacobson had made big strides in ridding the membership of its fear of the Mafia and creating conditions for free elections.

I knew what my story would say: Here's what an earnest, energetic reformer can accomplish in the war against mob domination of unions. If the Mafia stench can be removed from Local 560, it can be done anywhere.

When I got back in the office, I phoned a U.S. Labor Department investigator, who gave me the names of Jacobson's secret supporters among the shop stewards. I reached one on the phone and asked for an interview.

"How'd you get my name?" he demanded.

The shop steward sounded surly.

I said I got his name from the Labor Department investigator.

"You're with The Wall Street Journal?"

"Yeah."

"How can I be sure of that?"

"I'll show you ID when we meet."

"Anybody can get phony ID," the shop steward said.

Chrissakes, he was awfully suspicious.

I said the Labor Department investigator would vouch for me.

Finally, he relented, but only on condition that I didn't quote him by name, didn't describe in the article what he looked like, and would never reveal to anyone that I spoke to him.

I said to myself, If this shop steward is typical, it could be a long time before a reformer has enough guts to come out of the closet to run for Local 560 office.

It was my first premonition that Jacobson mightn't be making the headway at Local 560 that I imagined.

We met for lunch in a hotel restaurant that he picked out near the Newark train station. Ordering a steak sandwich and french fries, he glanced around nervously to see if he spotted anybody from Local 560.

"You think you were followed?" I asked.

"Not really," he said, "but you never know. Those guys never sleep."

"What guys?" I said, pretending not to know what he meant.

"You know who."

"They're that tough?"

"I'll tell you how tough," he said, leaning toward me and speaking softly. "You ever hear of Anthony Castellitto?"

I had. Castellitto, a Local 560 dissident, had been murdered in 1961. In 1978, Tony Provenzano was sentenced to life in prison for ordering the hit.

"Tell me," I said, "do you feel you could get up at a union meeting and criticize Tony Pro?"

"To be honest," he said, "I don't think I could."

"Tony Pro is still that strong in the union?"

"You don't understand," the steward said. "Tony Pro was Robin Hood to them. Because of Tony Pro, they have medical benefits and good wages. Whatever he may have done that the government charges him with, the members remember that he took care of them."

"What's the feeling about Jacobson?"

He shrugged. "They think he's okay, but not tough enough to stand up to the employers the way they think Tony Pro did. Look, the feeling is, 'It's our local, and no damn judge has the right to take the local away from us.'"

"How long you think before free elections can be held?"

His answer surprised me. "Not for three, four years, at the least."

"Are you saying, if Tony Pro weren't in prison, and he ran for office, he'd be elected?"

"No question in my mind," the shop steward said.

"That's pretty damn discouraging," I said.

He told me to go to the Newark federal courthouse, and look up what Tony Pro's daughter, Josephine Provenzano, told Judge Ackerman during the trusteeship hearings in 1984. As much as he hated to admit it, he said, Josephine's statement accurately reflected how most of the membership felt about Tony Pro.

I looked up her testimony. According to her, this was the rank and file's attitude:

"What did the press ever do for me? What did the government ever do for me? Look what Tony did for me. He gave me pensions, eye glasses. He gave me dental. I have welfare payments. He saw me in the street and took me in the bar. We had a drink. He remembered my wife's name. He asked me how my daughter was who had the concussion."

Tony Pro's daughter said: "He has an uncanny ability of making people relax, and making them know he cares. He is not a big deal. He is not very well educated, book-wise. He might have gone to the fourth or fifth grade. But you give him a contract, he can read it. My girlfriends, they call me on the phone in tears. How could they say that about your father?"

Tony Pro's backers had formed a committee, "Teamsters for Democracy," and were demanding immediate union elections. Their candidate for president was Michael Sciarra, who owed his career in Local 560 to Tony Pro. Sciarra had been a member of the local's executive board that Judge Ackerman removed.

Over drinks in a tavern near Local 560 headquarters, I interviewed Tony Pro's backers—heavyset, muscular men, some with tattoos on their forearms.

"You gonna quote us?" one asked.

"Yeah, unless you object."

"Is it OK to call you "Stosh" (Polish for Stanley)?" another asked.

"I don't mind."

"Stosh," the guy said, "you quote us all you like, just so you spell the names right."

They all laughed, then turned serious.

I was told to put in my article that "Teamsters for Democracy" hadn't anything personal against Jacobson, that he was a fine old gentleman. I should put in my article that it was the trusteeship they hated.

"A trusteeship is a waste of time and money," complained Anthony Valdner, a shop steward, who wore a baseball cap with the inscription "Free 560. I want my officers back."

Some 5,300 members, nearly 70% of Local 560's total 7,600 membership, had signed petitions urging Judge Ackerman to grant elections now, according to Valdner. He offered to show me the signatures.

"Nobody was intimidated, coerced or threatened," he said. "Anybody says they were is a liar!"

Nunzio Spano scoffed at my suggestion that the rank and file was afraid to speak out. "I've been a shop steward 11 years," Spano said. "The last time I was re-elected by a 79-to-29 vote. They can vote any way they like."

Spano said if I wanted to get a real feel for the union, I should interview rank and filers at Pacific Intermountain Express, where he was the shop steward.

I took him up on it. Next morning, I took the train to Jersey City, where Spano met me. We drove to the PIE terminal. Union members were packed into a second-floor meeting room, waiting for The Wall Street Journal reporter to show up.

They crowded around me, all saying essentially the same thing: Jacobson must go, and elections should be held so "Mikey" Sciarra could be president.

"I been in this local 36 years," an angry Ed Taglieri said. "If the government thought the local was being intimidated, why didn't they ask us, 'Do you want a change?' We weren't asked!".

Spano stood at one end of the room, watching them harangue me.

It was pretty clear that the former corrupt regime still had a lot of rank-and-file support. Which raised a question: Could it be that Jacobson was over-optimistic in assessing his progress in cleaning up Local 560?

Judge Ackerman had told me that the mob was waiting to get back in. "They're there," he said. "I know it. It's like squeezing dirty water out of a wash rag. There's still a lot of dirty water in that rag."

Particularly disquieting was that the Local 560 members who opposed Tony Pro's people were afraid to do so publicly.

A veteran truck driver, a longtime dissident, who didn't want to be identified, said: "There's 20 different ways they can get rid of you. You can have an 'accident,' like getting a pipe in the head. Or they plant stuff in your truck and say you were stealing."

Playing devil's advocate, I said, "But you can elect a reform candidate when the election comes. You're guaranteed a secret ballot. Nobody'll know how anybody voted."

"You gotta be kidding," he laughed cynically.

"What do you mean?"

"Tony Pro'll know."

"How, for chrissakes?"

"They have ways," the dissident said. "They'll pay off the election inspectors to show them the ballots. Or there'll be a camera hidden in the booth. Or a peephole in the ceiling to see who you voted for." According to him, "Mikey" Sciarra would be the only candidate for president if elections were held today.

I visited the 51-year-old Sciarra, who was working as a driver at Ward Trucking, in Little Falls, N.J.

He made no secret of the fact that Tony Pro was his idol. "I don't know anything bad about the guy," Sciarra said. "He was great for labor. He might be a tough guy, but that's what this union is."

The story was assuming a different look. It seemed that nothing much had changed at Local 560. As in the past, the dissidents were afraid to go public, and reformers were afraid to run for office. That Jacobson was giving 100%, I didn't doubt. But, in attempting to reform the local and smash the Provenzano influence, maybe he was doing it the wrong way.

I began hearing criticisms about Jacobson from his own supporters, who faulted him for failing to publicly denounce Tony Pro and his cronies.

For example, Jacobson's supporters said, he'd blundered when, immediately after he became trustee, he visited the terminals with Sciarra as his escort.

"It sent the wrong message," said one, who didn't want to be named in the article. "He should attack Mikey Sciarra. The word is, 'Mikey's out but he'll be back.'"

The man added, "Jacobson is there, but Mikey's running the show. The attitude is, Jacobson's just babysitting the local."

Said another Jacobson backer, who insisted on anonymity, "He's got to make the guys wake up, show them what's going on."

Otherwise, a third supporter said, "Mikey Sciarra's a shoo-in. And when he gets back, it'll be the same old story."

Jacobson was sharply criticized for retaining Joseph Sheridan, a former Local 560 vice president, on the union payroll. Sheridan was a Tony Pro fan. Of Tony Pro, Sheridan had testified: "I don't think there is a man in our union or in the labor movement that can say anything against him."

In describing Sheridan, Judge Ackerman said he was "decent, devoted, blind and bought."

I talked to a Washington attorney, who represented dissident Teamsters.

He said Jacobson made a big mistake: "Retaining Sheridan strikes the wrong message to the rank and file if you're expecting real leaders to come out of the woodwork to clean up the union."

Suddenly, Jacobson had warts. His strategy for creating conditions for a free democratic election didn't seem to be working. His own supporters were asking, Was Jacobson afraid to attack Tony Pro and Sciarra?

This left me uncomfortable. Originally, Jacobson was going to be the hero of my piece—a tough old geezer cleaning up the union. Now, it looked as if I might have to throw mud at him.

He sounded on the defensive when I asked about Sheridan.

He said Sheridan was kept on the payroll for "humanitarian reasons," that Sheridan would shortly become eligible for a union pension and retire.

Why didn't Jacobson denounce Sciarra as an agent for Tony Pro?

That would be bad strategy, Jacobson said. "You force the Sciarra loyalists to come to his defense. The candidate running against Sciarra—that's the guy should be scoring points, not me."

I wasn't entirely pleased with the story when it came out, faulting myself for not having been tougher on Jacobson. I had buried his supporters' criticisms of him at the bottom of the piece. They should've had a more prominent spot.

Also, I didn't give enough analysis of why Jacobson was having such difficulty in getting the dissidents to overcome their fears and speak out. As I saw it, the piece focused too much on Jacobson's efforts, and not enough on his weaknesses.

The story is on page 152. Here is the headline:

Mob's Legacy

Teamster Local Greets Court Trustee Angrily After He Takes Reins

---

But Joel Jacobson Tries Hard
To Prevail in New Jersey;
Getting Rid of a Law Firm

Is Rank and File Intimidated?

Jacobson didn't call me. That was surprising. Did he dislike the story? He hadn't any reason to, as far as I could see. The criticisms of him represented only a small part of the piece. The bulk of it dealt with Local 560's legacy of corruption, and the obstacles confronting Jacobson in setting the stage for free elections.

I phoned him, asking how he liked the story.

70

He said coldly, "My friends think it made me look weak."

He hated the piece. To this day, I don't see why.

A short time later, I got an inkling of his bitterness toward me. In a letter to an acquaintance of his, a copy of which the Journal received, Jacobson wrote:

"In my judgment, while almost savagely researched, the article was poorly written, unbalanced in its treatment of a very controversial problem, and on more than one occasion, not the whole truth."

Three months later, Jacobson was ousted as trustee by Judge Ackerman. Jacobson hadn't made enough progress to suit the judge. Free elections were a pipe dream until Local 560's dissidents felt secure enough to become candidates for union office.

Jacobson, who took the ouster hard, accused Judge Ackerman of bad judgment in replacing him.

Edwin H. Stier, a former prosecutor of organized crime and corruption cases, became the new trustee. Stier would later testify before a U.S. Senate panel that he found a portrait of Tony Provenzano on the wall at Local 560 headquarters when he took over. He took it down. Stier, at the Senate hearing, was asked why Jacobson was removed. "The judge decided that my presence might be more confrontational in dealing with the problems of racketeering," he said.

An angry Jacobson told the Senate panel, "In the parlance of the working man and woman, the judge had replaced a trade unionist with a cop."

On Dec. 6, 1988, Local 560 held elections—its first under the trusteeship. Mikey Sciarra, a candidate for president, had been removed from the ballot by the court, on the ground that the union would once again fall under the control of the Genovese crime family if Sciarra won.

Ever resourceful, the old regime's backers turned to Daniel Sciarra, Mikey's younger brother, who was elected president over a union dissident by a 2-to-1 margin. Jacobson blamed the results on Judge Ackerman's action in switching trustees, declaring that Sciarra's victory "will henceforth be accurately known as Ackerman's folly."

I interviewed Stier, who had a different view. True, Daniel Sciarra won, he said, but it must be remembered this was Local 560's first contested election in 25 years. Union dissidents not only showed up at political rallies, they also permitted their names to be used on leaflets. "You're trying to change values," Stier said. "The change will come about in small increments."

CHAPTER 9

WILLIAM CASEY'S SECRET

ANAGING EDITOR FRED TAYLOR called me into his office and said to see what I could dig up about William J. Casey. Casey had just been nominated by President Richard Nixon to head the U.S. Securities and Exchange Commission. The appointment needed the Senate's ratification.

According to Taylor, there were rumors in Washington that Casey had defrauded shareholders of a company. Taylor didn't know the company's name, or indeed if it really existed.

I had no leads. What to do?

It could be an important story, if true. The man chosen by the president to regulate the nation's securities laws was himself accused of violating the same laws? Wow. An expose of Casey could conceivably torpedo the nomination.

This was 1971. Ten years later, Casey would become head of the Central Intelligence Agency under Ronald Reagan. Later, Casey would be accused by critics of being an intriguer, who doctored facts, had contempt for the press, and made secret deals with Iran's terrorist regime behind Congress's back.

But in 1971, not a lot was known about Casey. Taylor had heard he'd been active in Nixon's 1968 Presidential election campaign. Casey had a reputation as a wheeler-dealer.

The tip had come from our Washington bureau. Cynic that I am, this made me suspicious. Why did Washington offer New York a potentially good story? Something fishy here, thought I. Maybe Washington suspected it was a bum tip, but wanted to look good in the managing editor's eyes by making a gift of it to New York.

This would be a tough piece to pull off, I warned Taylor.

In effect, I was saying, "Don't blame me if I don't get a story."

I looked for clues in Casey's background. He was a graduate of St. John's University Law School. During World War II, he was based in London for the OSS, the U.S. spy branch, a forerunner of the CIA. After the war, he became a tax lawyer, teaming up with Leonard Hall, a Republican Party bigwig, in the Wall Street law firm of Hall, Casey, Dickler & Howley.

Casey became an investor in go-go companies. He published manuals for businessmen on how to legally evade income taxes, including an epic called "How Federal Tax Angles Multiply Real Estate Profits." He was wealthy, a sloppy dresser, and mumbled when he talked.

But nobody seemed to know if he'd cheated shareholders.

The Senate Banking Committee, which held hearings on Casey's nomination, had dug up some dirt. In 1959, Casey and a publishing company on whose editorial board he sat, had been defendants in a $175,000 plagiarism suit, accused by a business writer, Harry Fields, of pirating parts of a Fields manuscript and using the material in a publication Casey edited. Casey and the publisher denied the charges. Fields won, after a New York trial, and got $15,000 in damages.

This was sleazy stuff, yet it caused hardly a ripple. The Senate committee voted 15-0 for the nomination, with only William Proxmire, a Wisconsin Democrat, abstaining. Casey seemed a sure bet to be ratified by the full Senate.

Even so, the fact Casey lost a plagiarism case gave me a lift. It showed he was tricky, doing whatever he thought he could get away with. If I looked hard enough, I might come up with the goods. I phoned my best sources—a prosecutor, an SEC investigator, an FBI agent, and a former SEC lawyer, now on Wall Street. They weren't of any help.

An idea—born of desperation—struck me. I'd search the archives in courthouses to see if Casey were being sued by the shareholders he supposedly cheated. Never before had I done a random search of courthouse files. Maybe it would be a wild goose chase. But it was all I could think of.

A fair and accurate report of a suit, of course, is privileged information. It can be used without fear of libeling anyone. And, often, a court complaint is more than just a bare-bones collection of allegations. It might include denials by Casey and decisions by the judge in Casey's favor. A suit against Casey would likely be accompanied by affidavits, exhibits and by pretrial testimony, describing in detail what he did wrong.

Another thing: In court complaints, the victims don't pull any punches—unlike press interviews, when they're usually wary of publicly denouncing their adversaries, fearing they could be sued for slander.

Problem was, had a suit been filed? If so, in what city? In what court?

Casey was a venture capitalist, one of those people who invest in fledgling companies which dream up new products but often don't have enough capital to bring them to market. Investing in these infant outfits can be risky. But the payoffs for wheeler-dealers such as Casey can be big.

The electronics field was filled with fledgling companies, particularly in Boston and Silicon Valley, which is near San Francisco. I phoned courthouses there, inquiring if a William J. Casey had been sued. The court clerks didn't tell me to go to blazes, but made clear they weren't getting paid to do my work.

It meant I must inspect the court files myself. But that could be expensive. I didn't have the chutzpah to ask the paper for expense money so I could spend a week in San Francisco rummaging through court files on the remote chance a suit against Casey would surface.

I would limit my search to Manhattan. After all, Casey had been based in Manhattan. There was a large concentration of companies in Manhattan.

I dropped into the state courthouse downtown. Civil suits were filed in the public reference room. They were listed alphabetically in big ledger books. Each suit was identified by a docket number. You give the clerk a requisition slip with the docket number on it. The clerk, after searching the stacks, returns with the case file. That simple. Yet, a hitch developed.

In this particular court, the ledger books listed complaints only in the plaintiff's name—not the defendant's. I was defeated before I started. I didn't have the plaintiff's name. Without it, I couldn't get the docket number. Without that, the clerk wouldn't be able to locate the case file.

It was frustrating. Surely, I said to a clerk, a defendant's name should be enough to find the complaint.

Not here, the clerk said.

What a damn silly way to file complaints, I protested. I stalked out, intending to inform Managing Editor Taylor the situation was hopeless. But, heck, I'd been on the story only a few days. It would be awful if the New York Times or Washington Post dug up the story I gave up on.

Across the street from the state court was the federal courthouse. It dawned on me that a complaint charging securities violations would be far more likely to be filed in federal court than a state court.

Happily, the federal court filed suits in the defendant's name, as well as the plaintiff's. I looked in the microfiche file for "Casey."

The gods were smiling on me. Casey was a defendant. But I mustn't get my hopes up. It might not be the complaint I was looking for. Or Casey might have won the suit. Or the suit against Casey could have been thrown out for failure to state a cause of action.

The microfiche showed that a Roland H. Boggs, of New Jersey, was the plaintiff. He had sued Casey in 1962. A settlement had been reached in 1964. This was seven years ago. The microfiche didn't describe the allegations. It didn't say who won the suit. To get that information, I must examine the Boggs vs. Casey file.

This was exciting. If it panned out, my story might cause the Senate to kill Casey's nomination. Probably other reporters were digging into Casey's background as well. There was no time to lose.

But I faced more red tape. Files of completed cases, such as Boggs vs. Casey, weren't kept in federal court. They were stored in a government warehouse, in Manhattan's Greenwich Village. Moreover, a completed case file received a new docket number.

I went to the federal court office that processed completed cases. I gave the clerk the original docket number of Boggs vs. Casey. He looked in his ledger. Next to the original number was the new one. The clerk wrote the new number on a slip of paper. That was easy enough. I took it and headed for Greenwich Village.

It was a bitter cold day in February. The red brick, multi-story warehouse was near the Hudson River. I found the public reference room. A handful of visitors sat at long tables examining documents. I scrutinized their faces, wondering if some sonofabitch reporter had beaten me to the story.

I handed the slip to a clerk. She gave it to her assistant, an elderly man, who shuffled off into a back room, where the case files were stacked. The clerk resumed reading her newspaper.

While waiting, I noticed a woman at the visitors' table furiously scribbling in a notebook. Could she be a reporter? If so, would she be willing to share the case file with me? Probably not, and I couldn't blame her.

Visitors were required to sign in, and list their affiliations. I scanned the names. Nobody from the press. The visitors listed themselves as law firm employees. I was relieved. I had the story to myself.

About 15 minutes went by. Where was the file? I informed the clerk I was a newspaper reporter with a deadline to meet. The clerk said the department was short-handed, and that her aide was doing the best he could. I must be patient, the clerk said with annoyance.

More time went by. I said to the clerk that maybe her assistant was looking in the wrong place. I suggested she help him.

The clerk looked offended. She informed me federal regulations forbade that the counter be left unattended.

I offered to stand guard. But the clerk would have none of it. Just then, the old gent returned. He was empty-handed. Something was wrong. The two of them held a whispered conversation.

Turning to me, the clerk said the Boggs vs. Casey file wasn't in the stacks. The clerk asked if I had the correct docket number.

I said it had to be correct. The clerk in the federal courthouse had written it down.

"I don't know what else to tell you," the clerk shrugged.

I was ready to explode. The file had to be in the warehouse. Would I lose what could be a great story because of this clerk's ineptitude?

I asked if she'd phone the federal courthouse to see if I'd been given the wrong docket number. The clerk refused: If she did it for me, she must do it for everyone.

The clerk offered the thought that a judge in the federal courthouse might be reviewing the file. I should track down the judge, and ask if I could be allowed to examine the file, the clerk suggested.

I said there'd been a settlement of the case seven years ago. It was unlikely any judge was reviewing it.

"It's not here," the clerk repeated.

I said maybe the file had been misplaced.

This angered her. I was casting aspersions on her department. The clerk said it could not have gone astray.

Would it would be all right if I looked for myself?

Federal regulations forbade visitors to search the stacks, the clerk said.

Clearly, she was losing patience. If I had a complaint, the clerk said, I should see the supervisor. She pointed to the supervisor's office.

The supervisor eyed me warily. I told him my tale of woe. He said it was unthinkable that a case file in the warehouse had been misplaced. He got up from his desk, and went over to the clerk. A discussion ensued.

The supervisor then went into the back room, where the stacks were. He emerged a few minutes later. He could definitely assure me the file case hadn't been misplaced, he said. If somebody made a mistake, he added, it was not anyone in the warehouse.

It was about 3 p.m. Any hope I had of getting a Casey piece in the next day's paper was dashed. I was furious. I had followed proper procedure, and had nothing to show for it.

What should I do? I could return to The Wall Street Journal and see if I could find Roland Boggs in a New Jersey phone directory. If I reached him, he could put me in touch with his lawyer, who, hopefully, could send me a copy of the case file. But several days could go by. There was also the possibility that Boggs's lawyer—for whatever reason—might not want to help me.

Back to the federal courthouse at Foley Square I went. The clerk who'd given me the new docket number was still on duty. I asked him to recheck it. He had erred. He'd given me the wrong docket number. He proceeded to give me the correct one.

I wanted to smash my fist in his face. I said instead that his mistake had cost me an entire day. He looked indifferent. Next time, be more careful, I said.

This upset him. I hadn't any right to talk to him that way. He said I should see his supervisor if I had a complaint.

"All right, where is he?" I said in a fury.

His supervisor was on sick leave, and wouldn't return till the following week, the clerk said smugly.

It was 4 p.m. now. The warehouse closed for the day about 4:30—not time enough to examine the file. Fate seemed to be conspiring against me. With my lousy luck, a competitor might beat me to the file.

Next morning, I got to the warehouse before it opened. No reporter was going to make me look foolish. I was the first visitor in the reference room. The same clerk was on duty. I gave her the the docket number. Not a word between us was spoken. In short order, the file was produced.

I sat down with the file. A quick look showed I had struck gold. Well, what do you know? The Washington bureau hadn't given me a bum tip after all.

In the suit, Boggs accused Casey of using false information to dupe investors into buying unregistered stock of Advancement Devices Inc., a small electronics company. This allegedly violated the Securities Act of 1933—a law that Casey, as SEC head, would be sworn to uphold.

Boggs charged that Casey—chairman of the board, general counsel and owner of 6.8% of the stock—had dominated the company. Boggs said his purchase of $10,000 of company shares had been based on promises in the prospectus that Advancement Devices was introducing a wide range of new products, including a "High Speed Clutch and Brake," an "Integral Calculus Computer" and an "Aircraft Anti-Collision System."

The company failed to develop any of these, Boggs charged. Nor did the prospectus disclose that the company was losing money and didn't know when, if ever, it would become profitable, said Boggs. He charged the stock was worthless, the company bankrupt. In court papers, Casey said he was innocent of any wrongdoing, and that he played only a tiny part in the company's affairs.

"They called me chairman of the board of directors," Casey said in pretrial testimony. "But it didn't mean anything. What constitutes a title? I don't know. I don't know that there was anything in the bylaws or charter that called for a chairman of the board. I acted as secretary, and I used to write out the minutes and the (company president) would run the meetings."

In short, don't blame Casey. Even so, Casey chose not to go to trial. Boggs collected $8,000, equal to 80% of his investment, in an out-of-court settlement.

The head of the SEC, which regulates the nation's securities markets, must be squeaky clean. Did Casey measure up to that standard? My story would raise doubts about his integrity. It could give the Senate a reason to reject him.

I finished taking notes about 2 p.m. Next step would be to go back to the office to write the story.

But I was uneasy. What if a New York Times reporter at this very moment was on his way to the warehouse to examine the Boggs' suit? The Times reporter would have time to get his story in tomorrow morning's edition, destroying my chance for an exclusive.

I could prevent this. I could employ the same tactic that Reuters news service once used against me. This was at an MGM annual meeting in a Times Square movie house. As soon as the meeting ended, I had rushed to a phone in the lobby to give the story to the Dow Jones news ticker. But two Reuters reporters had grabbed the two available phones. I was stymied.

To block the Times reporter, I could arrange for the Journal to send a reporter to the warehouse. Our reporter would not let the file case out of his grasp till closing time. Meantime, my piece would appear the next day. The Times would be out in the cold.

Under the circumstances, it seemed justified. The story could bring about the rejection of a president's nominee. Letting the scoop slip away from me would be folly.

Still, it seemed a shabby thing to do. Plus, it was highly unlikely the Times even knew about Boggs's complaint. I was pretty sure I had the story to myself. I returned to the news room. Reporter George Nikolaieff helped me by phoning people for reactions.

We got Casey on the phone. He dismissed the Boggs's complaint as a "nuisance."

Just "a piece of civil litigation," said Casey.

Had Casey, before being nominated, informed the Nixon administration he'd been accused in a lawsuit of securities' violations?

"I'd forgotten about it," Casey said. "I don't think it's relevant. If you led an active business life, as I have, people are going to make claims against you."

We told Sen. Proxmire about Boggs's charges against Casey. Proxmire said he'd request Sen. John Sparkman, an Alabama Democrat, head of the banking committee, to reopen confirmation hearings.

Said Proxmire, "The revelations that Mr. Casey was involved in civil action involving a violation of our securities laws casts new doubts" on whether he should be the SEC head. He added: "Perhaps there are other cases which would shed additional light on Mr. Casey's nomination. Until the matter is fully resolved, he should not be confirmed." Another senator on the committee echoed Proxmire's comments.

The piece appeared as a page-one story the following morning.

The headline said:

Nominee to Head SEC
Was Sued for Breach
Of Securities Laws

Casey Settled Out of Court
In 1964; Two Senators Seek
To Reopen Hearings on Him

The hearings were reopened. Shortly before they began, Casey had been called to a secret meeting by Len Hall, his law partner and a Republican bigwig. Attending was Jack Wells, a senior partner in another Manhattan law firm, which included William Rogers, then Nixon's Secretary of State.

According to author Joseph E. Persico in his 1990 biography, "Casey," Hall and Wells prepared a statement in Casey's name, saying he hadn't done anything wrong, but didn't want to embarrass President Nixon, so he was withdrawing his name from consideration.

Casey, not easily intimidated, refused to sign it. He said he wanted to think about it. He phoned John Mitchell, Nixon's attorney general, who later would be imprisoned for his criminal actions in the Watergate cover-up. Casey told Mitchell he hadn't done anything wrong and wanted the SEC job.

"OK," Mitchell said. "We'll stick by you," according to the Persico book.

Reappearing before the Senate panel, Casey made light of Boggs's complaint. He was a venture capitalist, he said, and venture capitalists got sued all the time. Besides, said Casey, a civil suit wasn't a crime, just a dispute between private parties.

Proxmire introduced a surprise witness—Judge J. Braxton Craven Jr., who had presided at the 1959 plagiarism trial, when Casey was accused of pirating part of someone's manuscript and a jury ruled against him. Braxton told the senators that Casey had made false statements about the plagiarism case during the initial Senate confirmation hearings.

The Boggs case, together with the plagiarism suit, made it clear to me that Casey was a manipulator, a trickster and a bender of the rules. No matter; the Senate committee voted 9-3 for Casey. The nomination then went before the full Senate. On the floor of the Senate, Proxmire said: "Mr. Casey has cut corners when he considered it to be necessary to his business profit. He has wheeled and dealed his way into a personal fortune, sometimes at the expense of his clients." Brushing Proxmire's criticism aside, the Senate ratified the Casey nomination.

The Casey affair revived memories of Joseph Kennedy, the SEC's first chairman, who was chosen by President Franklin D. Roosevelt in 1934. Kennedy, father of President John Kennedy, made a fortune as a stock speculator in the 1920s, and his selection dismayed New Dealers. FDR, by way of explanation, said, "Set a thief to catch a thief."

Ironically, Casey proved to be a tough regulator. The New York Times economics analyst wrote, "(Casey) has shocked his fellow lawyers by naming some of their group as defendants" in fraud cases involving clients, and has "forced stockbrokers to live by somewhat stricter rules than many of them really wanted."

After 20 months at the SEC, Casey was named by Nixon to be undersecretary of State for economic affairs. Once again, Casey's past caught up with him. He was the founder, and a director, of a company, Multiponics Inc., which was forced to file for protection against creditors in bankruptcy court.

Prior to Senate hearings on whether to confirm Casey, I got a tip that the court-appointed trustee for Multiponics was getting ready to sue Casey, and other directors, on behalf of aggrieved shareholders for mismanagement and violating their obligations. Some of Multiponics's transactions were so questionable, "that this may be a matter that should be referred to the Department of Justice," according to the judge in charge of the case. I rushed out a front pager on Casey's role in Multiponics. (This story and the other Casey stories are reprinted on pages 155–159.)

The headline said:

A Breach of Duty?

SEC Head to Be Sued
For Role as a Director
Of Small Firm in '68-'70

Trustee of the Concern Says
Casey, Others Mismanaged;
Judge: "Inconceivable Acts"

Casey Denies Wrongdoing

The SEC, which had known of Multiponics's collapse before Casey became head of the SEC in 1971, often investigates bankruptcy cases for securities law violations. Yet, despite a judge's allegations of possible corruption at Multiponics, the watchdog agency showed no interest in the company. In defending its inaction, the SEC said Multiponics hadn't sold stock to the general public. That Casey was involved in Multiponics in no way influenced its decision not to investigate, insisted the SEC. At the Senate hearings, Casey denied any wrongdoing, and once again was confirmed, this time as undersecretary of State.

But Multiponics wouldn't go away. The trustee's suit on behalf of Multiponics's investors dragged on. In 1981, the federal judge handling the case said it was his opinion that Casey, in a 1968 Multiponics prospectus, misled investors through false statements.

Casey had just been cleared by the Senate as Reagan's CIA director. The judge's denunciation of Casey triggered demands in the Senate that Casey resign. "He should go—now," William V. Roth Jr., a Republican on the Senate Intelligence Committee, said.

The Senate held hearings to see if CIA Director Casey was fit to remain in the job. At this critical juncture, Stanley Sporkin, the highly respected, former head of the SEC enforcement division under Casey, came to Casey's rescue. Sporkin, selected by Casey to be CIA general counsel, helped sway Senate opinion by publicly defending his boss's integrity.

The dump-Casey effort failed. Casey managed to disentangle himself from the Multiponics mess by agreeing to give Multiponics's investors $117,000.

As CIA director for nearly six years, Casey was credited by supporters for rebuilding the spy agency. But his penchant for secrecy and willingness to manipulate facts got him into more trouble. He became enmeshed in Iran-Contra, Reagan's secret scheme in 1985-86 to sell arms to Iran. Senate-House investigating committees charged that Casey was deeply

80

involved in the covert operation, despite his earlier denials in congressional hearings of any knowledge of an arms shipment to Iran in 1985.

He died in 1987 at age 74, after surgery for a malignant brain tumor. If Casey had lived, he might have been criminally prosecuted for testifying falsely with regard to Iran-Contra.

CHAPTER 10

MEXICO'S SIERRA MADRE

I N THE MOVIE, "Treasure of the Sierra Madre," Humphrey Bogart, playing a down-at-the-heels rummy, prospects for gold in the rugged Sierra Mountains in northwest Mexico. He finds the yellow metal, and feverishly fills up his sacks with it, only to be murdered by marauding bandits before he can reach safety.

These days, the bandit-infested Sierra Madre yield a different treasure: opium poppies. The opium paste is turned into heroin, then smuggled into the U.S. to feed addicts.

The red-petaled poppies, growing in small plots on the sides of the mountains, are unreachable by road and protected by growers with automatic weapons. The U.S. Congress, complaining that heroin was a major cause of inner city crime in America, demanded that Mexico act against its heroin traffickers. But Mexico needed help. Putting their heads together, U.S. and Mexican officials came up with a plan: The Mexican poppies would be sprayed from helicopters with deadly herbicide so they'd be destroyed while still in the ground. The U.S. would finance the project; Mexico would provide pilots and mechanics. It seemed like a terrific idea.

The project got under way, and soon was hailed a success. Mexican government press handouts claimed that thousands of acres of opium—and marijuana—fields were being eradicated. The U.S. State Department declared: "The air eradication program represents the single most effective means of lessening the availability of drugs in the U.S. and Mexico."

The story I heard was that the project was plagued with mismanagement; pilots' low morale, lack of replacement parts, corruption. In short, crop eradication was being bungled.

This would be a good story, one I was eager to do. But I had to resolve a question. If I got the opportunity, should I accompany an aerial-spray pilot on his search-and-destroy mission?

No question about it, on-the-scene coverage would enliven the piece. But color, I told myself, is not vital. And it could involve physical danger. I wasn't a coward. But neither was I a war correspondent. To me, being an investigative reporter had always been clean, safe work. Flying in a helicopter through narrow mountain passes in search of poppy fields guarded by gun-toting growers seemed foolhardy. Helicopters had crashed from the gusty winds rattling through the Sierra Madre. Wire mesh concealed in trees overhanging the poppies could ensnare the copters' landing gear, causing them to crash. Copter pilots, in positioning themselves to spray the poppies, had been shot out of the sky by traffickers hiding in the thickets.

From time to time I'd be asked: Didn't I fear being murdered by the bad guys I wrote about? I had no such fear. Racketeers weren't fools. Murdering a reporter would generate a flood of articles—publicity mobsters didn't want.

True, investigative reporters had been victims of reprisals. Years ago, a top New York newspaper reporter, Victor Riesel, who'd exposed waterfront corruption, lost his eyesight when a hoodlum threw acid in his face. In 1976, Don Bolles, an Arizona Republic reporter, died after a bomb exploded under his car, triggering allegations he was murdered to stop him from writing a story about the mob's ties to powerful Arizona business figures. And in 1992, Manuel de Dios Unanue, editor and publisher of two Latino magazines in New York, was shot in a Queens restaurant; a cocaine cartel in Columbia apparently ordered his killing.

But such occurrences were rare. A rule of thumb for reporters was: Don't get friendly with racketeers. Don't accept dinners from them, tickets to sports events, gifts of any kind. This way, if a reporter exposes a gangster, the gangster won't have reason to feel betrayed, and won't seek vengeance. To me, it made sense.

I decided I didn't want to risk my life by taking a cockamamie ride in a helicopter in the Mexican badlands. So—honorable reporter that I am—in seeking story approval, I made no promises to the editor of a firsthand account of a helicopter wiggling through a mountain canyon searching for illicit opium poppies.

Instead, in my story proposal, I hit hard on the subject's significance. The U.S.-Mexico venture was the largest of its kind. More than 90 aircraft, plus 600 pilots, mechanics and others were involved. Yet, despite the massive effort, Mexican narcotics output kept increasing, prompting congressional demands to punish Mexico by reducing U.S. economic aid.

A congressional staffer for a committee that monitored U.S.-funded, anti-drug programs in foreign countries, gave me the idea for the story. It was my custom to phone the staffer every few months to see what was going on. The staffer trusted me to not reveal my source.

The staffer told me that testimony before the Democratic-controlled committee showed that the U.S.-Mexico crop-eradication effort was in disarray. The testimony had been made publicly available in a committee report. But I hadn't noticed any mention of it in the press.

"It just isn't working," the staffer said. "Everybody is blaming everybody else."

The U.S. was shelling out more than $100 million a year in 12 drug-producing nations to wipe out heroin, cocaine and marijuana. Mexico's share—$14.5 million—went for helicopter maintenance, replacement parts and pilot training. In addition, U.S. funds paid for nearly all the helicopters. Mexico ran the project, on the ground and in the air, with the U.S. State

Department acting as adviser.

According to the staffer, Mexican officials didn't take kindly to U.S. advice. The State Department, not wishing to ruffle Mexican sensibilities, largely kept its hands off the program. Meantime, bumper crops of opium were being produced, raising the question of just how workable these crop-eradication programs were.

With anger and sarcasm, the staffer described the foul-ups in Mexico. The staffer, a Democrat, would of course be delighted to see a story zeroing in on a Reagan administration foreign policy weakness. But motives didn't concern me. All I cared about was, could the staffer's assertions be substantiated?

I got in touch with an American pilot, whose name and phone number the staffer had supplied. The pilot had been among a small group of U.S. pilots who, for a brief period, flew aerial-spray missions in Mexico.

The American said he'd received $9,500 a month from the State Department to destroy drug crops. Mexican pilots, by comparison, got $800 monthly from the Mexican government—less than one-tenth what the Americans got. This was causing low morale and heavy turnover among the Mexican pilots.

"The Mexicans took the same risks as us, but they got paid this corn-bread living," the American said. A good quote for my story, thought I.

According to a former U.S. adviser on the project, whose name and phone number were supplied by the staffer, the sharp wage disparity badly affected the Mexican pilots' work habits.

"American pilots took off at daybreak, flying two aerial-spray missions by lunch time," the ex-adviser said. "The Mexicans wouldn't take off till 9. When they got back, that was it for the day." Nobody flew in the afternoon, he said, because of the stiff, hazardous winds in the mountains.

Theft at the main air base at Culiacan was a major problem. "They'd have fuel trucks sitting there," said the ex-adviser, who'd visited the base frequently. "I asked why the trucks weren't being used. They'd tell us: 'no battery, no generator, no tires.' Guys would tell us someone took it. They'd just shrug, 'that's the way it is.'"

Because of a lack of parts, helicopters couldn't fly. "The parts they had were obsolete," this man said. "New parts had to come from the U.S. A plane would sit at a base for weeks."

Thus far, I'd interviewed the congressional staffer, the American pilot and the former State Department adviser. Their information seemed solid. But all insisted on anonymity. I doubted I could get a 2,500-word story in the paper based strictly on anonymous sources.

Who could I quote by name to criticize the project? The namby-pamby State Department would be highly unlikely to bad-mouth Mexico for the record. The Mexicans, when I confronted them, likely would accuse my anonymous sources of seeking to wreck U.S.-Mexico relations. The Mexicans would probably contend the aerial-spray project was right on schedule.

Unknown to me, the U.S. General Accounting Office, an investigative arm of the Congress, had previously reported that large numbers of aerial-spray aircraft in Mexico had been grounded through lack of parts, thereby limiting the time the opium poppy patches could be sprayed. I was on the GAO's mailing list. Probably, I had received it, and thrown it away without looking at it.

I asked for a copy after hearing about the report during the course of my reporting. It had good, hard specific stuff: Aerial-spray pilots were logging 46 flight-hours a month—far below the targeted 80 hours monthly.

No way the Mexican government could brush this aside as gringo propaganda.

According to the GAO, Evergreen Helicopters Inc., a Portland, Ore., company hired by the State Department, had sharply criticized the aircraft maintenance program. Evergreen found that the mechanics, angry at their lousy pay, engaged in work slowdowns. I phoned Evergreen. "The mechanics aren't putting in a full day's work," Robert Fox, a senior vice president, told me.

Harder to nail down was that corruption was hamstringing the project.

The ex-U.S. adviser had found it awfully suspicious that certain Mexican drug fields looked to be off-limits to aerial-spray pilots. "Pilots got their assignments from zone coordinators," he said. "Certain sectors they wouldn't let us work in. Our pilots would fly over these (drug) fields. After they got back, they'd (inform) the zone coordinator, who said he'd have them sprayed. He never did."

He couldn't prove that air base officials took payoffs to protect the drug fields from being sprayed. Even so, I published his remark in the piece, feeling justified in doing so. Widespread narcotics corruption in Mexico was common knowledge. A State Department report quoted U.S. Customs as saying: "The level of official corruption with the Mexican government" was undermining U.S. narcotics cooperation with the Mexicans.

The piece needed a U.S. official to give an on-the-record statement that Mexican crop-eradication was being bungled. Rep. Lawrence J. Smith, the Democrat who headed the House Foreign Affairs Committee's anti-drug task force, was happy to oblige.

"The whole thing has turned into a shambles," Rep. Smith said. "Cajoling, pleading, begging, diplomatic inquiries—none of them works."

I was ready to face the Mexican government. I told the Mexican Embassy in Washington what I was writing about; that I'd read the GAO report; had interviewed Evergreen Helicopters, and that Rep. Smith called the project a failure. Surely, Mexico wanted to give its side.

You betcha, the embassy PR man replied. Come to Washington, and all my questions will be answered.

In his high-ceilinged office on Embassy Row, embassy officer Jose A. Gonzalez conceded there'd been problems. Anyone who thought that such a path-breaking venture against wily international gangsters wouldn't face difficulties was naive, he said.

But Mr. Gonzalez insisted the problems had been overcome. As he told it, allegations of pilots' low morale were greatly exaggerated. Even so, salaries of Mexican pilots and mechanics had been sharply raised.

The mechanics' slowdowns had ended, Mr. Gonzalez went on. The pilots' roster, which admittedly had shrunk, was rebounding sharply. As a result, big gains had been chalked up in eradication. Reading from a government document, Gonzalez said 6,200 acres of poppies were destroyed last year—up from 5,900 acres the previous year. More gains were expected for the current year. No country fought the drug war harder, or more effectively, than Mexico, said Mr. Gonzalez.

He asked if I were aware that 60% of Mexico's anti-crime budget was devoted to the drug fight; "154 Mexicans have lost their lives in the fight," he said grimly.

Since all the problems had been corrected, he added, there wasn't anything to write about. Nonetheless, he said, he could see I would not be dissuaded. In that case, I must go to Mexico City to interview Deputy Attorney General Jose Maria Ortega-Padilla, who, even though he was very busy, would squeeze me in. While there, said Gonzalez, I must inspect the hangar, where the helicopters were repaired.

Because of The Wall Street Journal's importance, hangar officials would personally show me around, Mr. Gonzalez said.

I said to myself that poking around in a greasy hangar won't yield fresh revelations. Gonzalez had given me the government's side. In the back of my mind was the fear that, once in Mexico City, I'd be urged by the Mexicans to inspect the Culiacan air base. In Culiacan, I'd be pressured to get a firsthand look so I could appreciate the difficulties the pilots faced.

I told my boss, Barney Calame, that Mexico's deputy attorney general was willing to be interviewed. I was half-hoping he'd say the interview wasn't necessary.

Accept the offer, Calame said. Otherwise, the Mexicans could claim we didn't give them fair treatment. Calame had a point.

Mexico City, 7,300 feet above sea level, and ringed with mountains, has a severe pollution problem. Because of the hazy brown smog, which made the air taste like grease, you can't see the snow-covered peaks of Popocatepetl, once a part of the city skyline.

Treating me with the importance accorded a Japanese businessman, Mexican officials met me at the airport and deposited me at my hotel in the Zona Rosa. Next morning, a government chauffeur drove me to the hangar, which was alive with activity.

Inside the hangar, a Bell helicopter, which had been in working condition, had been stripped to its skeleton. Because of the parts shortage, it had been dismantled to provide parts for the repair of three other helicopters.

Cannibalizing a perfectly good helicopter for spare parts seemed ridiculous. Who was to blame for the shortage? I asked.

American workers were at fault, Rafael Garcia-Delgado, in charge of aviation services, said angrily. "Parts are sent to the U.S., but aren't repaired properly. We have to send them back!"

This told me that the project, contrary to Gonzalez's assertions, was still floundering.

Nor did Deputy Attorney General Ortega pull any punches.

When I asked if the U.S. State Department should play a greater role, Ortega said scornfully, "The U.S. attitude is, 'Father knows best.' We're not little kids who need a tutor."

I said the State Department had offered to pay part of the Mexican pilots' salaries to bolster their morale, but that Mexican officials rejected the offer. Why?

"The pilots cannot have two bosses," Ortega said stiffly.

He criticized a Dallas company, E-Systems Inc., which advised Mexico on maintenance and parts procurement. "In '86 and '87," Ortega grumped, "I never got spare parts in timely fashion, or I didn't get the right amounts."

E-Systems, which was later dropped by Mexico, denied it was to blame, claiming funds from the State Department weren't always available. The State Department said the criticism was unfair.

I had a pretty good story, and was ready to return to New York. But Ortega had other plans for me.

Was I aware, he said somberly, of how many Mexican lives had been lost so far in the drug war?

I said, "Mr. Gonzalez told me."

As if not hearing me, Ortega said, "154 lives."

Reaching across his desk, he handed me black-and-white photos. They showed wrecked helicopters and dead pilots.

Pilot Emmanuel Olea had been shot down by drug growers, Ortega said. Another pilot, while attempting to rescue Olea, was killed when his plane smashed into the mountain. Olea survived, but both his legs were paralyzed.

I said nothing.

Ortega said a government plane would fly me to Culiacan, where arrangements had been made to show me how poppies were sprayed.

I didn't know if I could spare the time, I said lamely.

How could I write about crop eradication if I didn't see how it was done? Ortega demanded. He assured me I'd have an armed escort, so there'd be no danger.

No danger, eh?

Earlier, hangar officials sought to impress upon me how fragile, and complicated, the helicopters were, which was why they broke down so frequently.

I'd never flown in a helicopter. There could be engine failure. A sudden gust of wind could fling the helicopter into a mountain. The thought occurred to me I might be murdered to keep me from writing my story. In Colombia, home of the Medellin and Cali cocaine drug cartels, dozens of reporters, judges and others had been slain by the narco terrorists.

It was far-fetched to think I was important enough to be targeted for murder. I only did two or three articles a year on drug trafficking. The drug lords never heard of me.

Still, this was Mexico. In Mexico, police officials took payoffs to protect opium growers from arrest.

My mind was alive with wild imaginings. The traffickers had been tipped off about me. They would kill me to keep the piece out of the paper.

I accepted Ortega's offer to visit the Culiacan air base. I would interview the pilots there. I hadn't any intention of going up in a helicopter.

But I could see problems ahead. I'd submit the piece to the paper, and an editor would find fault with it for its paucity of color. "A pretty good story, Stan," the editor would say. "But it could've been better. You were in Culiacan. Why didn't you watch them spray the poppies?"

Culiacan, a city of 700,000 on Mexico's west coast, is a center of the cocaine trade. It is 140 miles north of the beach resort town of Mazatlan. A guide book warns tourists who drive to Culiacan, "Don't buy drugs. And do not stop for hitchhikers, and you should not have any trouble."

A government plane brought a group of us to the helicopter base on the city's outskirts. Five Bell helicopters were on the tarmac. To the northeast loomed the Sierra Madre, a jagged mass of purple peaks.

The pilots were in a shed, waiting for us. They were a cocky, laughing bunch. Through a translator, I asked a pilot, "Destroying many poppies?"

Yeah, yeah, he nodded his head vigorously.

It was 10 a.m. Pilots were supposed to fly two missions in the morning, since dangerous winds precluded afternoon flights.

I asked if he'd flown today.

He said he hadn't. According to him, flight schedules had been rejiggered, because of the presence of the dignitaries from Mexico City.

Did the pilot regularly fly two missions a day?

He shrugged. Sometimes yes, sometimes no. The helicopters broke down a lot, he explained. The right parts weren't always available.

Through an interpreter, Enrique Arenal, Deputy Attorney General Ortega's aide, informed me the helicopters were ready. Arenal wore a handgun in his belt. Dutifully, I followed him onto the field.

It was a warm, hazy day, with a slight breeze. From the ground, it looked like good flying weather. But in the Sierra Madre, the winds could be gusting 30, 40 miles an hour.

I was introduced to the head pilot. He had black hair, bronze skin, and looked to be in his mid-20s. He opened the cockpit door, and, smiling—he spoke no English—motioned for me to climb in.

I looked around me. The rotor blades of the five choppers were thrashing round and round, ready for liftoff. A Mexican reporter, who had accompanied me from Mexican City, had already boarded a helicopter.

Seeing I had misgivings, the pilot pointed to a matting that covered the cockpit floor, gesticulating that I hadn't anything to fear. It looked to be bulletproof padding.

I got in. We lifted off at 10:20. There wasn't a cloud to be seen. Higher and higher we climbed. The engine roar was deafening, despite cotton in my ears. We were flanked by two helicopters in front of us, and two in back.

The gringo from New York would be well protected.

Soon, we were above the peaks, which were 7,500 feet high. The mountaintop was covered with boulders, rocks and underbrush. Sudden gusts of wind caused the machine to lurch. I looked to the pilot for reassurance.

Nothing to worry about, he grinned.

An opening in the mountain appeared below us. Slowly we descended into it. Wooded slopes with overhanging trees were on both sides of us. Ever so slowly, the whirling 33-foot rotors propelled us through the pass.

Then the pilot spotted what we came for. In a garden-size clearing, red petals gleamed in the sun, partly concealed by leafy trees. A hut used by the drug dealers was nearby. Near the cabin was a dried-out stream. Coils of water hose lay on the ground.

Any fear I had that I'd be shot out of the sky proved baseless. The deputy attorney general had taken precautions. The mountainside was blanketed with soldiers. Evidently, the drug dealers had fled, for the time being at least.

A helicopter near us got into position above the poppy patch and shot herbicide at it. That was it. Later, we turned and headed back, reaching the base shortly before noon.

We gathered in the shed. There were smiles all round. The gringo had witnessed the destruction of poppies. The day was counted a success.

The headline said:

Crop Busters

U.S.-Mexican Project For Planes to Wipe Out Drug Crops Is Faltering

Illicit Narcotics Keep Flowing
As Problems With Pilots,
Aircraft and Parts Pile Up

Many Acres of Dead Poppies

The story I turned in had 10 paragraphs of firsthand color.

Too much color, the rewrite man decided. He compressed it into three paragraphs, which served as the lead:

> CULIACAN, Mexico—The five Bell 206
> helicopters began threading their way
> through narrow 7,500 foot mountain passes.
> Suddenly, a telltale hint of scarlet in the
> underbrush ahead betrays a target.
>
> One chopper eases in at treetop level.
> Pilots have learned to be wary: They some-
> times find wire mesh waiting to snare
> them. And occasional gunfire. Today there
> is neither. An empty tin-roofed hut and
> some hastily abandoned tools, blankets and
> a ratty cowhide below indicate no one stuck
> around. The pilot opens fire—with a herbi-
> cide spray—and the airborne armada then
> whirls back to base.
>
> The kill: A garden-sized plot of flower-
> ing poppies.

I was pleased with the story, which is reprinted on page 163. It proved that the much-ballyhooed drug-eradication project was floundering. Not only that. I had ventured into the dangerous Sierra Madre, and—unlike Humphrey Bogart in the movie—returned to tell about it.

Then a colleague in the New York office spoiled everything. Having read the piece, he asked if I actually flew through those narrow mountain passes.

I looked at him in disbelief.

"Of course I did," said I. "Isn't it clear from the story?"

No, it wasn't, he said. Readers might get the impression I got the color from interviews with the pilots at the air base.

I reread the top of the story. He might be right. It wasn't absolutely clear I had participated in the action.

Probably, the lead paragraphs should have been in the first person, elim- inating any doubts I was there.

Damn. Why hadn't I suggested it to my editor? On the other hand, it should have occurred to the editor. What are editors for?

90

CHAPTER 11

THE INFORMER

ACCORDING TO RON FINO, there were certain hotels in Boston the Mafia didn't patronize, the Ritz-Carlton being one of them. It may be that the Ritz, with its tradition of serving afternoon tea, was too snooty for the Mafia, or the Mafia hated the Ritz's gourmet cooking. Whatever the reason, the mob would never think to look for Fino at the Ritz, which was why we met there.

He was seated on a couch in the lobby—a black-haired, middle-aged man, with wire-rimmed glasses, reading the Boston Globe, seeming oblivious to the comings and goings around him. In a well-tailored navy suit, white shirt and black shoes, the 44-year-old Fino blended in nicely.

His father, Joe (Ebe) Fino had been boss of the Mafia organization in Buffalo from 1968 to 1972. Through the Mafia, Ron Fino wound up in a cushy job as head of Buffalo Local 210 of the Laborers International Union of North America. Joe Fino died in 1984 at age 69—never aware that his son, during the 15 years he headed the local, was an undercover informant for the Federal Bureau of Investigation, giving evidence of the union's links to the mob.

Now, the mob boss's son was offering me an inside look at life in the Mafia.

Fino was articulate, had a thoughtful manner and seemed eager to talk. That he was willing to be interviewed didn't surprise me. He had time on his hands. He was cut off from family and friends, and the Mafia had put a price on his head. Through me, people would learn of the hell he'd been through.

He was a tormented guy, agonizing aloud about whether he did the right thing in helping the FBI expose Mafia crimes. He'd paid a fearful price—his marriage in ashes, and separated from his son and daughter, who lived with their mother in Buffalo. Using an alias, and changing residences from time to time, he took care not to let the Mafia spot him. But he couldn't overcome a deeply rooted pessimism that Mafia trigger men would find him.

Here we were, the hunted man and the reporter. Fino's concern was to stay alive, while my only interest was to get a juicy story on how a mob boss's son shook himself loose from the underworld's grip. Why did Ron Fino betray his Mafia birthright? What was his wife's attitude toward his working undercover for the FBI? How did the mob learn he was spying on them? The story must show that his personal life was in a shambles.

I would get most of the story from Fino. It sounds ghoulish to say it, but it crossed my mind that he could be murdered before I finished interviewing him, and I might not have any story. Well, it was a risk worth taking.

Could he be believed? How could I verify what he told me? Those were my overriding concerns. He had none of the look or manner of the Mafioso portrayed in the movies. What hoodlum would say that when he was in high school he dreamed of becoming an archaeologist? Or that he regretted not staying in college long enough to earn a bachelor of arts degree? Fino seemed decent and sincere.

Even so, his personality could have a dark side that was concealed from me. I mustn't forget that he'd been shaped in the shabby world of the Mafia. The mob mentality—the lies and deception—could have rubbed off on him.

I'd have egg on my face if the piece contained major errors of fact.

Fino gave me names of friends and associates who, he said, would attest to his good character. But most of them refused to discuss him, including his wife, who had just divorced him.

His enemies were talkative. A lawyer for a Local 210 officer, whom Fino implicated in a crime, said Fino was bitter, that he had resigned from the union because he couldn't run it the way he wanted to. In Washington, a spokesman for the Laborers International, the parent union, implied Fino was unstable: "Very flaky, some sort of shadowy character, always by himself."

I told myself, if I catch Fino in just one lie, no matter how tiny, I drop the story.

Early on, I established three key facts, which gave me the confidence to pursue the story to the end.

Fact No. 1: Joe Fino had been in the Mafia. This was a fact, according to a 1963 U.S. Senate report on organized crime. The report showed mug shots of the Buffalo Mafia hierarchy, Joe Fino included. Fino then was a "section leader," with leadership capabilities, according to the Senate report. It said: "He has grown in the organization from hoodlum status to upper echelon rank."

Fact No. 2: Joe Fino did indeed head the Buffalo Mafia for a time. A 1988 report of the Senate Permanent Subcommittee on Investigations, page 324, said so. The report said the information came from the FBI and Buffalo police.

Third, Ron Fino was credible—this from G. Robert Langford, head of the FBI in Buffalo. Langford said Fino helped to bring about the indictments of three officers of Laborers Local 210. Fino was aiding in FBI investigations of Mafia infiltration of labor unions in other cities, Langford said.

I found Fino by chance, while working on a story about Mafia-controlled unions. For the story, I was hoping to find an ex-Mafioso who knew firsthand the subject of mob unions and would be willing to talk.

There were 26 Mafia families in approximately 21 cities. The FBI operated in most of those cities. I phoned the FBI offices at random. When an agent came on the phone, I asked if he knew of any Mafioso-turned-informant who'd be willing to talk to me.

I got lucky in Buffalo, where the FBI's Paul Moskal said I should talk to Ron Fino. Fino phoned me, at the FBI's request.

He told me about the Mafia control of Laborers Local 210, how he headed the local at the same time he was an FBI informant. Fino would be perfect for my story on Mafia unions.

In fact, it occurred to me, I could probably get clearance from the front page to do a profile of him.

Wait a moment, thought I. If Fino were quoted in my article on Mafia unions, he'd be sure to attract the attention of the national media. The news magazines might attempt to snatch him from me so they could do their own profiles of him before I did mine. This mustn't happen.

With the guile of a Machiavelli, I left Fino out of my piece on Mafia unions. The media would not hear about him till my Fino profile came out.

In doing the profile, I was fully aware that ex-mobsters who snitch on the Mafia are popular subjects for movies and books. But, in pitching the story to the front page, I argued that Fino was different from other informants. The others were mostly Mafia turncoats, who swapped information for reduced prison sentences or immunity from prosecution. Ron Fino was never a Mafioso. And he was never coerced by the FBI into giving evidence. As an unpaid informant, he served voluntarily.

Besides showing the Mafia closeup, the story would also be newsy: It would inform readers that the FBI, using Fino's information, was attempting to smash the Buffalo Mafia's leadership, headed by reputed crime boss Joey Todaro Jr., and clamp a court trusteeship on Local 210, to rid it of its Mafia influence.

As I saw it, the story must answer the question of why Ron Fino—this exemplary citizen, loving father and churchgoer, who seemed to be at peace with the world—risked everything for the dubious privilege of exposing Mafia crimes. As Local 210 head, he lived comfortably on $85,000 a year in salary and benefits, drove a union-supplied Chrysler, and took expense-paid trips to Miami and Hawaii in the winter. He was popular in the community for his civil and humanitarian projects. The local NAACP honored him at a black-tie dinner one time.

Fino's answer to the question: He hated his Mafia birthright. "I could never get rid of the feeling that I was one of them," he said. "You have this original sin that never washes away."

It sounded pretentious, yet I believed him. A hoodlum never would say it or think it. Moreover, he backed up his statement with anecdotes from his past.

In high school, he had dated a new girl. The next time he called up for a date, her parents refused to let her go out with him. They'd read about mobster Joe Fino in the newspaper.

Another time, 11-year-old Ron Fino watched his father, who was an illegal bookmaker, pay off two police detectives, so they wouldn't arrest him and put him out of business. It was Ron Fino's first realization that his dad was a crook.

What drove him into the FBI's embrace was his awareness, after he become head of Local 210, that he was just a figurehead. He was then just 27 years old, one of the youngest labor leaders in America. He ran on a "reform ticket," denouncing the leadership of the local union for its "laziness, favoritism and mismanagement." He promised the 2,000 rank and filers to protect their interests if elected.

His running on a reform ticket sounded ludicrous. I bet the Mafia bosses laughed till their bellies ached. Let Ronnie Fino have his fun. He'd be set straight soon enough.

Fino told me it didn't dawn on him till he became head of the local how thoroughly it was dominated by the Mafia. The Mafia bosses told him who to put on the union payroll and who should control the union benefit funds. The Mafia controlled the union hiring hall. When employers needed new workers, the Mafia's friends were the first ones hired.

Fino said he'd been invited to join the Mafia, but turned it down. He wasn't able to prove it, but he did show me that he'd been treated by the secret society as one of its own. In 1976, Fino had met with Anthony D. Liberatore, a reputed "capo" in the Cleveland Mafia. "Liberatore thought I was a member of the Buffalo 'family,' so he spoke freely," Fino said. "He told me the mob had a leak into the FBI's office in Cleveland—someone in the FBI feeding stuff to them."

This disclosure by Liberatore shook Fino. If true, it showed how far reaching the mob's tentacles were. It meant the mob had access to the FBI computer, which had a list of informants, Fino included.

Fino, whose FBI code name was "Mike Stitt," reported the leak to his FBI handler. The FBI corroborated this. In 1978, a file clerk in the FBI office, together with her husband, pleaded guilty to receiving $15,000 from Liberatore in exchange for the FBI list. Happily, Fino's name wasn't on the list. Liberatore was also convicted.

The portrait in the piece on Fino's father shows a side of the Mafia that not many know about. Fino Sr. was a failure as a Mafia boss, a far cry from the stereotype of the domineering Mafia despot.

Poor Joe Fino. While other crime families were generating new income by expanding their empires, Joe Fino's crime family largely confined itself to the traditional rackets, such as gambling and loan sharking. "Family" members groused about Joe Fino's lack of vision, comparing him unfavorably to the late, dreaded Stefano Magaddino, founder of the Buffalo mob.

As No. 1, Joe Fino was entitled to a healthy cut of the crime family's profits but, out of weakness perhaps, he didn't take it. He was ridiculed behind his back. His own wife complained what a lousy breadwinner he was. Finally, he was ousted as Mob boss by the Five Families in New York.

In disfavor, Joe Fino returned to his old job as a bookie. While the Buffalo leadership looked the other way, he lost customers to rival bookies.

According to Ron Fino, his father became financially hard up and had to live off handouts from his son. Following are perhaps the best quotes in the piece:

"Toward the end of his life," Ron Fino said, "I made him a member of the union. I got him work as a laborer. I said, 'As a union member you're entitled to a pension.' I explained to him the strength of legitimacy."

In depicting Joe Fino as a failure, I didn't want to sentimentalize him. To hear Ron Fino tell it, "My father was a very caring man. He gave me money if I needed it. He never hit me—I never saw him hit anyone." In summers, Joe Fino took his wife and four kids to Maine for vacation.

How idyllic. But Joe Fino wasn't your basic, everyday daddy. In his criminal career, Joe Fino served as a Mafia enforcer, its "muscle." Only a violent, brutal man is so honored by the mob.

I asked Ron Fino, Did his father ever kill anyone? It would make a nice morsel for my story if he did.

Ron Fino could've said he didn't know, or that it wasn't any of my business. Instead, he revealed that his father murdered the lover of a Mafioso's wife, on the mob's orders. The killing was never solved, and Ron Fino never told anyone till after his father died.

I interviewed Fino about 20 times, all by phone, except for the face-to-face meeting at Boston's Ritz-Carlton. Fino would phone me at the office, at a prearranged time, usually 9:30 in the morning. I didn't ask for his phone number, and he didn't offer it. I couldn't blame him for that. How could he be sure I wouldn't sell it to the Mafia?

Ron Fino is the hero of the piece. After all, he did a brave thing in exposing Mafia crimes. But he isn't depicted as a saint.

For example, he never confided to his wife, Donna, that he was living a double life. She heard about it from him only after he went into hiding and gave her a call from a pay phone. Nor was she aware, till a Buffalo paper reported it, that he was accompanied by a female companion when he fled.

The events had to have ripped her apart emotionally. Patrick Fino, Ron's brother, in a brief interview, said angrily, "Shame on him because he left his wife and kids."

Because of his wife's refusal to be interviewed, I couldn't give a firsthand account of her feelings. Even so, in hindsight, I should have dug into the ambiguities of their relationship. The piece could've raised questions about his judgment in not telling her he was spying on the mob and that he could be murdered, leaving her a widow with two fatherless kids.

Fino said that when he came home late at night after meeting with his FBI handler, his wife accepted his explanation that it involved business. I wondered about that. Did she really believe him, or did she suspect he was secretly seeing other women? They drifted apart. Finally, he moved out, renting a small apartment in town.

Fino was naive in believing he could keep hidden his role as FBI informant, and that he could resume a normal life when he chose. Everything unraveled after Joseph Rosato and John Catanzaro, Local 210 shop stewards, were indicted in Buffalo's federal court in 1988, charged with taking illegal payments from employers for work not performed.

Fino didn't realize the jam he was in till he was confronted by a high Mafia official, who ordered him to be an alibi witness for Catanzaro, who was scheduled to go on trial first. The Mafia official was an old friend of Fino's. They, and their wives, had taken trips together to Las Vegas and San Francisco on union business.

The Mafia official said to Fino, "You got to do something for 'Catz' (Catanzaro)," never dreaming that the no-show indictments of Catanzaro and Rosato had been triggered by Fino's information to the FBI.

"I don't see how," Fino stalled. "The FBI had surveillance on the job site. They know Catz wasn't there."

"You can do it," the Mafioso insisted.

"How do I do it?" Fino said irritably.

"You say Catz had permission to leave the job. You say you gave him permission."

Fino asked his FBI handler if it would be OK if he lied on the witness stand on behalf of Catanzaro, in order not to draw suspicion on himself. The FBI agent said Fino mustn't lie on the witness stand.

Shortly before the trial was to start, Catanzaro entered a guilty plea, and got a 27-month prison sentence. So Fino didn't have to testify.

But now Fino was pressured by the mob to be Rosato's alibi witness. "I kept ducking them," Fino said. "I was evasive. Then the mob decided something was wrong."

Perhaps the most vivid scene in the piece involves Fino's showdown with the Mafia. It took place in a coffee shop in the Veterans Administration building, downtown Buffalo. An elderly Mafioso, a longtime friend of Ron Fino's father, told Ron: "I'm going to have to frisk you."

Fino, wearing a wire recorder concealed in a pack of cigarettes in his pants pocket, feigned anger at being treated so shabbily.

"Shame on you," he said.

His bluff worked. "Out of respect for your father, I won't do it," the Mafioso relented. But he warned Fino he was no longer trusted by the 'family.'

Shortly after, "I got word from a relative of someone in the 'family' that I had a 'problem,' and I should get out of town," said Fino.

Fino was tipped off that his life was in danger in the Ragtop, a restaurant-bar in downtown Buffalo, This incident, rich in detail, isn't in the story. I didn't put it in. Why? I felt it would be chopped out by the front-page editor, on the ground the piece was already too long. Foolishly, I was trying to anticipate what an editor would do.

The meeting at Ragtop with the relative of a Mafioso was made to appear as a chance encounter. The man was standing at the far end of the bar, sipping a whiskey, when Fino showed up. The roar of the disco music would prevent the two from being overheard.

Fino ordered a Heineken. They exchanged pleasantries.

Then the tipster said, "They know about you. You should leave town."

Fino felt sick. "You sure?"

"There's no doubt about it," said the tipster.

"I suppose I shouldn't waste any time," Fino said glumly.

"You should go now. Don't waste a minute."

Fino paid for the drinks, then signaled to an attractive 27-year-old blonde, who was seated at a table chatting with friends. They had come in together, and she was waiting for him to finish his meeting.

At Fino's request, I didn't identify his girlfriend in the story. He'd been romantically involved with her since breaking up with his wife. The blonde, a former graduate student at the University of Buffalo, worked for a small toxic-waste company as a junior executive. Fino had revealed his double life to her after they began going together.

Fino told me his mind was in a whirl as they drove back to his apartment. His entire life, except for a stint in the army, had been spent in Buffalo. Where would he go? What would he do? Would his companion accompany him? It would be unfair to ask her to do it, and yet he dreaded the prospect of being alone.

He didn't realize he was speeding till she told him to slow down.

"What did he say?" the blonde asked.

"They know all about me," Fino said. "I have to leave as soon as possible."

"What are your plans?"

"I don't have any."

"Well," she said lightly, "I'm ready whenever you are."

Fino was elated. Still, he felt he owed it to her to warn her she could be in physical danger if she accompanied him.

She wasn't worried, she said. Her job bored her, and, anyway, she had no desire to spend the rest of her life in Buffalo.

Fino had a small, second-floor apartment near the university. Photos of his son, 19, and daughter, 17, enlivened the living room wall. Fino bolted the front door and he and the woman began packing. Her stuff went into a suitcase. He filled up two large plastic bags with 15 shirts, two pairs of slacks and toilet articles.

From the bedroom closet he removed a high-powered rifle and put it against the wall next to the bed. His .357 Smith & Wesson pistol was under the bed within easy reach.

The woman slept soundly, but he kept waking up, listening for suspicious noises. It was unlikely the mob would try to break into the apartment. The noise would bring the police. His guess was they would tail him, and pounce on him when he was getting in or out of his car.

The thought of his daughter kept recurring. She was bitter at him for walking out on her and her mother. When word got out publicly that he was an FBI snitch, his daughter would be taunted by schoolmates about her crazy father.

Next morning, a Saturday, Jan. 13, 1989, they left in a rented black Thunderbird, skipping breakfast. He had on a windbreaker and slacks. She wore a yellow ski jacket and blue jeans. He took his pistol with him. They stopped at the bank, where she removed $2,600, all her savings. Fino said he couldn't relax till they got on the thruway and saw they weren't being followed.

They drove to California. Fino decided he didn't like California, so they drove to a different part of the country.

This was no life for his companion and they broke up, parting on friendly terms. Fino was invited by the FBI to join the federal Witness Security Program. But he would be required to relocate to a community designated by the U.S. Marshals Service. He didn't want this. He chose to be on his own, even though it entailed greater risks.

The FBI said the mob offered $200,000 for Fino's murder. He was guarded by FBI agents whenever he testified in court. Fear for his safety kept Fino from attending his mother's funeral in Buffalo in December 1989.

Ironically, Fino's public exposure was a boon to the FBI. No longer a secret informant, he now could be used as a prosecution witness, testifying in open court about Mafia ties to the 500,000-member International Laborers Union, as well as Local 210.

On May 30, 1991, I sat in on the racketeering trial of John M. Riggi, in Newark federal court. The 65-year-old Riggi, reputed Mafia boss of New Jersey, was charged with shaking down contractors as a business agent for a laborers local in Elizabeth, N.J.

The spectactors' benches were packed with union members—many in T-shirts and baseball caps, some with tattooed forearms. They glared at Fino, muttering curses at him when he was sworn in as a government witness.

The prosecutor asked: Did Riggi belong to the Mafia?

Yes, Fino said.

How could Fino be sure?

In a firm, clear voice, Fino said the Mafia bosses in Buffalo—including his own father—told him that Riggi was in the Mafia.

The defense attorney tried to discredit Fino, bringing out that he was getting $6,000 a month from the government to give dirt against reputed Mafia figures.

Fino, not wishing to leave the impression he was getting rich at government expense, pointed out that one-third of it went to his ex-wife for support payments.

To drive home the point, Fino said hotly, "I lost my family! I lost my home! My way of life!"

To me, he was quite convincing. But what did the jury think? The jurors looked either expressionless or bored. For my own selfish reasons, I hoped the jurors believed him. A finding of guilty against Riggi would reinforce the point of my piece—that Good Guy Ron Fino had firsthand knowledge of the Mafia.

Riggi was convicted on seven counts of extortion and labor bribery.

I received compliments for the story. Talent agents phoned, making my head swim with talk that the article could be the basis for a book or TV miniseries. Nothing came of it.

Life went on. Each morning I rode the subway to the office, and had my cup of coffee before starting work for the day.

Fino's routine is different.

First thing each morning he examines his car's undercarriage for sticks of explosives, so that he won't be blown up when the ignition is turned on. Then he goes jogging, keeping an eye out for suspicious strangers. "If somebody looks like he's checking me out, I report it to the FBI," he says.

He toys with the idea of moving to Europe, thinking his chances of staying alive are better overseas. On the other hand, he may remain in the U.S., if the FBI can find a company willing to hire him. He considered plastic surgery, but doctors told him he can't change his features enough to make him unrecognizable.

When last we spoke, he was taking a course in a nearby college. He had a new girlfriend. I didn't ask if she knew he was hiding from the Mafia.

The pathos of Fino's life is summed up—nicely, I think—in the last sentence of the story:

"One night, he says, as he listened to his daughter weep recriminations into the phone, 'I began to feel I was the evil one.'"

The story is on page 166. The headline:

Family Rift

An FBI Informant
Gives Rare Inside Look
At Life With the Mob

———

Ron Fino Tells of Growing Up
As the Son of a Mafia Boss,
And 15 Years Undercover

———

Star Witness Against a Union

———

CHAPTER 12

THE WORLD ACCORDING TO ARI

I WAS A GUEST for dinner at the Caffe Cielo on Manhattan's West Side. Ari Ben-Menashe, who described himself as a former Israeli secret agent, was the center of attention. Ben-Menashe, 39, was black-haired, swarthy, and spoke fluent English. He wore blue jeans, a shirt open at the neck and needed a shave. He had an intense, nervous manner. He hardly touched his pasta. It was November 1990.

With us were Ben-Menashe's two attorneys, plus a former Time magazine reporter, and Gary Sick, of former President Jimmy Carter's National Security Council staff. Sick, an expert on Iran and a former Navy officer, had been involved in efforts to free 52 American hostages seized at the U.S. Embassy in Tehran in 1979. President Carter's failure to gain the hostages' freedom was widely believed to have contributed to his defeat in the 1980 election.

The hostages were freed only minutes after Ronald Reagan's inauguration in January 1981. The timing looked suspicious, feeding rumors that the Reagan campaign and Iran's mullahs had agreed to delay the hostages' release till after Election Day, thereby assuring Carter's defeat. For all anyone knew, it might be true, except there was no proof.

Ben-Menashe said he had proof.

The way he told it, Reagan's aides held secret meetings with Iranian officials in Madrid in July 1980, then sealed the deal October 15-20, in Paris, just weeks before the election. In return for an agreement to release the hostages, Iran was promised massive arms shipments, to begin immediately after Reagan took office. William Casey, Reagan's campaign manager, later appointed by Reagan as boss of the Central Intelligence Agency, masterminded the conspiracy, with George Bush participating, Ben-Menashe said.

If Ben-Menashe were correct, the actions of the 1980 Reagan campaign team were despicable. Not only had the 1980 presidential election been rigged, but also the hostages' safety had been jeopardized by delaying their release. George Bush's 1992 re-election chances could be damaged— deservedly so—if it could be proved.

After we left the restaurant, Sick and I got on the subway. I asked what he thought of Ben-Menashe's story. Sick, in a deep resonant voice, said he found it fascinating, but doubted it could ever be corroborated.

He must have changed his mind. On April 15, 1991, the New York Times carried an Op-Ed page piece by Sick, echoing Ben-Menashe's conspiracy allegations. In a four-column article, titled "The Election Story of the Decade," Sick said he was convinced the 1980 Reagan campaign stole the election. What convinced him? According to Sick, he had interviewed numerous individuals who claimed knowledge of the conspiracy by virtue of their "official duties or access to intelligence reports."

Stories of a 1980 Reagan-Iran conspiracy had been kicking around for years. But Sick, a man with impeccable credentials and an impressive manner, gave the tale a mainstream credibility. Sick was on TV talk shows. He and Ben-Menashe beat the drums in an hour-long documentary on Public Broadcasting's "Frontline." He appeared before a congressional committee.

Congress stirred. Citing the "seriousness of the allegations" and "the weight of circumstantial information," the lawmakers voted to investigate.

Sick had beaten me. I'd been left at the starting gate. But it wasn't as if I hadn't tried. I'd had numerous interviews with Ben-Menashe before and after the dinner at Caffe Cielo, fully aware that his disclosures could trigger the biggest scandal since Watergate.

It had all sounded farfetched. But, I reminded myself, political scandal stories often sounded improbable at first, only to be proved true later. Take the 1985-86 Iran-Contra scandal. A shocked world learned that the Reagan White House secretly sold arms to Iran, and used the profits to arm Nicaragua's anti-government rebels illegally.

I asked myself about Ben-Menashe's motives. Why did he make his revelations now, 10 years after the event? Was he attempting to perpetuate a hoax, hoping to cash in by writing a book about it? Was he unstable, suffering from delusions?

He sounded convincing. He spoke in rich detail, rattling off names, dates, places. His tone was—"I know, I saw it happen."

When I first met Ben-Menashe, he was facing trial in Manhattan federal court, accused by the Justice Department of unsuccessfully conspiring in 1989 to sell three U.S.-built military cargo planes to Iran. Ben-Menashe contended he had been acting for the Israeli government, which denied it.

He later would be acquitted in a jury trial. But when we first met, the criminal charges against him made me uneasy. Could there be a dark side to this guy I knew nothing about? The safe thing would be to walk away from him.

Ex-Time reporter Raji Samgabhadi eased my concern. Ben-Menashe had been a Samgabhadi news source during Iran-Contra. "You can trust Ari," Samgabhadi said.

I decided I would pursue the story. If I caught Ben-Menashe in a lie, I'd walk away from it.

My first meeting with Ben-Menashe was in the apartment of attorney Mark Anthony Cristini, on Manhattan's Central Park South. During the interview, Cristini made no attempt to censor his client.

Ben-Menashe said his parents were Iraqi Jews, who moved to Iran, where he was born. The family resettled in Israel when he was 15. He spoke Arabic, Farsi and Hebrew. He said he served in Israeli intelligence from 1977 to 1987.

How did Ben-Menashe know Bush had been involved? I asked. Ben-Menashe said he was told by Israeli intelligence officials who took part in the conspiracy meetings in Europe. As he himself conceded, his knowledge was secondhand, since he hadn't attended any meetings. But he said he had been in Paris during the fateful October 15-20 week and, with his own eyes, saw Bush in a hotel lobby.

Obtaining corroboration of secret meetings in Paris wouldn't be easy. Both Bush and Reagan had denied any knowledge of a conspiracy. Iran said such talk was rubbish. William Casey, the alleged mastermind, was dead.

Could he prove he'd been a secret agent? I asked.

He couldn't, he admitted. Secret agents, he said, never carried ID, to ensure they wouldn't be tortured for their secrets in the event they were captured.

That made sense to me. If he were an impostor, I reasoned, he would try to dupe me by displaying a phony ID that said, "Ben-Menashe, Secret Agent."

Instead, he showed me documents that said he'd been employed by the Israeli Defense Forces' external relations department. According to him, external relations was a cover for Israeli agents.

I could believe that. CIA operatives often hid their real roles by posing as employees of U.S. embassies. Ben-Menashe hadn't proved he'd been an undercover agent, but could I accept his claim that he'd served in the Israeli government?

Ben-Menashe gave me copies of typewritten letters from three Israeli military officers. The letters were on Israeli Defense Forces' stationery. All were dated in September 1987, shortly after Ben-Menashe said he'd quit as a secret agent. The letters appeared to be character references. Addressed "To Whom It May Concern," they lavished praise on Ben-Menashe.

A Colonel Yoav Dayagi called Ben-Menashe a "gifted person," and said he'd held "key positions." Ben-Menashe was lauded for his "exceptional analytical" talents in "complex and sensitive assignments" by Colonel Pesah Melowany. Colonel Arieh Shur predicted Ben-Menashe would "excel" in any career he chose.

The testimonials failed to specify what work he did in the external relations department. I mentioned this. Ben Menashe shrugged. He asked with sarcasm if I expected his superiors to reveal to the world he'd been an intelligence operative?

Although admitting he hadn't attended the meetings in Europe, Ben-Menashe said he had firsthand information of U.S. arms sales to Iran. As he told it, $80 billion in U.S. arms was sent to Iran in 1981-87. That was a lot of weapons. Perhaps he exaggerated. I pushed the thought aside.

According to Ben-Menashe, weapons had been flown from a U.S. Air

Force base in Arizona to Iran, by way of Israel. A London-based front company, the Ora Group, acted as broker. Ora billed Iran for the weapons; Iran reimbursed the U.S. through Ora.

Could Ben-Menashe prove this? Sure. He had headed the Ora Group.

He showed me a letterhead that said "Ora Group" on top and, at the bottom, "Ari Ben-Menashe, Director."

Fine. But could he prove Ora Group had been the go-between for the shipments?

No problem. Ben-Menashe handed me copies of two telexes to high Iranian government officials. They seemed to show that Ora Group had supplied Iran with arms.

One telex was addressed to "His Excellency President of the Republic Representative of Imam Khomeini, Ayatollan Ali Akbar Rafsanjani." It said: "Able to supply 4,000 units...at a price of U.S. $13,800 each. Inspection upon arrival. Funds have to be deposited in a prime European bank."

The other telex, addressed to "His Excellency Minister of Defense," said: "We have made two attempts to present a $50,000 bank check to your embassy in Vienna and it has been refused due to their lack of information about the subject. We propose that subject be discussed while (our representative) is in your country."

The telexes troubled me.

They were dated February 1987—six years after the 52 hostages were released by Iran. This didn't prove that the freeing of the hostages triggered U.S. arms shipments. I needed to see documents showing that the massive arms sales alleged by Ben-Menashe took place right after the hostages were let go.

Another thing: The telexes, even if they were authentic, didn't prove the involvement of the U.S. government. Nor did they establish that Ora Group was an Israeli government company. For all I knew, Ora Group was a private venture and Ben-Menashe was an opportunistic arms dealer.

I raised these points. Ben-Menashe said he had documents that would overcome my doubts. I would like to see them, I said.

Unfortunately, said Ben-Menashe, they were in safekeeping overseas. It would take a few weeks before he could get them.

I told myself this would be a tough story to crack.

Ben-Menashe had warned me the Israelis would bad-mouth him. I phoned the Israeli Embassy in Washington. He was right.

"Have you heard of an Israeli named Ari Ben-Menashe?" I asked embassy spokeswoman Ruth Yaron.

"We know about him," she said coldly.

"He says he was a go-between for the Israelis in shipping U.S. arms to Iran."

Yaron replied, "Menashe had no involvement in actual or potential sales of arms to Iran."

I said, "He claims to have been an Israeli secret agent."

Yaron was ready for that.

She said, "Menashe is known to the Israeli defense department as a pretender, who introduced himself in the past under many different identities as a high-ranking official of the defense department. The defense department has warned certain countries about him and his record."

Pretty strong stuff.

"I'm sending you some documents," Yaron added. "You'll find them interesting."

I read them. If they were correct, Ben-Menashe had never been a secret agent; he'd been a translator in the external relations department for his entire career.

Included in the documents was a letter from the external relations chief, dated July 23, 1987, to the head of the manpower branch, accusing Ben-Menashe of "taking too many leaves abroad," and returning from one leave "later than the authorized date."

Said the letter: "No more leaves will be authorized (to Ben-Menashe) in the future as they interfere with office work. If this is unsuitable, employee should consider his future in the department."

According to the documents, Ben-Menashe had testified before a government committee that he was quitting as a translator because he hadn't been promoted. In his testimony, he demanded severance pay.

Was Ben-Menashe an impostor? Had he never lived a life of danger and mystery? Was he basically a drone, trapped in a dead-end job?

Walk away, I said to myself. Stop wasting your time. Conspiracy theory stories are a quagmire.

But the letters from his military bosses backed up his claim of having been employed in external relations. Moreover, his last civilian rank as translator was equivalent to that of army captain, proving he hadn't been a cipher.

Maybe the Israeli government was lying about Ben-Menashe. Governments lied all the time, using national security as a pretext. It was too soon to throw in the towel. There was a possibility his story was correct.

Trouble was, he hadn't yet showed me any solid evidence that arms were swapped for the 52 hostages.

I said to Ben-Menashe that my editors would pull me off the story if I didn't come up with hard information pretty soon. Was there no one at Ora Group willing to verify that the company was involved in U.S. arms shipments as a go-between?

Ben-Menashe said Nicholas Davies could confirm it, but that he wouldn't talk to me.

"Who's Nicholas Davies?"

Ben-Menashe said he wrote for the London Daily Mirror.

I was stunned. "This guy is a newspaperman and he was secretly working for the Israelis?" I asked.

Ben-Menashe produced an Ora Group telex, dated February 25, 1987, to the Iranian Defense Minister. It said Davies was an Ora Group representative, with authority to sign contracts in Iran.

I asked for Davies's phone number. Ben-Menashe gave it to me, warning I'd be wasting my time calling him.

Nicholas Davies was the Mirror's foreign editor. The paper's owner was Robert Maxwell, who later would die at sea under mysterious circumstances. Maxwell's many properties also included the Macmillan Publishing Co.

On the phone, Davies denied ever serving as an Israeli undercover agent.

"Why would Ben-Menashe make up such a story?" I asked, puzzled.

Davies said he had no idea what went on in Ben-Menashe's mind.

"Do you know him?" I asked.

"I know him as a news source."

"How long have you known him?"

"He's been a source since the '80s," Davies said.

According to Davies, Ben-Menashe had come to him 18 months earlier, saying he wanted to write a book about Iran-Contra. Would Davies ghost the book, and would Macmillan publish it?

Davies said, "I introduced him to Mr. Maxwell. He put it up to Macmillan. A few weeks later, they said (to Ben-Menashe) 'Thank you, but no thanks.'"

Could Davies be believed? Then why did Davies's name appear on an Ora Group telex? Was the telex phony?

I had opened another can of worms.

I decided not to pursue the Davies angle, else I'd be on the story forever. My spirits sank.

I was still without hard proof the Ora Group brokered the shipments. Nor could I show arms had been sent in the wake of the hostages' release.

But I kept on because he had convinced me he'd worked for the Israeli government

And there was still an angle I could pursue. Ben-Menashe had said that the Israeli government, as the middleman in the arms sales, reaped a $1 billion profit. The money should have gone into the Israeli treasury. Instead, if Ben-Menashe was correct, it was diverted to secret foreign bank accounts by the right-wing Likud government, in cahoots with the Mossad, the Israeli spy agency. The "slush fund," as Ben-Menashe called it, had been used for payoffs to U.S. officials in connection with the Reagan-Iran arms deal, and for new housing for Jewish settlers on the occupied West Bank.

How did Ben-Menashe know? I asked.

He said the Israeli government had appointed a three-member committee to handle withdrawals from the slush fund. According to Ben-Menashe, he was a committee member.

105

"Why you?" I asked

Iran was his area of expertise, Ben-Menashe explained.

Who gave the orders to make withdrawals? I asked.

"We withdrew when told to by the controller of the Mossad," Ben-Menashe said. "We took instructions from the prime minister's office. The signatures of all three members were needed to make a withdrawal."

"The money was used for bribes?"

"Among other things."

"U.S. officials received bribes?"

"They, and others," Ben-Menashe said.

"Which U.S. officials?"

He named five former Reagan Administration officials.

"I don't understand," I said. "Why would they get payoffs?"

"Because they helped in the arms sales."

Could he prove it?

Yes, he had documents. But, he said, he wasn't ready to show them to me.

Didn't it bother him serving on a committee that dished out payments to U.S. officials?

It did, he said. As he explained it, he and the other two on the committee, as an act of conscience, refused in the summer of 1987 to sign any more withdrawal slips. It was agreed by the committee that Ben-Menashe should have power of attorney for the fund, he said.

"Do you still control the fund?" I asked.

He did, he said.

What did he do with the money?

He had transferred the $600 million left in the slush fund to secret bank accounts in the U.S., Europe and South America, Ben-Menashe said. Only he knew the identity of the banks. He had a coded list of the bank accounts. Only he could decipher the list.

I asked why the Yitzhak Shamir government hadn't attempted to recover the money.

As Ben-Menashe explained it, the Israeli public wasn't aware of the slush fund. The Likud government feared it could be kicked out of office if the public knew money had been used for questionable purposes. "The government has to pretend the money doesn't exist," Ben-Menashe said with a smirk.

I asked to be taken to the banks so I could verify the $600 million existed.

If he refuses, I told myself, I'll quit the story.

Ben-Menashe said he'd be happy to accommodate me. There was just one problem. He intended to transfer the $600 million to special Iran-Contra prosecutor Lawrence Walsh. As soon as this was done, he'd let me see the bank records.

I asked how long it would take.

"We're hoping not too long," Ben-Menashe said.

I was shown a letter from attorney Mark Cristini, dated October 29, 1990, to Walsh aide Greg Mark, requesting a meeting "in the safety and security of (Mark's) office" so Ben-Menashe could hand over the profits from the sale of a "massive quantity and variety of arms, airplanes, jets, ammunition, etc."

Ben-Menashe told me he was willing to testify about the 1980 "October Surprise," and to name U.S. officials who accepted bribe payments. In return, he wanted U.S. citizenship to prevent his being deported to Israel where, he said, he feared being murdered by his enemies.

He also wanted a finder's fee—a tax-free $60 million, representing 10% of the $600 million.

I said it sounded like a pretty big fee. He seemed offended.

He said look at the risks he took to ensure that the $600 million didn't fall into the hands of the "corrupt Shamir government." Ben-Menashe added heatedly that he was broke, hadn't any job prospects, and was saddled with debt. Furthermore, he'd promised to split the $60 million with his two former committee colleagues.

Although $60 million sounded excessive, it wasn't my affair. What interested me was the slush fund. If I could prove it existed, I'd have a terrific story.

I didn't want to wait till he and Walsh worked out a deal. I wanted to see the secret bank accounts now, I said.

He refused. He said Walsh might get upset if he found out.

I'd have to drop the story, I warned.

Ben-Menashe wouldn't budge.

I'd been on the story for weeks with nothing to show for it. I said, "Be reasonable."

He still wouldn't budge.

I offered a compromise: He should show me the list of bank accounts, so I could satisfy myself that he was telling the truth. I'd wait till Walsh received the $600 million from Ben-Menashe before publishing the slush fund story.

Again, he refused. He reminded me he was about to go on trial in connection with the alleged conspiracy to sell Iran three military planes and that he was barred by court order from going outside the New York area.

I felt my gorge rising.

I offered to go to the banks alone. I said, "Give me letters signed by you that authorize the banks to show me how much is in each account."

There were 35 bank accounts scattered over half the globe, he said. "It would take you weeks to do it."

"I'm ready," I said stubbornly.

It was a bad idea, he insisted. The banks wouldn't show me the accounts unless he was with me.

You sonofabitch, I thought to myself.

"I'm stymied," I said. "I'm gonna have to drop the story. I see no other choice."

Ben-Menashe relented. He would show me the coded list.

"When?"

"Whenever you want."

"Tomorrow," I said.

He agreed to drop by my office in the morning. But first, he told me, I must go to a bookstore and get "Heart of Europe, a Short History of Poland." This book, he said, contained the key to decipher the coded list of banks.

I was excited. Could it be that the story of a $600 million slush fund was within my grasp? I'm getting close to the Promised Land, I said to myself.

There was such a book. I paid $10.95 for a paperback edition at Barnes & Noble. A blurb on the front-cover of "Heart of Europe" said: "A marvelous read—a great achievement in political writing."

As promised, Ben-Menashe showed up the next morning. I met him when he got off the elevator, and led him to my desk. He wore his usual blue jeans and open-neck shirt. He carried a large manila envelope.

He said not to tell his attorneys he was showing me the coded list. I promised.

He took a sheet of white paper from the envelope, and put it on my desk. I counted 35 rows of numerals, presumably representing the 35 bank accounts he said contained the $600 million. Each row had 12 numerals.

I handed him "Heart of Europe." He turned to Page 245, and pointed to the first word on line four, "compulsory".

"It has 10 letters," he said.

Yes, that was so.

Using a pen, he wrote 1234567890 in consecutive order, above each letter in "compulsory."

Next, he referred to the top row of numerals on the sheet of paper. They were: 172012340273.

With fascination, I watched as he translated 172012340273 into CSOY-COMPYOSM, using "compulsory" as the key.

This reminded me of one of my favorite short stories, Edgar Allen Poe's "The Gold Bug." In it, a pirate chief leaves behind a coded note, giving the exact whereabouts of a treasure he buried. The note—filled with asterisks, parentheses and numerals—looks undecipherable. But Poe's hero unravels it, and unearths the treasure.

But what did CSOYCOMPYOSM stand for?

Ben-Menashe said it was the code name of a bank account.

I was baffled. I thought 172012340273 was the code name for the account. Now he was saying CSOYCOMPYOSM was the code name.

Exasperated, I said, "I don't get it. It's all hocus pocus to me."

I gave him an ultimatum. "I want to go to the banks and see the accounts with my own eyes. Give me letters of authorization. Otherwise, as

108

far as I'm concerned, there are no accounts."

He said he would discuss my request with attorney Cristini.

After Ben-Menashe left, I got on the phone to Cristini. I poured out my frustrations. He listened patiently. He said he'd see what he could do.

Next day, a handwritten, unsigned message came to the office. It was on yellow, legal-size paper. It said:

"Confidential.

1. Chicago-Tokyo Bank
   Chicago, Illinois U.S.A.
   Last Date of Activity 1988
   Amount on deposit $20,000,000
   #66068204
   Account name. Ora Ben-Shalom
   (Power of attorney in safe deposit box—key available)

2. Chicago-Tokyo Bank
   Chicago, Illinois U.S.A.
   Last date of activity 1988
   Amount on deposit $18,000,000,
   Account name: Shula Livney
   (Power of attorney in safe deposit box—key available)

3. Bank of Hungary
   Main Branch—Budapest
   Amount on deposit $15,000,000
   Account #341226633
   Code: Orah
   Name on account: Eitan Levadi"

Hallelujah! Ben-Menashe had come through.

True, I had only three bank accounts to work with. But it was a start.

I'd worn Ben-Menashe down. My persistence had paid off. I was proud of myself. Other reporters would've given up long ago. Not me. I was a bulldog.

Thanking Cristini for his efforts on my behalf, I asked what my next move should be.

He said I should write a letter to Chicago-Tokyo Bank in Chicago, authorizing the bank, in Ben-Menashe's name, to give me the information; that Ben-Menashe would sign the letter, and that he, Cristini, would hand-deliver it to the bank.

Was there ever an attorney in all of history as helpful as Cristini? He was taking time from a busy schedule to fly to Chicago to see that the bank got the letter. What a nice guy Cristini was. I would buy him a dinner after this was over.

In Ben-Menashe's name, I typed a letter instructing Chicago-Tokyo Bank to verify for Stanley Penn, A Wall Street Journal reporter, that Ari Ben-Menashe was empowered to withdraw $38 million from the Shula Livney

109

and Ora Ben-Shalom accounts.

After Ben-Menashe signed it, Cristini, good to his word, took it to Chicago.

He phoned me from O'Hare Airport, saying he'd just arrived. A few hours later, he called to say Ben-Menashe's letter had been delivered and he was grabbing the first plane back to New York.

Excitedly, I phoned Chicago-Tokyo. Bank officer William Bond came on the line. I identified myself, and asked if he had received Ben-Menashe's letter of authorization.

Yes, he had it. Then silence.

"Anything wrong?" I asked.

Bond said the bank hadn't any accounts in those names.

There must be some mistake, I said.

No mistake, Bond replied.

"You're telling me you don't have a Shula Livney or Ora Ben-Shalom account?"

Bond said he'd gone through the bank records. There simply were no accounts in those names.

I hung up. I was ready to explode. .

I left a message for Cristini to call me when he got back from Chicago. To calm my nerves, I left the office and walked the streets. I had lunch. A message from Cristini's secretary awaited me when I returned.

It said: "Gave Mark message regarding Ari. Ari has several aliases."

What did it mean?

Did the bank accounts exist, or not? I didn't bother to ask. I no longer cared.

There were too many unresolved questions. Ben-Menashe couldn't be trusted. My patience exhausted, I gave up the story.

Ben-Menashe's story of numbered bank accounts had also tantalized the Feds. FBI agent Michael Foster had interviewed him in Manhattan in January 1990, shortly after his arrest in the cargo plane conspiracy for which he was later acquitted.

In the interview, according to a transcript, Ben-Menashe never referred to the 1980 "October Surprise." Instead, he focused on Iran-Contra. He claimed he had incriminating new information about bribe payments, including numbers of five European bank accounts in the names of "at least" three U.S. government officials. The documents, said Ben-Menashe, were given him by one Amiram Nir, a former Israeli government adviser on anti-terrorism, who assertedly "stole" them from the office of Likud Prime Minister Shamir. Nir died in a 1988 plane crash in Mexico.

FBI Agent Foster asked Ben-Menashe if his allegations could be corroborated. Ben-Menashe said he'd given assistant U.S. attorney Baruch Weiss a coded list of the European bank account numbers. Those records, he said, would prove bribes had been paid to U.S. officials. All Weiss had to do was decode the numbers.

There was just one hitch. Ben-Menashe had designed the code by using a page from a book entitled "A Short History of Poland."

"No one can decipher the code except Menashe," Foster said.

I'm no longer in touch with Ben-Menashe. But I read about him from time to time. He supplied information for Gary Sick's book, "October Surprise," and for a book by investigative reporter Seymour Hersh, "The Samson Option," about Israel's nuclear weapons program.

In January 1993, the edifice built by the conspiracy theorists came crashing down. After an 11-month investigation, a bipartisan panel of the U.S. House of Representatives found that a conspiracy never existed. The panel's report called Ben-Menashe's "October Surprise allegations...a total fabrication."

AFTERWORD

WHEN STANLEY PENN retired from The Wall Street Journal staff at the end of 1990 he threw away a pile of the file folders and notebooks accumulated during his career of distinguished reporting. Some of the notes he threw out were more than 30-years-old and some of those he still has go back 25 years. "It pains me to get rid of them," Stan told a colleague.

It is a painful act for many reporters, it seems, and the single question that I am asked most often by reporters in my role as counsel for Dow Jones and The Wall Street Journal is: "How long should I keep my notes?"

There is no pat answer to that question; but here, in a nutshell, is what I explain time and again to reporters concerning the retention of notes.

If we're sued, good notes from the reporter are the cornerstone of our defense. Notes establish the care that went into the reporting and a map of how the reporter put the story together.

The statute of limitations for bringing a libel action is two years from publication in most states, so it would be ideal if reporters saved notes that long. The most important thing, however, is that reporters be consistent.

If a reporter always holds notes for one year, he or she shouldn't throw out the notes from any story before then. Should we ever have to explain why the notes are missing, a jury might well infer an evil motive, presuming that the notes included some damaging details, and not understand that the destruction was inadvertent or resulted from a lack of space. If the reporter usually holds notes for six months, but decides to hold notes from an investigative story for two years, he or she should apply this policy to all of his or her notes.

—STUART KARLE
Counsel
Dow Jones & Company

RECOMMENDED REFERENCE SOURCES

Following is a list of federal and state agencies, which issue periodic reports on organized crime, drug trafficking, and other criminal activities. Ask to be put on the mailing lists.

Pennsylvania Crime Commission (yearly report) 1100 E. Hector Street, Suite 470, Conshohocken, PA. 19428. (215) 834-1164

New York State Commission of Investigation (yearly report) 270 Broadway, 26th Floor, New York, N.Y. 10007. (212) 577-0700

New Jersey Commission of Investigation (yearly report) 28 W. State Street, CN 045, Trenton, N.J. 08625. (609) 292-6767

U.S. State Department's Bureau of International Narcotics, 2201 "C" Street N.W., Room 7333, Washington, D.C. 20520. (202) 647-8464

Senate Permanent Subcommittee on Investigations, 100 Russell Senate Office Building, Washington, D.C. 20510. (202) 224-3721

California Attorney General's Office, Bureau of Investigation, 4949 Broadway, Room C217, Sacramento, CA. 95820. (916) 445-9555

U.S. Postal Service (monthly report) Main Building, 475 L'Enfant Plaza West S.W., Washington, D.C. 20260. (202) 268-3864

U.S. Justice Department, 10 Street & Constitution Ave. N.W., Washington, D.C. 20530. (202) 514-2007

U.S. General Accounting Office, 441 "G" Street N.W., Washington, D.C. 20260. (202) 512 3000

Two published reports that are worth a look:

President's Commission on Organized Crime 1985-86 Report, Washington, D.C. (Available at the New York Public Library, 42nd Street and Fifth Avenue, Room 228, and at many other public libraries. It is no longer available for purchase.)

Organized Crime: 25 Years After Valachi, issued by U.S. Senate Permanent Subcommittee on Investigations, Washington, D.C. (Also available at the New York Public Library and others. It may be purchased for $30 at the Government Printing Office, 26 Federal Plaza, Room 110, New York, N.Y. 10278. (212) 264-3825)

SOME STORIES BY STANLEY PENN

'Get the Giant'

Computer Rivals Try New Tactics to Lessen The Dominance of IBM

Some Step Up Development, Realign Staff, Concentrate On Certain Market Areas

RCA Sees Bonanza in 1970s

By STANLEY W. PENN

The nation's "other" computer makers are regrouping their forces in an effort to unloose the industry grip of International Business Machines Corp. They hope the tactics will hasten the day that their computer operations pay off.

At the moment, IBM holds an estimated 65% to 70% of the computer market, now running at $3.6 billion a year and still growing. Of the eight big companies making computers for business and science, it alone is making a substantial profit from the business. At least four, and possibly five, of the other seven are losing money on their computer operations.

IBM's competitors face several big problems. To compete effectively, they must allocate huge sums for research and development. Because most customers prefer to lease rather than buy the systems, the recovery of this investment is slow. Also, IBM dominates all marketing areas of the business. To compete effectively on all fronts, the other companies must build marketing staffs that some right now can't profitably support.

One alternative, of course, is to quit the business. This, however, is unlikely. IBM's rivals are finding that the mere fact they have a computer line is helping sales of their other office products. And they expect big earnings

from computers eventually. Radio Corp. of America predicts computers will be as vital to it in the 1970s as color television is today.

Anyway, the companies aren't in real straits. Most have ample funds from their other operations to carry them through this expensive phase in the computer age.

The other alternative is to take the attack. This is what is being done. Among other things, the major competitors of IBM are:

-Concentrating sales efforts in fewer markets. "It was a problem trying to meet IBM on all fronts," says J. Frank Forster, president of Sperry Rand Corp., the Univac maker. "We decided we should be more selective in the markets we cover," he adds, declining to identify the markets Univac plans to play down.

-Committing large sums to research and development. One IBM competitor has been spending 10% of total company revenue for R&D work to bring out new equipment and develop new uses for computers. (IBM spends 6% on research and development.)

-Realigning sales staffs and increasing their productivity. Burroughs Corp. has found that a salesman does a better job if he concentrates on computers rather than on a variety of office products including computers. RCA says each of its nearly 200 computer salesmen booked nearly twice as much business last year as in 1962 because they now are more knowledgeable.

-Bringing out computers one or two at a time, as need dictates, rather than introducing a whole family of computers at once. This tack, being followed by Univac and Burroughs, spreads research and development costs over longer periods.

-Altering the traditional pattern of short-term leasing contracts. The typical contract has been for 12 months; at the end of that time, a customer is free to turn in the machine to the maker and switch to a competitor's model. Because of high marketing and installation costs, short-term contracts are far from lucrative for the maker. Honeywell, Inc., among others, has revised its price policies to give cost advantages to customers agreeing to four-year or five-year leases.

These moves, the computer makers reason, will lead eventually to computer profits. For some companies, it may be a long road. At the moment, Control Data Corp. is showing a modest profit after several years of fast growth. RCA has been showing a slight profit on computer operations since 1964. It isn't known whether National Cash Register Co. is making money on its computers. General Electric Co., Honeywell, Inc., Sperry Rand and Burroughs are losing money on computers.

These other companies are narrowing their losses on computers. And some figure they would be making a profit now if computers, like cars or steel, were purchased rather than leased by most users.

"When you're developing your computer business largely on a leasing arrangement—and making progress in earning an additional share of the market—you temporarily postpone profitability," according to Fred Borch, president of General Electric Co. "The reason is that you have incurred high development and production costs within a short period of time, but you need a period of years to recover your investment from regular rental income."

GE, which entered the computer field in 1956, hasn't said publicly when it expects to earn money from the machines. One drag on GE's profitability has been its heavy investments in the European computer field. It has invested $55 million in France and Italy in the past two years.

Just this week IBM said it would have to raise money to finance the heavy production demands for its System 360 computers. The company authorized a common stock offering to shareholders designed to raise about $350 million. It also said it arranged a $160 million line of credit with several banks.

A key reason Control Data had been one of the few profitable producers in the industry in the past is that most of its computers were sold outright and not leased. The company, which has been slumping in recent months, is expected to show a sharp drop in profit in the fiscal year ending June 30, and this is due partly to the increasing ratio of lease orders to outright purchases.

"For most of our large computer systems, a switch of just one order from sale to lease can materially reduce current after-tax earnings per share," William C. Norris, president of Control Data, has said. The company's 6600 machine, one of its biggest, sells for upwards of $5 million.

Honeywell, Inc., also troubled by the slowness of recovering investment through the leasing of computers, recently decided to sell some leased-out computers to "a financial organization" and then rent them back from the company. The equipment, which Honeywell customers have on five-year leases, was sold to the finance company at list price; the customers aren't affected.

This tactic provided $2.2 million, or 16 cents a share, of Honeywell's first period profit of $8,636,429, or 60 cents a share, according to James H. Binger, chairman. This more than accounted for the company's 22% gain in earnings from a year earlier.

If industry shipments are any guide, the profit potential for computer makers is increasing each year. This year's expected total for domestic revenue (sales plus lease income) of $3.6 billion is up from $3 billion last year and $2 billion in 1963, according to the Business Equipment Manufacturers Association, a trade group. A level of $6 billion is predicted for 1970.

In addition, U.S. makers play a major role in supplying computers to the foreign market, which is growing even more rapidly than the U.S. market.

Even though the computer line itself isn't profitable to some companies, it is bringing in some business in other areas, they say. National Cash Register, which may or may not be making money on computers, says its computer line has stimulated sales of NCR cash registers, accounting and adding machines. "If we hadn't been producing computers, the other ends of our business would have suffered," says O. B. Gardner, vice president of the accounting machine and data processing division. The office machines are being used increasingly as peripheral equipment for computer systems.

One reason computer profitability has been so elusive is that the companies have to keep developing bigger and better computers to remain competitive. And the bigger the computer, it seems, the bigger the problems.

Control Data found to its dismay that a few of its 6600 computers—among the biggest and fastest in the industry—had some technical problems, including a few defective components, that didn't show up until after the machines were installed. Control Data didn't collect any revenue from the machines until the problems were overcome.

The switchover to new models is costly even to IBM. T.J. Watson, Jr., IBM's chairman, has said that the new micro-electronic modules, which are the basic building blocks in the circuitry of the new machines, required "totally new manufacturing concepts." IBM also has had to resort to costly overtime schedules at some of its plants to keep shipping delays down to a minimum.

One way to make money in the computer business apparently is to concentrate on one segment of the market. At least that's the secret of the success of Scientific Data Systems, Inc., a small Santa Monica, Calif., computer maker that has been profitable almost from its formation in 1962.

Scientific Data Systems has carefully skirted the large-scale computer market, in which IBM and Control Data are the major factors, and has concentrated on small computers priced at $29,000 to $150,000; most of these computers are sold rather than leased,

which also aids profitability. In addition, it concentrates its marketing in the scientific field, avoiding large areas of the competitive commercial business.

As a result, earnings last year jumped to $3.3 million from $2.1 million a year earlier, while revenue climbed to $45 million from $20.4 million. With such success in the small computer field, the company last month introduced the Sigma 7, a medium-scale computer designed for solving business and scientific problems. The system sells for $200,000 to $1 million.

—April 28, 1966

The Schenley Saga

How the Personal Life Of Chairman Entwines With Corporate Affairs

Firm Figures Prominently In Rosenstiel Legal Tiffs; 1965 Profit Moved Upward

Raiders Waiting in the Wings?

By STANLEY W. PENN

To an outsider, Schenley Industries, Inc., might seem ripe for a takeover.

Though it is still among the top U.S. distillers, Schenley's profits have mostly stood still for the past 10 years, while liquor consumption has surged. Its leader, Lewis S. Rosenstiel, is 74, is enmeshed in personal legal troubles, and has announced that by Sept. 12 he will step down as Schenley's $250,000-a-year president and chairman to become a $150,000-a-year consultant. For decades he has ruled Schenley as "the chief," according to subordinates (as a "dictator," critics say) and competitors can't see who might fill his shoes. "It's like asking who will replace de Gaulle," says one.

Still, a Schenley takeover is no cinch—as

several outsiders already have discovered. Even after he relinquished day-to-day management, Mr. Rosenstiel told a recent visitor to his Conyers farms estate in Greenwich, Conn., "I'll probably never retire." He has brushed aside several attempts by outsiders to acquire the estimated 29% of Schenley's stock that he and associates own.

In other ways, too, Mr. Rosenstiel shows undiminished vigor. A tall, husky man with thinning hair, he wears amber-tinted glasses, still smokes long cigars, and still displays a quick temper. In past years he has survived hot disputes with competitors and minority shareholders. Now he is fighting an exceedingly bitter marital battle with his 43-year-old fourth wife, into which Schenley's name has been dragged; another court struggle with his own daughter, involving control of a foundation owning much Schenley stock; and still a third court struggle with his former personal attorney, Ben Javits, who has rumbled about possibly starting a proxy fight for Schenley. As these entanglements suggest, Mr. Rosenstiel's personal affairs are so often intertwined with Schenley's that it is next to impossible to separate the two.

There are signs, too, that Mr. Rosenstiel has got Schenley profits moving again. In its last five fiscal years (they end Aug. 31) Schenley averaged $10.8 million operating profit a year, against a $10.9 million average in the preceding five years, though U.S. liquor consumption rose 35% over the 10-year period. But in fiscal 1965 operating profits jumped to $17.7 million, from $10.4 million the year before, on a gain in sales to $460.7 million from $405.7 million.

116

In August 1964 Schenley acquired 53% of the stock of Buckingham Corp. Thus Schenley's better performance in 1965 reflected in part Buckingham's contribution, whereas 1964 results did not. All Buckingham's sales for the full 1965 fiscal year were included in the Schenley sales for 1965, and Schenley's share of Buckingham's 1965 profits bolstered Schenley's 1965 profits.

With control of Buckingham, Schenley got exclusive rights to distribute Cutty Sark, the top-selling Scotch, in the U.S. Analysts say lack of a top-selling Scotch had accounted for much of Schenley's earlier lackluster performance.

Mr. Rosenstiel's reputation as a redoubtable foe has not kept several groups from covetously eyeing his position at Schenley—and his stock. Among its attractions: Schenley assets top $500 million, and its book value (excess of assets over liabilities) per common share is about $52—though the stock sold for only $12 a share at yesterday's close.

Some outsiders also feel Schenley could earn more with more aggressive and brand-conscious management than they think Mr. Rosenstiel has supplied. Current profits are a far cry from the $49.1 million Schenley earned in 1946 when it was the top U.S. distiller. Distillers Corp. Seagrams, Ltd., passed it in 1947, and today Schenley is bunched with Hiram Waler-Gooderham & Worts, Ltd., and National Distillers & Chemical Corp. in industry rank. Each is estimated to have 12% to 14% of the liquor market, against over 20% for Seagrams.

No Schenley brand—not even Cutty Sark—was among the top 10 in U.S. liquor sales in 1964, according to the most recent figures generally accepted in the industry. Mr. Rosenstiel, as creator of the Bourbon Institute, has done much to popularize bourbon. But National Distillers' Old Crow is the No. 1 bourbon. Schenley's Ancient Age is third among bourbons, and was eleventh among all liquor brands in 1964.

Consequently, the outlines of not one but several possible future bids for Schenley control can be seen in these recent maneuvers.

In January 1965 Schenley reported to stockholders that an outside group had bid unsuccessfully to buy the Rosenstiel group's Schenley stock. This group has never been identified; all efforts to interview Mr. Rosenstiel about attempts to buy his stock—or about other aspects of his role in the company—have been rebuffed in the last several weeks.

In early 1965 Glen Alden Corp. made a bid to buy out the Rosenstiel interests. It has $50 million or more available to renew that bid if its chairman, financier Meshulam Riklis, chooses to do so. At current prices that would buy nearly 1.2 million Schenley shares, or 24% of the total.

Another suggestion of outside interest in Schenley stock occurred in December 1964, at the annual meeting, when Ben Javits turned up. He was no stranger either to Schenley or Mr. Rosenstiel, having represented both in times past. In 1961 Mr. Rosenstiel had hired him to aid the Schenley chief's marathon efforts to dissolve his marriage to his blonde wife Susan, but by the time of the 1964 meeting his client-attorney relationship had gone extremely sour. Indeed the two men were, and still are, personally suing each other—Mr. Rosenstiel contending that Mr. Javits did not represent him properly, and Mr. Javits contending Mr. Rosenstiel had not paid him for all his legal services.

At the meeting, Mr. Javits asked a series of questions that angered Schenley's management. Among them: Whether a certain journalist was on Schenley's payroll. Then Mr. Javits asked for a Schenley stockholder list. Months later he explained he was considering starting a proxy fight for control of Schenley.

All these maneuvers have met a cold reception from Schenley. In the same letter reporting to stockholders the unidentified group's bid last January, Schenley made a tender offer to buy for its treasury 1 million of the approximately 5.9 million common shares it then had outstanding, reducing the total by about 16%. Nat Gluck, a minority shareholder, filed suit to block the offer, saying it would increase the Rosenstiel group's percentage ownership of Schenley (then estimated at 24%, against 29% now) and thus "cement their position." His suit failed, Schenley spent $32 million on the buy-in, and common outstanding has been reduced to about 5 million shares now.

When Mr. Javits asked for a stockholder list, Schenley got a New York court to order him to submit to examination to see if the company had grounds for suing him. This questioning brought hints that still other outsiders had been interested in the liquor company.

Roy Cohn, counsel for Schenley and a controversial figure himself, conducted the examination last April. Under his questioning, Mr. Javits said he had talked about Schenley with Herbert Allen, a partner in Allen & Co., Wall Street investment house. "I think Herbert Allen told me they were discussing the possibility of buying control of the company from Mr. Rosenstiel," he said. Mr. Allen says this was a "casual conversation," initiated by Mr. Javits, and nothing came of it.

Mr. Javits has stated, in papers on file in New York Supreme Court, that Schenley between 1956 and 1959 paid him $100,000 to keep an eye out for any groups trying to move into Schenley—and specifically for any purchases of Schenley stock by Samuel Bronfman, president of Seagrams and an old adversary of Mr. Rosenstiel. Under examination by Mr. Cohn, Mr. Javits conceded that his brother, U.S. Senator Jacob Javits, "has a close personal relationship" with Mr. Bronfman's son Edgar. But he answered "no" to questions about possible relationships of the Senator, Seagrams or the Bronfmans to his disputes with Schenley and with Mr. Rosenstiel.

Mr. Javits will not say now if he is still considering a Schenley proxy fight. Schenley has dismissed his questions at the 1964 annual meeting as being "motivated by a personal desire to . . . improve his bargaining position in (his) unrelated litigation" with Mr. Rosenstiel. A representative of Mr. Javits has retorted that, in Schenley's efforts to find grounds for suing the lawyer, "Mr. Rosenstiel is using his corporation as a vehicle" to harass Mr. Javits.

This exchange illustrates how difficult it is to disentangle Mr. Rosenstiel's personal affairs from his role in Schenley—or from his ability to continue in that role. Nearly all the extensive personal litigation he is enmeshed in has produced testimony about his conduct at Schenley. And much criticism of the way Schenley has been run turns into criticism of Mr. Rosenstiel.

Given the long time Mr. Rosenstiel has been the dominant figure in Schenley, it would be difficult to assess the company without considering his personal characteristics. Born in Cincinnati in 1891, Mr. Rosenstiel went to work as a floor sweeper in an uncle's distillery in Kentucky as a 17-year-old.

During Prohibition, Mr. Rosenstiel had the foresight to buy an idle distillery in Schenley, Pa., and also to buy up stocks of aged whisky, which other distillers didn't want to keep holding, against the day its public sale might again become legal. He incorporated Schenley as a distilling company when the "Noble Experiment" was repealed in 1933. The company began life with a bigger inventory of liquor to sell than most of its rivals, and thus a long head start on them.

The Schenley boss had other triumphs since. In 1959 the industry gave him much credit for leading a lobbying drive that produced a change in Federal liquor tax laws. This eased the tax burden on distillers who wanted to hold whiskeys for aging up to 20 years, an important gain in competing with premium-priced liquors from abroad.

When Schenley set out to acquire Buckingham Corp., and the U.S. distribution rights to Cutty Sark, in 1964, competitors were angling for Buckingham, too. "But they couldn't move as fast as Rosenstiel," says a former Schenley executive, with grudging admiration. "That's because he's his own boss. He doesn't care what hour of the night he calls somebody in," says a former subordinate. "He'll go, if he has to, until 5 in the morning."

But critics of Mr. Rosenstiel contend his leadership hasn't been very consistent. "He has brilliant ideas, but he doesn't have the patience to build brands over the long pull," says a former aide. "He may have a faltering brand. He'll try a new merchandising campaign. If it doesn't get results in a short time, he'll drop it."

"Rosenstiel is not a sharp merchandiser," says an official of a liquor company. "He goes all over the lot. There's no continuity to his (promotional) campaigns."

In dealing with subordinates, former Schenley executives picture Mr. Rosenstiel as domineering and suspicious—a combination several have found unnerving.

"He screams at you one minute and then loves you the next," says one former aide. "It became too much of an emotional thing working for him. I remember I was in his office one day and he began screaming at me for something in the presence of people who were under me—and I mean screaming. I wouldn't take it, certainly not in front of the others; I walked out and went back to my office. He followed me, angry that I'd walked out. Later, we were good friends again. He loved me."

Former Schenley executives may tend to see Mr. Rosenstiel in an unfavorable light, of course. But present executives, who might be more friendly, are unavailable. Attempts to reach them directly or through Schenley's corporate vice president for public relations, Paul Lockwood, or through Schenley's outside public relations advisers, the Carl Byoir agency, have been fruitless. No one wants to talk.

One possible explanation of this reticence is suggested by a former aide of Mr. Rosenstiel, who says: "He's suspicious of the world. He's concerned that people are trying to undermine him."

Susan Rosenstiel, the liquor executive's estranged wife, said in a 1962 affidavit on file in New York Supreme Court that "our house at E. 80 St. (New York) is a veritable electronic maze, with concealed microphones, wiretapping equipment and recording instruments throughout the entire house. Practically every telephone call or conversation with visitors was recorded while plaintiff (Mr. Rosenstiel) lived there." Former Schenley executives often were summoned to the townhouse for business conferences.

On file in the same court is an inventory of property found at the E. 80 St. townhouse July 1963. It shows $1,225 worth of "microphones, telephone taps and wires for tape recorders, etc.," listed as having been found in the library, Mr. Rosenstiel's bedroom and other rooms.

Whether or not Mr. Rosenstiel is hard to work for, nine of 14 vice presidents Schenley had in 1956 are no longer there. They include Mr. Rosenstiel's son-in-law, Sidney Frank, who stepped out as vice president and a director in 1961.

No. 2 man at Schenley for several years was W. Earle Blakeley, executive vice president. He came to Schenley from Bankers Trust Co. and was greatly respected in the financial community. But he left recently; Schenley said its board accepted his resignation after he "requested early retirement."

Mr. Blakeley was succeeded by Louis B. Nichols, who joined Schenley in 1957 after 23 years with the FBI, where he had risen to be administrative assistant to J. Edgar Hoover. Mr. Rosenstiel is known to have a high regard for Mr. Hoover and the FBI. Liquor industry sources say Mr. Nichols also was recommended by Roy Cohn, who has become a close friend of Mr. Rosenstiel as well as the Schenley chief's personal attorney. One source who knows both says "Rosenstiel idolizes Roy. He looks on Roy as a son."

Mr. Cohn and Mr. Nichols had become friends in Washington when Mr. Cohn was chief counsel for the late Sen. McCarthy's investigating committee. Mr. Nichols was a witness for Mr. Cohn in 1964, when Mr. Cohn was tried by the Federal Government on charges of conspiracy and perjury arising out of his association with key figures in the United Dye & Chemical Corp. stock fraud case. Mr. Cohn was acquitted.

At least one Schenley competitor questions whether Mr. Nichols' FBI training would enable him to take over the top spot after Mr. Rosenstiel bows out. This liquor executive says: "They tell me he's an able man," but the questions whether Mr. Nichols' experience in the industry qualifies him for the top post.

An analyst for a large brokerage house asserts: "I have some doubts about the depth of Schenley's management." Mr. Nichols is 60, and some of Schenley's other nine current vice presidents are aging. James B. O'Rear is 73; Frank Sundstrom is 65; James Woolsey is 61 and Theodore Gommi is 60.

Whatever Mr. Nichols' talents as a liquor executive, Ben Javits has stated that Mr. Nichols has assisted Mr. Rosenstiel in his personal affairs. In a bill of particulars supporting his litigation against Mr. Rosenstiel in New York Supreme Court, Mr. Javits said Mr. Nichols wrote him at least one letter, demanding an accounting of money Mr. Javits had spent while acting as Mr. Rosenstiel's attorney in the Schenley chief's marital dispute.

According to Mr. Javits' bill of particulars, John Harrington, another Schenley official (assistant to Mr. Rosenstiel) also became involved in Mr. Rosenstiel's dispute with Susan Rosenstiel. Mr. Javits said in the court papers that Mr. Harrington had ordered him, while he was acting as Mr. Rosenstiel's attorney, to investigate various aspects of Mrs. Rosenstiel's personal life.

Schenley's name has popped up in other litigation related to the marital dispute. The Rosenstiels were married in 1956, when the Schenley chief was 65 and Susan was 34. They separated five years later. After that Mr. Rosenstiel sought an annulment, claiming that Mrs. Rosenstiel's Mexican divorce from a previous husband was invalid. New York Supreme Court once granted an annulment but higher New York State courts reversed it last year, so that the Rosenstiels legally are still married.

Now, Bonwit Teller, a department store, and more than 20 other shops are suing to collect $40,000 to $50,000 in allegedly unpaid bills from the Rosenstiels. Mr. Rosenstiel contends that his wife should pay; he says he gave her more than enough money when they lived together. Mrs. Rosenstiel claims her husband should be held liable. The trial, in New York Civil Court, is now in progress.

In December, Mrs. Rosenstiel testified at this trial that between Dec. 1, 1960, and January 31, 1961, she had entertained at a cabana at the Fontainebleau Hotel in Miami, with Mr. Rosenstiel present. "It was Schenley Industries' cabana," she said. The Fontainebleau management says a cabana of that type rents for $125 a week in that season.

Of course, Mrs. Rosenstiel can hardly be described as a friendly witness. But a witness much more sympathetic to the Schenley leader also has testified at the trial to connections between Mr. Rosenstiel's living expenses and the corporate coffers of Schenley. He is Seymour Roberts, Mr. Rosenstiel's personal accountant.

Mr. Roberts has produced figures showing that, from 1956 through 1961 (the period when the Rosenstiels lived together) Mr. Rosenstiel had gross household expenses of $626,000. According to these figures, Schenley paid $355,000 of that, while Mr. Rosenstiel paid $271,000.

In the same years, Mr. Roberts figures showed, Mr. Rosenstiel's gross yacht expenses were $366,000. Schenley paid $216,000, and Mr. Rosenstiel $150,000. Mr. Roberts testified that Mr. Rosenstiel often uses his various homes—the Manhattan townhouse, Conyers Farms in Greenwich, and a residence in Miami Beach—for business purposes.

The extent of Schenley's reimbursement of Mr. Rosenstiel for certain expenses had earlier been an issue in litigation between the Schenley chief and Annette Abramson, a minority Schenley shareholder. Mrs. Abramson charged in a Delaware court that some of Mr. Rosenstiel's business expenses were excessive and that his employment contract was unreasonable.

Mr. Rosenstiel denied the charges. But in a settlement made effective September 1960, he agreed to take a pay cut from $300,000 a year to his present $250,000; to reduce his vacation period to two months from three months a year; to increase by $3 a share the price he would pay for Schenley shares acquired upon the exercise of certain options, and to refund Schenley $135,000 he had received in the past.

In the settlement, Mr. Rosenstiel also gave up five months of accumulated vacation time and surrendered claims of $38,423 for reimbursement for business expenses incurred from Aug. 29, 1955, to September 1960. Mrs. Rosenstiel said in her 1962 affidavit in New York Supreme Court that, as another result of Mrs. Abramson's suit, these items were returned to Schenley from the Rosenstiels' Manhattan townhouse: $200 worth of soup plates; two statuettes each valued at $75; a $65 vase; a $185 porcelain box, and some cups and saucers.

The settlement has not noticeably diminished Mr. Rosenstiel's personal wealth. His total worth isn't known, but information on the record indicates it is quite extensive. Mr. Roberts has testified at the current trial in New York Civil Court that the Schenley chief's total capital assets at book value at the end of 1961 were $6.6 million. Of that, some $3.4 million was represented by securities which had a market value then of $18 million.

At present, Mr. Rosenstiel's 690,790 Schenley common shares have a market value of $29 million; his 112,876 Schenley preferred shares have a value of $1,128,760. The 1,700 acres of land he and members of his family own in New York and Connecticut are assessed at over $1.4 million, and the six-story Manhattan townhouse that has figured so prominently in his litigation with Susan Rosenstiel is estimated to be worth about $400,000. His Miami home is valued at $113,000 and the Conyers Farms residence at $139,000.

Mr. Rosenstiel's income has been high, too. Figures produced by Roberts at the current trial in New York Civil Court show the liquor executive's gross income for the six years 1956 through 1961 totaled $9.1 million. It ranged from a low of $1 million in 1958 to a high of over $2.6 million in 1961.

However, Mr. Roberts testified, Mr. Rosenstiel had heavy expenses on oil and gas operations in which he had an interest, heavy interest expenses and losses on operation of Conyers Farms—so that his total provision for Federal income taxes for the six years was held to $642,000. It ranged from a high of $337,000 in 1961 to a low of $20,000 in 1956—a year in which Mr. Rosenstiel's gross income, Mr. Roberts testified, was $1.1 million. Mr. Roberts testified that the Internal Revenue Service is auditing Mr. Rosenstiel's returns for several years. This, of course, does not mean the IRS will find anything wrong.

Even apart from his marital dispute and the New York Civil Court trial, not all the Rosenstiel personal litigation in which Schenley's name has popped up has been concluded. The litigation with Ben Javits has not come to trial. Also pending is a dispute between Mr. Rosenstiel and his daughter, Mrs. Sidney Frank, over the running of the Dorothy H. and Lewis S. Rosenstiel Foundation, which holds 494,782 Schenley shares, worth $20.7 million at current prices (Dorothy H. Rosenstiel, Mrs. Frank's mother, was Mr. Rosenstiel's first wife; she died in 1944).

Mrs. Frank in 1961 brought suit in Los Angeles Superior Court to prevent her father from naming three new directors of the nonprofit foundation. She accused her father of using the foundation's holdings, along with his own and those of trusts under his control, to "dominate" Schenley.

Mr. Rosenstiel said that, as a result of deaths, the directors of the foundation were reduced to his daughter and himself. So, he said, he proposed adding Francis Cardinal Spellman of New York; Rabbi Nelson Glueck, president of Hebrew Union College—Jewish Institute of Religion (Cincinnati); and Russell G. Smith, executive vice president emeritus of Bank of America and a Schenley director. Since his daughter opposed the plan, Mr. Rosenstiel sought a declaratory judgment in the California courts as to his rights to carry it out; the litigation is still unresolved.

While such personal troubles pile up, and outside groups angle for his Schenley stock, Mr. Rosenstiel has carried on as a stormy petrel not only within Schenley but in the liquor industry at large. Even aside from his feud with Mr. Bronfman of Seagrams he has often provoked sharp industry disputes, and the past few years have seen no letup in these.

In 1962, Schenley led a group of liquor companies seeking permission from the Treasury Dept. to sell liquor in four additional bottle sizes, besides the eight now allowed. The Distilled Spirits Institute, a trade association to which Schenley once belonged, opposed the plan, saying it would cause confusion and lead to price increases that weren't called such. It feared Schenley and others would charge the same price for liquor in new, smaller bottles that was being charged for liquor in established, larger ones. The Treasury ruled against Schenley.

In 1964, Schenley jumped at the chance to broadcast liquor commercials over New York's radio station WQXR, which proposed to break an old broadcasting (and liquor-industry) taboo by accepting liquor-company sponsorship of programs for airing after 10:30 at night. The Distilled Spirits Institute again objected; it has long feared that airing of liquor commercials over radio and TV would arouse anti-liquor groups to push for restrictive legislation. Schenley relented to the extent of not using the air time it bought to advertise whisky. Instead, its commercials mentioned Schenley's name and then called listeners attention to cultural events in the New York area.

Says one liquor executive of Mr. Rosenstiel's role in industry council: "It's reached the point that when Rosenstiel makes a suggestion the rest of us steel ourselves against it. The man is prolific with ideas, but some of them are a little screwy."

—*January 26, 1966*

*   *   *

Fighting Back
Stock-Scheme Victim Is Still Seeking Redress After 9 Years in Courts

Ex-Broker, Now Hotel Clerk, Devotes Himself to Quest For the $250,000 He Lost

Just Deserts or Just Futility?

By Stanley W. Penn

Norman Oppenheimer is the night clerk on the four-to-midnight shift in an old hotel for pensioners and transients.

He lives at the hotel in a stark room with one window, a bed, a few pieces of furniture and a toilet that doesn't always work.

But he is better off than he was. In the past few years, he has been periodically unemployed, his third marriage has broken up and at one point he got kicked out of a fleabag hotel for failing to pay his rent. He has always managed to get back on his feet with odd jobs such as selling Christmas cards and working nights in a Bronx meat market.

Yet the 58-year-old Mr. Oppenheimer, with a dignified manner, well-tailored appearance and a distinguished mane of sandy grey hair, could pass for an executive or stockbroker.

In fact, he once was a $25,000-a-year executive with an electronic firm and before that an $18,000-a-year stockbroker. And in those days he lived in a luxury apartment building on Manhattan's fashionable East Side.

His riches-to-rags saga isn't a case of a scion who dropped out to Skid Row. Rather he is the victim of the stock scheme who has devoted every spare moment for the past nine years to his campaign—some friends and foes alike call it his obsession—to get back the nearly quarter-million dollars he feels he is owed.

This so-far quixotic quest has taken him through seven lawyers and more than $50,000 in legal fees. When he was out of money he became his own lawyer, drawing up motions and arguing his case orally in federal court.

As his debt piled up, his two daughters had to interrupt their education for lack of funds.

Recently, his resolve has been heightened by a few court victories, including a ruling that he was indeed the victim of a scheme. But he has regained only a token amount of the money he says is due, and he certainly isn't quitting now.

His persistence isn't always appreciated. A federal judge rebuked him for his "harrassing tactics" in filing "frivolous" motions, and more than one friend and relative has warned him he may be chasing a will-o'-the-wisp.

His reply: "I was shafted. They took something that was mine. I'm not going to let people get away with it."

But the "they" he refers to are being as elusive as his goal, and there's still doubt he will ever retrieve another penny, however justifiable his case.

Mr. Oppenheimer's tale has enough trial and travail for Messrs. Quixote and Odysseus combined. It all began on a happy note back in 1963, when Mr. Oppenheimer was a securities salesman with Loeb Rhoades & Co. on Wall Street. He helped find an underwriter for a public stock offering of Electro-Nucleonics Inc. of Fairfield, N.J.

In return for his services, Mr. Oppenheimer received a warrant, exercisable until February 1968, to buy 2,250 shares of Electro-Nucleonics at $5 a share, or a total of $11,250. Although that price was above the $3.50 market price of the stock at the time, Electro-Nucleonics was a growing company in a glamor industry, so the warrant was potentially of considerable value. The company has a classified government contract to try to develop a less costly way to produce fuel for nuclear power plants.

Later in 1963, Mr. Oppenheimer quit his job at Loeb Rhoades and went to Puerto Rico to try to start his own brokerage business. Unsuccessful in that effort, he purchased an operating lease on a San Juan hotel, giving his Electro-Nucleonics warrant as collateral.

For a time, everything was sunny in Puerto Rico. Mr. Oppenheimer fixed up the hotel, obtained a liquor license and was planning to apply for a gambling casino permit. But the clouds soon gathered ominously—the hotel owner declared the lease void for alleged nonpayment of rent.

This news was brought by Benjamin Rodriguez, then a principal stockholder in the hotel company. According to Mr. Oppenheimer's later allegations in a complaint in court, Mr. Rodriguez threatened to kill him if he didn't vacate the hotel quickly.

Fearing for his life, Mr. Oppenheimer did leave quickly, but he first demanded his warrant back. Rodriguez refused.

Mr. Rodriguez concedes he had "angry words" with Mr. Oppenheimer over the lease but says, "I had no occasion to threaten him." (Mr. Rodriguez over the years has had a number of brushes with the law. In 1958 he was found guilty of conspiring to violate narcotics laws, but a higher court overturned the verdict. In 1972, he was indicted on another narcotics charge, but the government later dropped the case. And in 1973, a jury acquitted him of narcotics conspiracy charges. He is currently awaiting trial on income-tax evasion charges that he profited from heroin sales.)

Because Mr. Oppenheimer allegedly failed to meet the terms of the hotel operating lease, Mr. Rodriguez claimed he forfeited the warrant, so the Rodriguez-controlled company kept it.

Thus began Mr. Oppenheimer's long quest to regain what he felt was rightfully his warrant. He sued in federal court in Puerto Rico. While the litigation dragged on, the stakes became massively larger. By February 1968, the deadline for exercising the warrant, Electro-Nucleonics stock had risen to $46 a share, and by July 1968 the market value was as high as $105, making the $2,250 shares worth $243,000, against the exercise cost of only $11,250.

Of course, Mr. Oppenheimer didn't then have the warrant to turn in for shares. But in 1969, the court ruled against the Rodriguez-controlled company, giving Mr. Oppenheimer his first cause to rejoice after his four-year struggle.

The rejoicing was short-lived, however, because Electro-Nucleonics wouldn't give Mr. Oppenheimer the shares represented by the warrant. Instead, it asked a federal court in Manhattan to determine the rightful owner of the shares and got and injunction against being sued for damages over the ownership questions.

Electro-Nucleonics's reluctance to turn the stock over to Mr. Oppenheimer stemmed from the fact that ownership had been claimed by another party, one Avelino Fiel, who became the newest adversary in Mr. Oppenheimer's odyssey.

Mr. Fiel, a Brooklyn garage attendant, told in the Manhattan court proceedings how he came by his claim to the stock. He said Mr. Rodriguez approached him for an $8,500 loan, offering $1,500 interest over two months. So Mr. Fiel obtained a bank loan secured by a mortgage on his Brooklyn home and gave Mr. Rodriguez the $8,500. As collateral, Mr. Rodriguez gave Mr. Fiel the Electro-Nucleonics warrant. When Mr. Rodriguez ultimately failed to repay the loan, Mr. Fiel kept the warrant.

In February 1968, the deadline for redeeming the warrant, Mr. Fiel sent it to the company with his check for $11,250. The company issued the shares in Mr. Fiel's name, but it says it didn't actually deliver the shares to him, pending a ruling by the Manhattan court on the rightful owner.

So now Mr. Oppenheimer had to await a ruling by the New York court, and the wait turned out to be long and costly. For a time, he worked for an electronics concern. Later, he worked again as a securities salesman, but he gave that up when he found he "couldn't function because of the mess" of litigation. With his days so involved in his legal crusade, he took only nighttime jobs, including the hotel clerk job he still holds. Without money to pay lawyers, he took his own depositions from Mr. Fiel and argued his own case for a time.

As the Manhattan litigation dragged on. Mr. Fiel at one point offered to give up his claim to the shares if Mr. Oppenheimer would drop the suit. At the time, the shares represented by the warrant were worth about $100,000—less than half the mid-1968 value that Mr. Oppenheimer believes he is entitled to, but a tidy sum for a destitute man whose debts were mounting daily.

Mr. Oppenheimer would have nothing to do with the settlement. "I wouldn't quit," he says. "I wanted justice done."

Mr. Fiel's lawyer, confirming that the offer was made and refused, puts it differently, saying Mr. Oppenheimer seems to be "an obsessed man."

The ownership litigation culminated after five years in another victory of sorts for Mr. Oppenheimer. Judge Constance Baker Motley ruled last year that the warrant belonged to Mr. Oppenheimer. She described Mr. Fiel's account of how he got the warrant as "incredible," adding that he should have known something was amiss because of the steep $1,500 interest over such a short period and the fact that this warrant was worth so much more than the $8,500 loan it backed.

In short, Judge Motley said, Mr. Fiel "knowingly allowed himself to be used in a scheme" to deprive Oppenheimer of his warrant.

With Judge Motley's decision, Electro-Nucleonics finally surrendered the shares (which had been split three-for-one by that time) to Mr. Oppenheimer. The irony, of course, was that the stock market decline had dragged the value of the stock to a fraction of the 243,000 the shares were worth in 1968.

Last September, Mr. Oppenheimer sold the shares for $25,000. "I paid off some loans, and I had my teeth fixed, which I had neglected for the past seven years," he says.

Now, Mr. Oppenheimer is pressing on with a separate suit. He is attempting to name as defendants Electro-Nucleonics, various company officers and directors, Mr. Rodriguez, Mr. Fiel and others in his claim for millions of dollars of damages, asserting they all acted wrongfully to deprive him of his warrant.

Although he formerly was on friendly terms with Electro-Nucleonics, and says he was on a first-name basis with the president, James Nowgard, and chairman, Vincent Abajian, Mr. Oppenheimer feels the company wronged him by blithely accepting Mr. Fiel as the warrant owner despite Mr. Oppenheimer's previous warnings about the litigation in Puerto Rico.

For its part, the company says it had no choice but to issue the shares originally in Mr. Fiel's name. James P. Duffy III, the company's lawyer, says, "Oppenheimer had endorsed the warrant. He put it in the stream of commerce, and it wound up in Fiel's possession. The company isn't a court of law."

The company says it originally had no reason to question the authenticity of the warrant, which was accompanied by a letter from Mr. Fiel's lawyer that it had been purchased for "good and valuable consideration."

(The lawyer, Irwin Germaise, gained notoriety later, in 1971, during the Knapp Commission investigation of corruption in the New York City police department. A tape played for the commission described a purported arrangement for Mr. Germaise to accept a payment in return for a promise to fix a court case. Mr. Germaise, who reportedly has settled in Israel, was disbarred by a court in New York last year on charges he took a $5,000 fee after representing that he could improperly influence a criminal case.)

Mr. Duff of Electro-Nucleonics says the company showed its good faith by not actually delivering the shares to Mr. Fiel, pending settlement of the dispute. But Mr. Oppenheimer says an April 1968 letter from the company said Electro-Nucleonics would defer issuance of the shares, whereas the company actually listed Mr. Fiel in its books as owner of the shares. The company says this was an accident, but it presented a legal roadblock for Mr. Oppenheimer.

Because the shares weren't turned over to him after the Puerto Rico court decision. Mr.

Oppnheimer feels the company is liable for damages. Mr. Duffy counters that Mr. Fiel also claimed to own the shares, and because Mr. Fiel wasn't a party in the Puerto Rico case, the ownership issue wasn't resolved between Mr. Fiel and Mr. Oppenheimer.

But he appealed, and orders were issued by the appeals court and Judge Motley that Mr. Oppenheimer interpreted to mean that the company would be reinstated as a defendant.

Reading one of these court orders in federal courthouse in New York's Foley Square recently, Mr. Oppenheimer broke into a broad grin and fished in his pocket for a dime to call his latest lawyer.

"I have to tell him we've just given birth to a baby," Mr. Oppenheimer said.

It may have been a stillbirth, however, because the appeals court largely left to Judge Motley's discretion whom to keep and whom to remove as defendants in the damage suit. That could mean she will again dismiss Electro-Nucleonics as a defendant before any subsequent trial.

The Oppenheimer opus today remains unfinished. Even if he wins the damage suit, he may have trouble collecting. Some of the people he named as defendants, including Messrs. Rodriguez and Fiel and some others connected with his Puerto Rican hotel troubles, may ultimately show they are unable to pay any damages. And appeals and legal fees could further dilute any of Mr. Oppenheimer's winnings.

Meantime, the night clerk continues his legal sleuthing by day with the same dedication as in 1965. "He's basically an optimistic person," says the first of his three wives. "He always feels that everything will be successful tomorrow."

—*February 28, 1975*

* * *

Of Love and Money
The Case of the Lady And the Stockbroker Could Affect Many

She Alleges Broker Churned Her Account of $600,000 While Holding Her in Sway

He Denies Any Illegal Trading

By Stanley W. Penn

Month after month, the weary woman sat in her broker's office, bitterly watching her stocks go down—and down, and down. "It got beyond human endurance," she recalls. "At the end of the day, I was so tired I'd stagger out."

At one point, she says, she thought of killing herself. "I didn't know how I could go on. One morning, I got up with a terrible case of jitters. My insides were shaking. I went to the brokerage office. I told Marvin (her broker), 'I just can't cope. You're going to have to look after me.'"

Judith Scofield, 56 years old, hazel eyes, reddish blond hair, was a victim of the 1970 stock market collapse, during which the Dow Jones industrial average dived 35% from its 1969 high. Many investors saw their fortunes cut in half, or worse. But few, if any, were wiped out as thoroughly as Judith Scofield was. Mrs. Scofield says she put well over $600,000 in stock and cash into her account over a 14-month period. When the brokerage firm finally froze her account—that is, refused to buy or sell stocks for her—as 1970 drew to a close, she had exactly $6,500 left in it. Today, she no longer has even that. She is broke, she says, and in hock to friends and relatives.

Mrs. Scofield still shows signs of the strain she has been under. "I can't speak civilly anymore," she says. "It's too much stress. My doctor says people can't take that much stress." During those grim months she spent in her broker's office watching her fortune vanish, she gobbled candy constantly to relieve her tension. As a result, she says, her dress size ballooned from 12 to 16. "I looked good two years ago," she says sadly. "I've aged 10 years in that time."

Mrs. Scofield's plight would be of small consequence were it not for a little known suit that she filed last July in Manhattan's federal district court. The outcome of that suit could conceivably affect investors and brokerage firms and the way they do business with each other.

124

Mrs. Scofield says she fell in love with her stockbroker, and according to her complaint filed in federal court she came "under the complete domination and control" of him. She had an affair with him, she says, and she was so crazy about him that she put all her trust and confidence in him, leaving him, in effect, in practical control of her account. In her suit, in which she seeks a $1.3 million judgment, she maintains that the broker and his firm illegally "churned" her account through excessive trading to generate commissions. She alleges they executed over 1,400 trades in her account—more than 100 a month—and billed her for over $122,000 in commissions, service and interest charges and transfer taxes.

Marvin Michael, age 53, handsome, successful, tanned, a product of Harvard Law School and a resident of Park Avenue, is the broker in question. He denies Mrs. Scofield's charges that he milked her account and says he prefers not to discuss her allegations of an affair. "I had no control over her account," he says in an interview. "All I did was make a suggestion when she asked me. She made the decisions. They were her own stock selections. In most cases, she did not ask for my suggestions. She was a compulsive gambler. I tried to get her out of the market and to get a job. I discussed this with her nephew and her sister. She wouldn't get out."

The important legal issue is the extent of a broker's responsibilities to a customer. The question is whether Mrs. Scofield, although never having given the broker "discretionary" power to trade stocks without her okay, had nonetheless relied so totally on the broker's advice that the broker in effect had practical control over the account.

In a case well known to securities lawyers, a California widow, Mrs. Bertha Hecht, was awarded $296,000 a few years ago after she filed a $1.7 million suit charging that her nondiscretionary account at a predecessor partnership of Harris Upham & Co. Inc. had been unfairly and grossly churned. The Hecht suit, of course, doesn't necessarily have any bearing on Mrs. Scofield's action.

What does have bearing is the question of who was really in charge of Mrs. Scofield's account. Hers was not a discretionary account in which a broker has permission to trade stocks for a client using his own judgment. But at least one brokerage official has offered the view that it is possible for a broker to exert control over an account without having been granted discretionary power. In May 1970, William Lerner, then a top executive for Cogan, Berlind, Weill & Levitt Inc.—

which, ironically, later became CBWL-Hayden Stone Inc., one of the parties Mrs. Scofield is suing—told a meeting of securities men that the relationship between customer and broker was a key determinant of who has true account control. If the customer puts his trust and confidence in the broker, the broker may have practical control over the account, no matter whether the customer ostensibly uses his own judgment in buying and selling, said Mr. Lerner who has since left CBWL-Hayden Stone.

So, the question is who had the final word on what stocks Mr. Michael bought and sold for Mrs. Scofield. The suit names three defendants—HS Equities Inc., formerly Hayden Stone Inc., where she opened her account in late September 1969; CBWL-Hayden Stone Inc., formerly Cogan, Berlind, Weill & Levitt Inc., which bought most of Hayden Stone's brokerage offices in September 1970, including the one Mrs. Scofield traded at; and Mr. Michael, who joined Hayden Stone about July 1964, and resigned in December 1970, about a month after Mrs. Scofield withdrew her account.

Besides the churning charge, the suit alleges that the three defendants arranged credit for her in the stock market in violation of federal rules on margin requirements. All of the defendants say they did nothing wrong or improper. CBWL-Hayden Stone adds that most of Mrs. Scofield's grievances deal with a period prior to the firms' takeover of the Hayden Stone branches.

Both Mrs. Scofield and Mr. Michael agree that she was in his office from early morning to evening. "She took over my office," he says. She used a desk next to his, looked up the latest market quotations on a nearby quote machine and eagerly scanned the ticker tape in the outer office. She watched the tape so intently, says a former colleague of Mr. Michael's, that when somebody unintentionally blocked her view of the tape she would impatiently urge the person to move aside. "She was one of Marvin's biggest customers," this man says. "People in the office generally stayed away from her—she was Marvin's territory."

Mrs. Scofield maintains that, with the exception of the first few weeks of their relationship, she didn't buy or sell a stock without Mr. Michael's okay. She says she was given a fistful of "buy" and "sell" tickets. "Marvin might be on the phone, and I might see something on the tape that looked good. I wrote the amount on the 'buy' ticket and showed it to him. He nodded his head yes or shook his head no," she says. One time, when she was visiting her sick father in the hospital, she says, Mr. Michael bought some stock for her without her knowledge. "Our relationship was such that he had carte blanche to do what he pleased," she says.

Nonsense, Mr. Michael replies. "I was unable to give her any advice on the stock market. She refused to follow the opinions of myself or the manager of the office."

Mrs. Scofield says that she came to Mr. Michael in the first place because she had heard he was an extremely savvy broker and she was displeased with the way her account was being handled at Goodbody & Co., her former brokerage office. "I had to produce a large amount of income on a small amount of capital," she says. (She needed income, she says, not only to live on but also to pay the bills of a nonprofit outfit called Save A Cat League Inc., of which she is founder and president. The league finds shelter for stray and abandoned cats.)

At the time Mrs. Scofield walked in the door, Mr. Michael was one of Hayden Stone's top producers. "He is an extremely bright individual," says a former colleague. "A super salesman. He also keeps himself in good shape physically. He's attractive to women."

Mrs. Scofield opened her account in the autumn of 1969 with $150,000 in cash and securities. Then, in March 1970, she added an estimated $350,000 in securities that she had inherited from the estate of her father. The portfolio included shares in such companies as Texas Gulf Sulphur, St. Regis Paper, AMF Industries and Seaboard World Airlines. Mr. Michael looked at these shares and decided none were worth keeping, Mrs. Scofield maintains. "They're too slow for you," she claims he told her. So, she says, those holdings were replaced with glamour stocks that it was hoped would generate big capital gains—stocks like Memorex, Telex and Natomas.

Mr. Michael, who now works for another brokerage firm, denies that story. "This business of owning glamour stocks was her own," he says. "She had owned the Syntexes and Solitrons in the past. She was always in glamour stocks."

Mrs. Scofield says her experience with Memorex illustrates the bad fortune that dogged her. In 1970, Memorex was one of the Big Board's most heavily traded stocks. Over a six-month period—from Feb. 1 to Aug. 1— the stock tumbled nearly 100 points from $144.50 to $48.125. Mrs. Scofield rode Memorex all the way down. "I remember saying at the time, 'If I should die of a heart attack, they'll put "Memorex" on my tombstone.'"

she says ruefully.

At one point, she held about 1,400 Memorex shares. "The stock started down, so Marvin sold 700 shares. The stock turned around and went up. He bought back 700 shares. Then he bought another 700 and sold another 700. We ended up with four trades on that." On the same day, she bought and sold shares in two other securities. Her tally for the day: a loss of $5,600. "I ended up selling off an extra 100 shares of Memorex to make up for the loss."

According to a former colleague, Mr. Michael had a reputation as an astute tape trader. "He was unbelievable. If a stock moved three points, he could be in and out of the stock twice. The tape appears to have a life of its own, regardless of the type of security. You see the buying building up and then the selling off. He could catch that ebb and flow. But you have to be careful when you do it. In a falling market, it's a dangerous technique when you do it with highly speculative stocks."

The atmosphere in the Hayden Stone office was depressing during the bear market. A man who worked there says, "You'd go to bed at night hoping the market would go up the next day. But it didn't. The phone wouldn't ring. The brokers were under pressure to produce. Then, too, the bad publicity about Hayden Stone's financial troubles caused customers to leave. People there were in a daze."

In March of 1970, Hayden Stone was forced to borrow $17.5 million. In May, it cut salaries and laid off people. By June, it was arranging for another loan. In July, stories were going the rounds that Hayden Stone was looking for a merger partner.

Meantime, Mrs. Scofield was renting a $23-a-day room at the Americana Hotel, one block from the Hayden Stone branch in which she kept her account. Back at the office, Mrs. Scofield says she took Mr. Michael's advice and bought 300 shares of Four Seasons Nursing at $11.25. A few days later, the SEC suspended trading in Four Seasons, the company collapsed financially and she unloaded the stock at 58 cents a share.

Mr. Michael says he doesn't recall giving such advice. He maintains that Mrs. Scofield had been in and out of Four Seasons many times in the past strictly on her own initiative.

Mrs. Scofield's account was in such bad shape, he says, that she begged Mr. Michael to call off a European vacation he had planned for August. She says she was worried that with him gone there would be no one to look after her stocks. But he wouldn't yield to her entreaties although, she says, he couldn't keep her woes out of his mind even in Europe. She says he wrote her: "I know how you are suffering in the market. It is now an almost seven months sickness. It seems to worsen no matter what you do. . . ."

For his part, Mr. Michael claims his absence didn't stop Mrs. Scofield from trading even more heavily than she did when he was on the scene. He also says that while he was on that vacation—in early August—Mrs. Scofield, at Hayden Stone's request, signed a letter to the effect that trading in her account was going on with her approval and knowledge.

Mrs. Scofield concedes she signed such a letter. "But it seemed so unimportant at the time," she says. "There was nothing I wouldn't have given Marvin. My feeling was he was going to come back from vacation and look after me and take care of me." "He had made no promises of any sort," she says, "but when you're sharing everyday life together, you assume he is looking out for you." It was her love for Mr. Michael, she says, that impelled her to keep him as her broker even as her fortune swiftly melted away. "Wild horses couldn't have dragged me out. You're so involved with a person it doesn't make any difference."

During the gloomy autumn days of 1970, Mrs. Scofield's spirits were occasionally buoyed by temporary rallies in the market. She recalls a trip she and Mr. Michael took one day to the Catskills where she had bought a barn for $8,000 to shelter her cats. On the drive back to New York City, the radio reported that Memorex had closed that day at $99.50, up $12.50. "I felt my troubles were over," she says.

Mr. Michael says that he lent Mrs. Scofield $10,000—against his better judgment—so she could buy the barn "for the 188 cats she'd kept in her apartment." She repaid that money, he says. But then, he adds, he lent her another $5,000 "because she had no money to feed the help and pay for the cats' upkeep. She still owes me the $5,000."

Mrs. Scofield says Mr. Michael's affection cooled as her account deteriorated. As she recalls it, "In the office, gradually, from playing up to me, he'd ignore me. Mostly he'd sit with his back to me and say nothing. Toward the end, he couldn't stand to have me near him. He said, 'Why don't you go outside and sit and watch the tape? Why don't you go talk to some of the other people?'"

The market decline, coupled with the collapse of her own account, caused him to go into rages and yell at her, she says. "Once he stood in the doorway and slammed his fist against the metal frame of the door till he had a lame hand. I just took it. I'd sit in the chair in his office and shrivel up."

A man who worked in the office at the time says, "It was a sick scene."

Mr. Michael concedes that he lost his temper during those dark days. "I told her please don't buy. Stay put. But the market made her desperate. When she got money, instead of putting it into a savings bank, she poured it into high flyers. Her philosophy was, keep trading, you've got to do something."

Mrs. Scofield was particularly vulnerable in the sinking market because she had a margin account. She was buying stock not just with her own money, but also with credit obtained from Hayden Stone—credit for which she had to put up collateral equal to 25% of the value of the purchased stock. For collateral, Mrs. Scofield used other stocks she owned. As those stocks shrunk in value, she was forced to come up with fresh margin—that is, cash—to stay within the New York Stock Exchange's margin rules.

As Mrs. Scofield's stock tumbled in price, she replenished her margin with fresh infusions of cash from the sale of jewelry and loans from friends and relatives. She was caught in a frenzy to raise money to avoid margin calls. "Things were desperate," she says, "so I asked Marvin to lend me $50,000" to put into her margin account. He told her he couldn't. So, she began selling off her stock. Finally, she ran out of stock to sell off.

In her suit, Mrs. Scofield contends the defendants violated margin rules by providing her with too much credit. At various times, she says, the New York Stock Exchange barred the purchase of certain volatile stocks, such as Memorex, Telex and Natomas, on credit. Yet, she maintains, these shares were bought for her account on margin.

The end for Mrs. Scofield came in November 1970. She says she was informed by the new CBWL-Hayden Stone management that she would have to increase her margin account to 30% from 25%. She said she couldn't possibly raise the additional margin, and she protested bitterly to Mr. Michael. "I just blew up," she says. "I said it wasn't fair for them to do this. He started to scream at me. Here I am, bleeding to death, and instead of being sympathetic, he's picking fights with me."

—April 21, 1972

Asian Connection

Chinese Gangsters Fill A Narcotics Gap Left By U.S. Drive on Mafia

Johnny Kon and His 'Eagles' Hit Paydirt as the Market For Quality Heroin Surges

But a Canary Puts Him in Jail

By STANLEY W. PENN

During the Vietnam War, Johnny Kon peddled fur coats to American soldiers through their PXs. Later, the Shanghai native arranged R&R tours of Hong Kong for battle-weary GIs. When the war ended, he turned to smuggling furs and selling stolen jewelry.

By 1984, he had gravitated to a more lucrative, and hazardous, business: heroin.

As always, he was in the right place at the right time. The U.S. heroin market, battered by cocaine, was picking up again. Poppy growers in the "Golden Triangle" of Laos, Thailand and Burma (now Myanmar) were producing a more potent heroin that could be smoked rather than injected, cutting the risk of AIDS; meanwhile, heroin was proving newly popular to ease the crash after a cocaine high. But thanks to a crackdown on the Mafia, this expanding U.S. heroin market was wide-open and promised easy entree for newcomers.

Mr. Kon's response to this opportunity was to form the Flaming Eagles, which would soon become one of the largest and most violent of the Chinese gangs that have rapidly seized control of the U.S. heroin trade. In less than four years, until his 1988 arrest, his organization shipped into the U.S. upward of 1,700 pounds of heroin, with a street value of nearly $1 billion, say agents of the Drug Enforcement Administration. That's enough to supply 1,000 addicts with a daily fix for 30 years.

The story of 46-year-old Johnny Kon, born Kon Yu-Leung and known to accomplices as Big Brother, offers a glimpse into the labyrinthine Chinese underworld that is feeding an ominous surge in U.S. heroin usage. It is a tale of greed, treachery and violence.

After he was arraigned in federal court in Brooklyn, Mr. Kon told two DEA agents: "Others will die, [then] you," according to Catherine Palmer, the assistant U.S. attorney who prosecuted him. Mr. Kon pleaded guilty to drug trafficking charges, and last Sept. 29 drew a 27-year prison sentence and $300,000 fine.

On Jan. 29, Ms. Palmer received in the mail a package containing a loaded, booby-trapped .22-caliber rifle. Opened by federal agents, it failed to fire. Mr. Kon denies threatening Ms. Palmer, to whom he says he bears no ill-will.

A muscular man of medium height with sleek black hair, Johnny Kon today portrays himself as a legitimate businessman whose generous nature enmeshed him in the heroin trade. "I have many friends," he says during an interview at the federal Metropolitan Correctional Center in Manhattan, with his attorney, Ivan Fisher, in attendance. "They asked me to help them, so I helped."

Clad in orange prison garb, bereft of the $30,000 diamond-studded Piaget watch he once sported, he greets a visitor courteously and smiles easily. He declines to discuss the workings of his organization, insisting he isn't an informant.

As a youth in Shanghai, Mr. Kon says, he joined his uncle's fur-coat factory, training as a tanner and dyer. The Vietnam War broadened his horizons. "In dealing with the Americans, he developed an international outlook," a DEA agent says. "He speaks English, plus Cantonese, Mandarin and Shanghai dialects."

After the war, Mr. Kon exported mink and rabbit coats to the U.S. and Europe through his Hong Kong trading company, Imperial Fur. He also took to smuggling furs to Japan to avoid import taxes.

It wasn't long before he acquired enough status in the underworld to join the Wo Shing Wo triad, one of the Hong Kong groups that deal in drugs, extortion, gambling and other rackets, a DEA agent says. "It was a sign of acceptability," according to the agent. "It opened doors for him." The triads, unlike the Mafia, welcome independent operators. "There was no obligation for Kon to kick money back up the line," the agent says. (Mr. Kon denies belonging to a triad.)

In the early 1980s he began assembling the Flaming Eagles. He signed up several former Chinese "Red Guards" who, after the end of Mao's violent Cultural Revolution, found an outlet for their energies in heroin and armed robbery. "He recruited the best of the worst," says Ms. Palmer.

From the recruits, Mr. Kon extracted an oath of silence. "If I betray the oath," each swore, "let the organization deal with me. I will even accept death without complaint."

For a time, the Flaming Eagles robbed Hong Kong jewelry shops and Mr. Kon fenced the booty abroad. When his fur-coat business soured, lawmen say, the allure of heroin proved irresistible. "It was a logical evolution for him," says a DEA agent formerly stationed in Thailand. "The supply side was increasing, and it was easy for him to tap in. He was moving up to make bigger profits with the same amount of risk."

Through his Hong Kong connections, Mr. Kon linked up in 1984 with high-level Chinese heroin brokers in Bangkok. These brokers are supplied by the two outlaw groups that control opium production and refining in the mountainous Golden Triangle: the Shan United Army and the Third Chinese Irregular Force. These renegades, who number in the thousands, move their product by armed caravan into Thailand, where it is readied for shipment to markets overseas.

As it happened, U.S. demand for high-purity Golden Triangle heroin, dubbed "China white," was just then beginning to explode. The abundance of the drug enabled dealers to increase its purity to over 40%, compared with 5% in the past, providing a more intense, addictive high.

Johnny Kon's trafficking career paralleled an abrupt shift in the heroin trade, during which Southeast Asia has overtaken Mexico as America's chief source. Over 40% of heroin in the U.S. now is China white. Opium output in Asia's Golden Triangle has soared fourfold in five years, to 2,400 tons annually, says Andrew J. Maloney, U.S. Attorney in Brooklyn.

During the mid-1980s, federal prosecution of mob leaders in the "Pizza Connection" and "Commission" cases loosened the Sicilian and U.S. Mafia's lock on heroin shipments into New York, the nation's wholesale distribution capital. Chinese gangsters moved in, grabbing 75% to 85% of the New York market, according to Mary Lee Warren of the U.S. Attorney's office in Manhattan. The Mafia now must buy from the Chinese, says Jules J. Bonavolonta, chief of the FBI's organized crime and narcotics division in New York.

Distrusting non-Chinese, the Chinese at first refused to do business with them. This reluctance has broken down in prison, where Asian, white, black and Hispanic heroin dealers have established ties. "Because of these contacts, Chinese traffickers now have a wide distribution network," says Robert M. Stutman, until recently the head of the DEA in New York.

Mr. Kon chose New York's Chinatown as his U.S. staging ground. There, gangs like the Ghost Shadows engaged in extortion and gambling and were eager to expand into heroin. "Kon hooked into their networks," a DEA agent says. "He sold heroin to them. They sold to the Hispanics. The Chinese made a marriage with the Hispanics."

While his New York operation was running smoothly, Mr. Kon had problems back in Hong Kong, where not all his gang members were adhering to their oath of silence. In late 1984, police seized 277 pounds of heroin concealed in a trawler near Hong Kong. A crew member, Ng Chieu-Ming, implicated Mr. Kon, who immediately fled to Taiwan. In an affidavit later given to U.S. authorities, Lau Shu Ming, a former Kon aide, said Mr. Kon told his henchmen: "We'll take care of Ng."

Mr. Ng was slain before he could testify, and the case against Mr. Kon collapsed. According to the affidavit of another Kon employee, Eric Luk, an exultant Mr. Kon told aides there were "no more witnesses against him in Hong Kong, so he and his associates were now able to go back."

Mr. Kon, who denies killing anyone, masked his illicit activities behind a front, Johnny Kon China Trading Ltd. In his affidavit, Mr. Luk, the company's ex-administrative executive, tells how gang members were put on the payroll. "Mr. Kon told me that ... I should not keep track of the employment hours of these individuals, because they had 'other business' to do."

Mr. Kon smuggled heroin to the U.S. in merchandise such as picture frames, vases and water buckets. After being flown into the country by commercial airline, the heroin was taken by car to New Jersey safehouses, where it was spooned into plastic bags for delivery to Chinatown wholesalers. One former accomplice recalled in an affidavit the overpowering odor of the drug as it lay in a heap on the floor: "After a while," he said, "I became lightheaded from the smell and went to lie down upstairs."

Kon couriers got up to $5,000 per pound of heroin brought to the U.S., earning as much as $50,000 for a typical 10-pound load. They smuggled proceeds back to Hong Kong in suitcases, each crammed with $300,000 wrapped in $10,000 bundles of $10 and $20 bills. Couriers were paid up to $15,000 per suitcase.

Mr. Kon's lush profit margins permitted such extravagance. He purchased a kilo (2.2 pounds) of heroin in Bangkok for $7,000 and resold it in New York for $90,000. The heroin, passing through other distributors, was bought by street gangs for $190,000 a kilo. Usually, a kilo is diluted, poured into 61,700 glassine bags, and sold to addicts for $10 a bag under various brand names: Red Heat, True Value, Black Magic and Day & Nite.

Mr. Kon's far-flung properties and investments gave him a pretext for frequent travel and helped disguise the movement of drug money. At one time his holdings included commercial property in San Francisco, part of a shopping mall in Queens, a movie theater in New York's Chinatown and a wristwatch factory in Paraguay. He owned a $1 million home in Gen. Manuel Noriega's Panama City neighborhood, and a more modest ranch-style house in the affluent New Jersey suburb of Short Hills, where his 47-year-old wife, Catherine Kon, lived unobtrusively with their two children. According to a DEA agent, Mr. Kon also purchased a Tokyo bar for his mistress, Helen Chow, a 27-year-old former Hong Kong actress who joined his heroin network. (Mr. Kon denies buying a bar for Miss Chow.)

The Kon drug empire was meticulously run. After studying airline security procedures, Catherine Kon instructed money couriers to fly China Airlines. "She said that the China Airlines examination is not very intensive," Mr. Luk said in his affidavit. (The airline says it is satisfied with its security procedures.)

While Mr. Kon spent most of his time in Asia, Catherine Kon supervised money shipments from New York. "These guys knew they couldn't cheat Johnny because his wife was here," Ms. Palmer, the prosecutor, says. "If there was a problem, she resolved it."

For all his attention to detail, Mr. Kon treated some underlings shabbily—a flaw that would come back to haunt him. "He reneged on promises," a DEA agent says. "For example, he promised new recruits that if they got arrested, he'd help their families financially. Well, one member was arrested, Kon failed to help out, and the guy's wife had to sell their house."

Though Mr. Kon himself had a weakness for gambling—he is reported by aides to have dropped $1 million at a casino in Macao—he coldly rejected a trusted associate's plea to help bail him out of a $50,000 gambling debt. The aide, Lau Shu Ming, was a pivotal member of his organization who hired lawyers for arrested gang members, received drug proceeds in Hong Kong and arranged for cash to be channeled to Bangkok to buy heroin. Disgruntled after Mr. Kon's rebuff, he tried to smuggle a load of heroin into the U.S. behind his boss's back. He was arrested, and ultimately cooperated with U.S. authorities.

U.S. lawmen had known Mr. Kon was a heroin dealer ever since the 1984 seizure of the trawler. But it wasn't until after June 1985, when two of his couriers were arrested at the Seattle airport, that the DEA connected him with smuggling into the U.S. The couriers were caught with 216 pounds of heroin stashed in metal ice buckets. "The amount blew our minds," says Ed Madonna, a DEA agent in Seattle. "Kon was the first one who woke us up to the fact that Southeast Asian heroin had become a major factor in the U.S."

Thus began the DEA's Operation Seahorse, a maneuver to plug this new heroin pipeline. "We knew that there was a big organization involved, and that it was probably one of many," says Michael J. Tobin, DEA boss in Newark, who then headed the operation.

They also knew that nailing the peripatetic Mr. Kon wouldn't be easy. "Kon had contacts with corrupt public officials all over the world," Mr. Madonna says. "He traveled with identification papers—or without papers—throughout Southeast Asia and Latin America."

It didn't help matters that Fang Han Sheng, one of the couriers arrested in Seattle, escaped—and soon afterward was shot dead in Bangkok. The killing is unsolved, but U.S. lawmen believe it was a warning to Tommy Chen, the other arrested courier, not to squeal. (Whatever the reason, Mr. Chen refused to cooperate. Convicted for trafficking, he got a 20-year sentence, later reduced to 10.)

The break finally came in October 1986, when a Kon associate, Antonio (Ronnie) Vacas, was detained at the Seattle airport on suspicion that his passport contained counterfeit departure stamps.

Though Mr. Vacas, a Eurasian, called himself a Hong Kong businessman, a search of federal files turned up his links to Mr. Kon. "I put handcuffs on him," a DEA agent recalls. "He was under arrest. I said I wanted to know about the ice buckets—a reference to the Seattle airport bust the year before. If he didn't tell us, he could stay in jail the rest of his life. He was pretty shocked."

Mr. Vacas knew plenty. He had smuggled drugs and money in and out of the U.S. for the Kon gang. And Mr. Kon had sought his help in obtaining phony passports for himself and his wife when they fled Hong Kong after the trawler seizure.

What's more, Mr. Vacas bore a grudge against Mr. Kon, whom he blamed for the murder of courier Fang, a close friend. Mr. Vacas turned informant. Federal agents agreed to drop any charges against him, provide expense money and give him a cash reward if his aid resulted in Mr. Kon's conviction.

"I don't think we could have gotten anywhere without Ronnie," a DEA agent says. "He gave us names. He gave us the aliases that Kon was using. He gave us photos of members, including Kon and Helen—Mr. Kon's mistress. He was able to corroborate what we had."

Allowed to return to the Far East, Mr. Vacas got off to a shaky start as an informant. Mr. Kon ordered him to supervise a heroin shipment to New York's John F. Kennedy Airport. But if Mr. Vacas complied, the DEA—through its paid informant—would be involved in narcotics smuggling.

On the other hand, the DEA didn't want to arouse suspicion by telling Mr. Vacas to beg off. So it leaked word of a U.S. drug investigation at JFK to the Hong Kong press. Mr. Kon scuttled the planned JFK shipment after Mr. Vacas showed him an article about the probe.

Mr. Kon, his wife and others were indicted by a federal grand jury in Brooklyn in December 1987. Because Mr. Kon still had to be lured to the U.S., the indictment was kept under wraps.

Back in Asia, meanwhile, Mr. Kon faced a liquidity squeeze. The previous year, Thai police had seized 301 pounds of heroin he had intended to sell in the U.S. for more than $12 million. His Bangkok heroin brokers tightened credit, demanding the bulk of payment up front instead of the usual 15% down payment.

Knowing Mr. Kon intended to liquidate some of his U.S. holdings to finance a big heroin shipment, Mr. Vacas flew to New York to lay a trap. He told his boss he had found buyers for the properties, and asked Mr. Kon to come to Manhattan to sign the documents.

Under the name Ricky Wong and using a Costa Rican passport, Mr. Kon flew to the U.S. He met Mr. Vacas at the New York Hilton coffee shop on Sunday night, March 13, 1988. Emerging later, Mr. Kon was confronted by 12 armed drug agents.

Awaiting trial in jail, Mr. Kon felt sorry for himself. In a letter to his mistress, he wrote: "I am just so mad that it was Foreign Boy [Mr. Vacas] who hurt me.... Tell him that there should be a limit trying to hurt me. ...In order for [me] to stay alive, it depends on one word of his. All he has to do is deny all the testimony that he has given in court." Further down in the letter, Mr. Kon added: "His heart is so vicious. He is not so softhearted like me, leaving people a chance to live."

Today, Mr. Kon becomes irate at the mere mention of Mr. Vacas, shouting an obscenity. "I saved his life twice," he says. "He was in the drug business, and he asked me for help."

Chinese drug lords like Mr. Kon have left a deadly legacy just now showing up in crime statistics. In New York—home of nearly half the nation's heroin addicts—heroin arrests by the police narcotics division jumped 80% in 1989, "reflecting the increased popularity of heroin on the street," says John J. Hill, the division commander. Nationwide, heroin-related deaths rose 8% between 1986 and 1988, the government says. In the same period, emergency hospital cases linked to heroin rose 18% to nearly 17,000.

High-purity China white is creating more hard-core addicts, says Raymond Moffett, a DEA agent in Providence, R.I. "When you're using weak heroin and shooting two days a week, you can withdraw," he says. "Using purer heroin, withdrawal is a lot harder." The Justice Department says high-potency heroin has been implicated in overdoses throughout New England. And heroin use by young crack addicts to abate the post-high depression "can give us a younger generation addicted to heroin," warns William Hopkins, of New York State's division of substance abuse.

Mr. Kon's 27-year sentence permits no parole. He complains that he won't be released until he's an old man. "It's not fair," he says. "They should have given me a chance for parole. They used me as an example." He contends that he pleaded guilty in hopes the court would go easy on his wife and his mistress. Mrs. Kon drew three years in prison. Miss Chow pleaded guilty to a heroin charge and awaits sentencing.

Last April, while the Kons were both being held at Metropolitan Correctional Center, Mr. Kon learned that Miss Chow was being extradited from Tokyo, and would be put in the same jail. Aghast that the two women would be jailed on the same floor, Mr. Kon decided to tell his wife about his relationship with Miss Chow. "She became distraught, wept, and attempted to throw a chair at him," Ms. Palmer says. Catherine Kon was transferred to a different jail.

Ronnie Vacas, meanwhile, was rewarded with an undisclosed amount of cash. Now living in Asia, he may be in danger. "We are looking for Foreign Boy," Mr. Kon wrote Miss Chow from jail, "and will continually do so."

Eric Luk and Lau Shu Ming, the former Kon aides who cooperated with the U.S. government, entered the federal witness protec-tion program.

Another Kon accomplice, Ah Chung, came to a grisly end. Arrested in Hong Kong, he agreed to turn against Mr. Kon. He was brought to the U.S. and placed in a Bayonne, N.J., jail. In July 1988, Ah Chung was found hanging by his neck.

He left a suicide note for his father in Taiwan.

"Please don't be mournful," he wrote. "I choose to end it all and I don't blame anyone." It was signed, "Your dishonorable son."

—*March 22, 1990*

FROM CHAPTER 3

Las Vegas East

U.S. Gamblers Prosper In Bahamas With Help From Island Officials

Top Local Political Leaders Grant Casino License, Also Receive Consultants' Fees

Is There Link to U.S. Crime?

By MONROE W. KARMIN and STANLEY PENN

Scene: the gold-papered, crystal-chande-liered Monte Carlo room of the luxurious Lu-cayan Beach Hotel. Roulette wheels spin their reds and blacks. Crap shooters roll their sevens and elevens. Blackjack dealers turn their aces and kings. Slot machines whirl their lemons and plums.

Surveying the quick play and quiet play-ers is the affable but cold-eyed man in charge, a runaway New Yorker wanted by American authorities. He is balding, 61-year-old Frank Ritter, alias "Red" Reed, whose natty appearance (mustard sports jacket with double vents, tapered beige slacks, brown suede shoes) fails to dispel the impression that he's familiar with the grime of the un-derworld.

Ritter's presence, and his suspected links

with the U.S. crime syndicate, cast a pall over this "island in the sun" just 70 miles off the Florida coast. Grand Bahama, largely barren a few years ago, today attracts hun-dreds of millions of dollars from U.S. tourists and investors. A big magnet: Gambling.

Now, newly discovered secret documents provide insight into how gambling came to Grand Bahama. The documents also tell a good deal about the ethical climate prevailing in the Bahamas, the multi-island British Colony.

The entrepreneurs on Grand Bahama, conforming to custom, did business in the early 1960s with the renowned "Bay Street Boys," the powerful group of merchant-politi-cians who dominate the colony from Nassau, the capital on New Providence Island, some 120 miles to the south of Grand Bahama.

To grasp the significance of these busi-ness dealings, a bit of background is neces-sary. Gambling is illegal in the Bahamas. Thus, to open casinos in Freeport took some doing—a special exemption from the colony's penal code. This exemption was granted in April 1963, not by the legislature, but by the governor's select, nine-member Executive Council which at that time was the most pow-erful arm of the government and pretty well ran the colony.

Executive Council deliberations are se-cret, and to this day there is no record of which members voted for or against gam-bling. But the result of the vote is no secret. The Council awarded a casino monopoly to Wallace Groves, a former Virginian who reigns as the "monarch" of Grand Bahama. He controls about one-half the total acreage on the island, is the dominant figure in Grand

Bahama Development Co., Grand Bahama Port Authority and Bahamas Amusements, Ltd. The three companies comprise the major commercial interests responsible for developing the island.

Mr. Groves has a blemish in his background. He's an old Wall Street operator who was convicted of mail fraud in 1941 and sentenced to two years in prison. Now, a quarter of a century later, Mr. Groves has wound up with the right to open any number of casinos on his island fiefdom.

But—on to the Bay Street Boys.

The most powerful is Sir Stafford Sands, the Minister of Finance and Tourism (a post equivalent to the U.S. Secretary of the Treasury). Sir Stafford also is the most respected corporation lawyer in Nassau. As such, he represented the Groves group in its quest for a gambling license at the same that he was a member of the Executive Council that granted the license.

Corporate records indicate Sir Stafford received for his services more than $1 million from a Groves-controlled company. This handsome fee was divided into several payments. Records of the company for 1964 show payment to Sir Stafford of $515,000 for legal services and also legal retainer payments of $10,000 per month.

Sir Stafford flatly denies payments of any such magnitude, although he does confirm he has done a good deal of legal work for Mr. Groves and his companies.

But the corporate records, disputed though they may be by Sir Stafford, also show consulting agreements with him, and two other members of the Executive Council—Sir Roland Symonette, the Premier, and Dr. Raymond Sawyer, a dentist. Besides Messrs. Sands, Symonette and Sawyer, still a fourth member of the Executive Council had personal business dealings with the Groves group—C. Trevor Kelly, the Minister for Maritime Affairs, who fittingly enough leased boats to a Groves company.

But business ties between the Grand Bahama entrepreneurs and the Nassau politicians weren't confined to members of the powerful Executive Council. Two other important political figures were quietly taken aboard as consultants. "Bobby" Symonette, the Premier's son and Speaker of the House of Assembly, was one. The other: Sir Etienne Dupuch, a member of the Senate and the editor-publisher of the Nassau Tribune.

Sir Stafford, according to a former official of one of Groves' Bahamian corporations, was to receive, under his consulting agreement, nearly $50,000 a year for 10 years, or as long as the Groves gambling license remained in effect. The official says the consulting fees were on top of the Sands legal fees. Again Sir Stafford denies he accepted any consulting fees.

Premier Symonette was to receive $16,800 a year for five years for his advice, the one-time Groves executive says. Not so, replies the Premier. Though a member of the Executive Council at the time of the gambling decision, it's reported the Premier voted "no." Besides being the head of government, Sir Roland holds extensive shipping, real estate, liquor and other business interests, and is regarded as the second most important figure in the Bahamas.

Dr. Sawyer, the dentist, again according to a former Groves executive, was to receive $5,600 a year for five years as a consultant. The dentist, who has since left government, denies any knowledge of the agreement. He says he was forced to give up his public duties because of the press of private business. Besides pulling teeth, Dr. Sawyer operates Nassau's Hobby Horse Hall racetrack. "Dentists don't make much money," he explains.

"Bobby" Symonette, the Premier's son, confirms that he was under contract to Grand Bahama Development one of the Groves-controlled companies, at $14,000 a year, but says he ended the agreement some months back. Besides being a man of rising influence, the House Speaker also is an accomplished yachtsman whose picture has appeared on the cover of Sports Illustrated. The 40-year-old sailor explains that, because of his experience at sea, he was retained by the Groves group to advise on marina construction to earn his $14,000 a year.

Mr. Kelly, the maritime minister, is a wealthy businessman (some say he's among the wealthiest in the Bahamas) whose widespread interests include lumber, hardware and shipping. A series of his ships are named Betty K., after his daughter. Mr. Kelly confirms he's done a continuing business, through the Betty Ks, with the Groves group. An ex-Groves executive says the towns have been highly generous to Mr. Kelly, but the maritime minister will only reply, "that's my private business."

Sir Etienne Dupuch, in a February 1964 letter to Mr. Sands, acknowledged receipt from Grand Bahama Development of "a cheque for one thousand pounds ($2,800) in payment of consultant services for January and February." Both Sir Etienne and his newspaper had opposed Grand Bahama gambling, and his letter said the consulting fee would be turned over to charity. It is understood that, before too long, Sir Etienne had second thoughts—and stopped accepting the fees.

Sir Etienne's doubts were not shared by some of the other Bay Street consultants. A former Groves official recalls the company received "letters of complaint" from at least one consultant when his checks did not arrive within "two or three days after the first of the month."

Premier Symonette, while denying any consulting agreement, does say he had a road-building contract with Grand Bahama Development Co. years ago. But he adds he gave it up in early 1964 when a new constitution took effect. The Premier says his contract with the development company "was nothing like" the reported $16,800 a year.

Sir Stafford Sands, vacationing in Europe, says he has acted professionally for Wallace Groves, president of the Grand Bahama Port Authority, since the late 1940s. But he adds: "In more than 15 years of this association, I have not collected a total of $1 million in fees from him or from the Port Authority, or from any other business with which we are jointly affiliated, or from all of them in the aggregate. Moreover, my records show that no checks approximating $500,000 were received for any purpose in the period you refer to."

Sir Stafford charges that his political enemies have falsely accused him in the past of accepting excessive legal fees.

He notes that some of his income is in the form of a retainer, "which you have termed a consultant fee."

Sir Stafford adds that his expenses include a legal office in Freeport, Grand Bahama, mainly serving the Port Authority and its associated companies. Also, much of his own time, as well as that of his staff in Nassau, is devoted to business for the same clients, he asserts.

Earlier this year, Sir Stafford unburdened himself to an English journalist about his double duty as lawyer and public minister:

"Ministers here are unpaid. As to the idea that I get a good share of the country's prosperity, of course I do. I would anyway since my family came over here 350 years ago, and I've been working here during the boom years. Anybody would come in for a share. I can't stop charging legal fees can I? But it's worth remembering that I've been a part of making all the islands a lot more prosperous."

This line of reasoning is echoed by many others. "We take the view that we should have unpaid government," explains Bobby Symonette, "because we couldn't afford to pay people in the government what they would earn privately." Indeed, the holding of public office by those possessing the greatest wealth has been the predominant style of government here since the beginning. This reflects the large educational and economic gulf that separates the ruling whites (20% of the population) from the colored majority. It also reflects the past ineffectiveness of the political opposition.

But it is getting harder to keep the lid on. Consider this episode, which has involved the highly regarded New York public relations firm of Hill and Knowlton, Inc., in what surely is one of the more curious arrangements in the history of publishing.

Hill and Knowlton operates the public relations department of the Bahamas' Ministry of Tourism under Sir Stafford. And it is a considerable operation: Last year the ministry spent $4.1 million, or 10% of the colony's revenues, to entice Americans and other tourists.

In the process of serving the interests of Bahamian tourism, Hill and Knowlton recently arranged for Exposition Press of New York to buy a manuscript entitled "The Ugly Bahamians." Exposition Press apparently thought highly of it—enough to pay the author $50,000 for the manuscript. Now, strange to say, Exposition Press has not the slightest intention of publishing its $50,000 property. It is safe to conclude, moreover, that the book will never be published. Hill and Knowlton has "no comment" on the incident.

Whether or not "The Ugly Bahamians" would have constituted an embarrassment to Sir Stafford and his ruling party, the United Bahamian Party, the winds of change are beginning to waft through the Bahamas.

Slowly the opposition Progressive Liberal Party is gaining strength, though probably not enough to come to power in the next election which must be called by the end of 1967. Nevertheless, the PLP's Negro leader, 36-year-old Lynden Pindling, is putting the pressure on the controlling party.

Last year Mr. Pindling, who knows a good political issue when he sees one, brought conflict-of-interest charges before the United Nations in New York. "The ministers in the Bahamas Government today own large shares in nearly every major local enterprise," he told the UN, "and are allowed to award themselves Government contracts and they do unlimited business with the Government they themselves control."

Last July, the Bahamian Government made public a code of ethics that requires a minister to withdraw from any case in which he has a private interest. Government officials contend they have followed this practice at least since a new Bahamian constitution took effect in early 1964. The decision to publicize the code in July may have been prompted by the conflict-of-interest charges raised by the opposition party.

Mr. Pindling's most potent political weapon is the Grand Bahama gambling, with its potential benefits of Government tax revenue and its potential dangers of mobster infiltration. A few weeks ago, Mr. Pindling journeyed to the UN again to charge that the 140,000 Bahamian people were being sold out to "gangsterism" by his political opponents.

That's why Frank Ritter, in the Lucayan Beach Casino, is such a focal point of attention. Along with two casino helpers—Max Courtney, real name Morris Schmertzler, and Charlie Brud, real name Charles Brudner—Ritter has been indicted three times in the U.S. for tax evasion and other offenses. Allegedly the three men operated a nationwide bookmaking business from New York before they skipped town.

Robert Morgenthau, the U.S. Attorney for the Southern District of New York, wants Ritter, Courtney and Brudner back, but the U.S. has no extradition treaty with the Bahamas. Trevor Kelly, acting Premier one day recently when he was interviewed, dismisses the thought: "The only charges the (U.S.) Government has on them is tax evasion," a crime that is not taken seriously by Bahamians who don't have to pay income taxes.

But U.S. Authorities are after bigger fish—Meyer Lansky, the notorious Florida mobster who ranks high in the U.S. crime syndicate. The Lansky reputation is so black that the Nevada Gaming Control board bars him from Las Vegas casinos. U.S. officials suspect that Lansky controls or gets a piece of the profits of the Lucayan Beach casino.

One bit of evidence: For many months, until Bahamian government officials invited them to leave the islands, Dino Cellini and George Sadlo were prominent figures at the Lucayan Beach casino. Both are known Lansky cronies.

One man in a position to know many of the intimate details of the casino operation describes the role of Cellini and Sadlo this way: "Cellini and Sadlo were Lansky's men. At the closing of the casino each night, all of the boxes were taken from the tables and brought into the counting room. There were three sets of keys to the boxes, but it was very important that either Cellini or Sadlo be present before a box was opened."

If indeed George Sadlo journeyed to the Lucayan Beach counting room on many a night to see to Meyer Lansky's interests, he was bringing with him a good deal of previous experience. Testimony before the Kefauver Committee in 1950 showed that Meyer Lansky and his brother Jake, along with George Sadlo, operated illegally the Club Boheme gambling casino in Florida. An accountant for the casino testified that, "At the end of the night . . . after they close each table, they take the money and put it in the cashier's cage and they count it down."

"Who counts it?" asked a committee investigator.

"Mr. Lansky," replied the witness.

"Personally?"

"Yes; or Mr. Sadlo, or whoever is there with him."

If some of the Lucayan Beach casino's profits are, in fact, being "skimmed off the top" by the Lansky crowd, U.S. authorities suspect they are being used to finance the activities of American hoodlums.

Such suggestions draw staunch denials from the Nassau police. Sitting in his office in the police barracks, S. R. Moir, assistant commissioner, is every inch the stiff, proper, tight-lipped Britisher. "No evidence," he replies to inquiries concerning mob infiltration of the casino and the possibility of skimming profits off the top.

The president of the company that operates the Lucayan Beach casino rejects reports of mob infiltration as "completely untrue." He is Keith Gonsalves, a former employee of Barclays Bank, and his company in Bahamas Amusements, Ltd., which is a part of the Groves group. Bahamas Amusements is required to pay all profits to the Grand Bahama Development Co., a land development firm, which is controlled by the Grand Bahama Port Authority, in turn controlled by Mr. Groves.

To confirm the integrity of the casino's operation, Mr. Gonsalves has ready a lengthy position paper. It mentions the presence of two security officers, hired on the recommendation of the police, who "have access at all times to all casino operations, including access to the countinghouse and records." Yet, the fact remains that the security officers are not policemen, are not employed by the government, but are employed by the company that runs the casino.

The Gonsalves paper also notes that the casino's books are audited by the accounting firm of Peat, Marwick, Mitchell & Co.

Despite Mr. Gonsalves' assurances, suspicion persists, favored by the presence of Ritter, Courtney and Brudner in the Lucayan Beach casino. Just when this presence began is not clear, but it certainly dates back to the spring of 1963.

Then the Lucayan Beach hotel was in an early construction stage. When the gambling license was issued in April 1963, meetings were arranged to convert a planned convention hall into the casino. Someone who attended a session in Miami recalls that Ritter and Courtney were brought in to help with the designing. "They were experts on casinos," he remembers. There are those unkind enough to suspect the convention hall was intended to be a casino all along.

Ritter and Courtney—along with Lansky crony Dino Cellini— were especially important in setting up the casino.

To remove any taint of Las Vegas and to give the Lucayan Beach casino "class" it was publicized widely that only European croupiers would be employed. Accordingly, a school was set up in London in early 1963 to train the European croupiers (they are not especially adept at the American game of craps). Apparently no effort was spared. The finishing school cost the casino $250,000.

"Cellini, Courtney and Ritter were sent over to start the school and to instruct the people," an insider recalls. "They returned to the Bahamas with 100 croupiers."

Ritter, Courtney and Brudner were allowed to remain on Grand Bahama, after Cellini and Sadlo departed. Mr. Gonsalves explains why: "It was necessary to have Americans in some key positions because more than 90% of the patrons of the (Lucayan Beach) casino are United States citizens; and Messrs. Ritter, Courtey and Brudner and other professionals were employed because of their previous professional experience in gambling in the United States."

Ritter bears the title of credit manager; Courtney, chief supervisor; and Brudner, casino floorman. But Ritter is obviously the key man. Credit is vital to casino profits. Most gamblers come to win, not lose, so they don't bring all their money. When the luck runs bad, the trick is to know just how much credit to extend to whom. That's where Frank Ritter shines. His knowledge of the financial status of American gamblers, plus his contacts with the Las Vegas casinos, make him an expert on "instant credit"—and where to draw the line.

This talent was observed at the Lucayan Beach casino recently. It was late, and only a handful of hard-core gamblers remained. Among them were two brothers from the States. One was playing with $100 chips in a closed game at the blackjack table. He was losing heavily; his brother already had lost quite a bit. They both came to Frank Ritter for credit. "You're all right," barked Frank to one, "but not him," jabbing his finger at the other.

The incident raises an interesting, but unanswered, question. Granting Frank Ritter's expertise at his job, he's still human. Suppose he makes a mistake. Suppose a borrower fails to pay up after he returns to the States. Who duns him for the debt? The mob? That's what U.S. investigators want to find out.

The casino is a sore point with many Bahamians. Mr. Pindling of the opposition party whose distress doesn't extend to favoring a shutdown of the casino, pledges: "If we came into power, we would renegotiate the entire casino license. Our concern is to eliminate all possible gangster influence."

Also distressed is the upper crust of Nassau society. Dining on the veranda of their spacious home, a banker and his wife view the distant Lucayan Beach casino as an "error of taste and judgment." They refuse to believe that American mobsters have infiltrated, but they fear the "potential" is there. The thought of an "offshore Las Vegas," as they term it, horrifies them.

And the man they blame for the mistake is Sir Stafford Sands, a huge man who, according to an acquaintance, "lives like an emperor." His Nassau estate, "Waterloo," comes complete with private lake.

Sir Stafford has a penchant for expensive lounging jackets and elaborate paperweights. He's addicted to the grand gesture too. "At a dinner for four, he'll have caviar for a hundred," says one friend.

Friend and foe alike regard Sir Stafford as the mastermind behind the Bahamas' tourist boom (this year a record 800,000 visitors are anticipated). And all descriptions of him, sooner or later, converge on the words "brilliant" and "genius." Even Mr. Pindling, who seeks to oust the United Bahamians, admits that, if successful, he'd like Sir Stafford to remain as minister of finance and tourism.

A tiny glimpse of the man's power, and the way he uses it, is provided by the letter that Sir Etienne Dupuch, the Senator and Tribune editor-publisher, wrote to him acknowledging receipt of his consultant's fee from the Groves-controlled Grand Bahama Development Co.

The letter would seem to suggest Sir Stafford shoved Sir Etienne, who had criticized gambling editorially, into accepting money from the casino crowd. Read:

"You had talked with me briefly on this proposal but I did not realize that it had been finalized.

"I am sure you know that I am not happy about having casinos in the islands but since a casino has been established at Grand Bahama, I am concerned to see that a high standard is maintained. If you think that my services in this way might be helpful, I shall do my best but I want you to feel that it is an arrangement that can be terminated at any time by either side.

"I told you at the time that this arrangement must not in any way be considered as influencing my decision in the Senate or the policy of the Tribune. You agreed to this condition.

"I would have readily given my services free of charge but since you insist on paying what you say is the normal fee for this kind of service I shall deposit the money to a special account I have in the Royal Bank of Canada for helping children and for other charitable purposes." —*October 5, 1966*

* * *

Kingdom in the Sun

Tough-WilledAmerican Turns a Bahamas Island IntoThrivingEnterprise

---

Wallace Groves Lures Firms And Tourists to Freeport, Enforces Rigid Controls

---

A Clash With Louis Chesler

By Stanley Penn and Monroe W Karmin

The sand is white, the sea emerald and the sun dazzling. Starting with these assets, a modest financial investment and the wholehearted cooperation of the Bahamian government, a mild-looking, balding American named Wallace Groves has carved out a prospering little kingdom on this island 80 miles east of Palm Beach, Fla.

Mr. Groves, who lives in a $1 million palace of blue-green tile, obtained his domain as a result of a 1955 agreement with officials of the British colonial government in Nassau, located 120 miles south of Grand Bahama on New Providence Island.

The agreement gave the 65-year-old Mr. Groves sweeping powers over Freeport, as he has named the half of Grand Bahama that falls within his purview. He alone can issue the licenses that are required for anyone wishing to do business here. He has wide power to remove persons who incur his displeasure. The agreement also contained broad, long-lasting assurances that Mr. Groves and other Freeport residents would be free of Bahamian taxes. At the same time, it empowered Mr. Groves to impose licensing fees of his own—ranging up to 10% of gross sales in some instances—on firms operating here.

In return, Mr. Groves, whose past is marred by a mail fraud conviction in the U.S., promised to develop Freeport intensively. He has delivered on his promise.

Americans and others have invested more than $200 million in the area so far. Largely desolate a decade ago, Grand Bahama now boasts flashy hotels and a gambling casino. Lavish vacation and retirement homes are springing up. More than 200,000 tourists, mostly Americans, will visit the island this year, up from 26,000 as recently as 1963.

Other types of business development also proceed apace. One of the biggest ship fueling facilities off the U.S. East Coast has been constructed here. U.S. Steel Corp. has built a $40 million cement factory that has a yearly capacity of 4.8 million barrels of cement, with most of the output going to the U.S. Active participants in the development of Grand Bahama—and beneficiaries of the profits the development is producing—are the "Bay Street Boys," the merchant-politicians who dominate the government in Nassau and whose cooperation enabled Mr. Groves to create his island kingdom.

But not every aspect of the transformation of Grand Bahama draws unqualified praise. Some of Freeport's 8,500 full-time residents (in 1960 there were only 250) complain that living costs are high, despite the absence of income taxes; it's suggested that the rigid controls on competition keep prices up. Strict rules on job changes—no employee may switch firms without a release from his employer—are irksome. Some residents also say

137

that the tight restrictions on development tend to limit the island's diversity, particularly in leisure-time activities.

"After a while you get a feeling of being imprisoned here," says English-born David Miller, a Freeport resident. "We call it 'rock fever.'"

But there are matters for more serious concern. Gambling may lure free-spending tourists, but it also attracts some unsavory characters. "It's drawing many types of people with criminal intent," says a Bahamian civil servant here. Three key employees of the Monte Carlo gambling casino in the Lucayan Beach Hotel—Frank Ritter, Max Courtney and Charlie Brud—are wanted by U.S. authorities in New York to stand trial on charges of tax evasion and illegal bookmaking; just last week, after a Wall Street Journal story described the trio's background the casino announced that the trio were resigning as of next Jan. 15 because of "unfortunate publicity." Prostitution and dope-peddling, unheard of in Freeport a few years ago, have popped up, according to a local newspaper editor.

Freeport comprises 211 square miles of the 430 square miles that make up Grand Bahama Island. Wallace Groves' basic vehicle for controlling Freeport is a multi-faceted company called Grand Bahama Port Authority, Ltd.

Island publicists describe Mr. Groves' company as a "modern day version of Hudson's Bay Co." It may well be true that the powers vested in the Port Authority are among the most sweeping given to a company since England's King Charles II awarded Hudson's Bay jurisdiction over a big stretch of Canada in 1670.

Before launching his Bahamian enterprise, Wallace Groves was a highly successful Wall street financier. But this career ended abruptly in 1941, when he was convicted of using the mails to sell stock at an artificially inflated price. He served a two-year prison term for the crime.

Late in the 1940s, Mr. Groves turned up on Grand Bahama. Initially, he bought and operated a lumber mill on the island. Then, in 1955, he reached the agreement with the Bahamian government whereby his Grand Bahama Port Authority would receive a wide range of concessions in return for building a port and bringing in industrial and commercial enterprises. The agreement, called the Hawksbill Creek Act after a creek running through the Freeport area, also awarded the Port Authority 50,000 acres of government land for $2.80 an acre. The land allocation was later expanded to almost 150,000 acres.

Besides his licensing powers, Mr. Groves received the sole right to plan, lay out and develop his half of Grand Bahama. He also got the right to import labor from outside the Bahamas.

The tax concessions enabled Mr. Groves to bill Freeport as a tax-free haven for businesses. Until 1990, residents and firms are assured of no taxes on corporate income, salaries, capital gains or property. They also are assured of no customs duties on imported business goods till the year 2054. Except for customs levies, residents of the rest of the Bahamas are free of taxes, too, but they lack Freeport's guarantees for the future.

Wallace Groves himself has been the chief beneficiary of the development of Grand Bahama. Through his Port Authority company and its affiliated firms, he owns Freeport's utilities, its only supermarket, its jet airport (nonstop flights from New York three times a week starting next month) and Freeport Bunkering Co., the big ship-fueling outfit.

Bahamas Amusement, Ltd., another Groves-controlled firm, holds an exclusive gambling license for Freeport, granted by the government in 1963; the government at that time exempted Bahamas Amusement from the law that prohibits gambling in the islands. Besides the highly profitable Monte Carlo casino in the Lucayan Beach Hotel, Bahamas Amusement is opening a second casino—called simply El Casino next New Year's Day. El Casino, a Moorish-style affair with gold-capped white towers, will be triple the size of the Monte Carlo room.

A Port Authority affiliate, Grand Bahama Development Co., was assigned 100,000 acres of land in Freeport and given the job of selling sites for homes, hotels, apartment buildings, golf courses and marinas. So far Grand Bahama Development has taken in more than $35 million, with some of the prime land for which Mr. Groves originally paid $2.50 an acre going for $40,000 to $50,000 an acre. Grand Bahama Development also built the Lucayan Beach—which charges a minimum of $40 a day per person without meals in season—though the Groves affiliate no longer owns the hotel.

The role of the Bay Street Boys in all this development has been substantial. Particularly important in Mr. Groves' operations has been Sir Stafford Sands, the Minister of Finance and Tourism. The most influential figure in the Bahamas, Sir Stafford has handled Mr. Groves' legal affairs since the founder of Freeport came to Grand Bahama.

The Bay Street Boys' activities in Freeport are varied. They control many of the local retail shops. Some of them have received consulting fees from Grand Bahama Development. Next year an elaborate new tourist attraction called the International Bazaar is opening in Freeport, and the Bay Street Boys are expected to operate many restaurants, night clubs and shops in it. The Bazaar, spread over a 20-acre tract, and featuring imports from all over the world, will be owned by a Port Authority affiliate.

Though Mr. Groves has always retained iron control over Freeport's development, right at the start he obtained extensive financial assistance from British and American interests. These backers have seen the value of their investments multiply many times over.

One of the principal investors was Charles W. Hayward, a British industrialist, who put up funds in return for a 25% stock interest in the Port Authority company. Another key backer was a group headed by Charles Allen, general partner of Allen & Co., a leading New York investment house; the Allen group purchased another 25% of the Port Authority. The 50% interest Mr. Groves still holds is ample to give him effective control of the company.

Groves also got some help from Daniel K. Ludwig, a New Yorker who is a millionaire shipowner. In exchange for 2,000 acres of land in Freeport and the right to build a shipyard (the right was never exercised), Mr. Ludwig dug a 30-foot harbor. This permitted Mr. Groves to fulfill his pledge to the island government to build a port. Mr. Ludwig promptly sold part of his real estate holdings to U.S. Steel for $1 million as the site for its cement factory. On another parcel of Freeport land Mr. Ludwig later obtained, he is now building a golf course and a luxury home development with houses priced up to $90,000.

Gulf Oil Corp. also lent a hand. It contributed funds for Freeport Bunkering's offshore fueling station. Gulf supplies the fuel for the station, which services ships that ply the major north-south Atlantic shipping lane off the Bahamas.

By 1960, both the port and bunkering station were in operation, but industry was still slow in coming in. So Mr. Groves' interests began to turn more to tourism. He decided to build a luxury hotel and gambling casino as a magnet to attract visitors. The tourism buildup apparently appealed to Bahamian officials: In 1960, when Mr. Groves promised to put up a 250-room hotel in Freeport, as well as to improve port facilities, the government sold Mr. Groves nearly 100,000 more acres of crown land, the great bulk of it at the old bargain price of $2.80 an acre.

The Lucayan Beach Hotel, which, along with the Monte Carlo casino, opened in January 1964, touched off a hotel-building spree. Freeport now has six luxury hotels with over 1,800 hotel rooms. Grand Bahama boosters are predicting that before many years Freeport will have more hotels than Nassau, the traditional center of Bahamas tourism.

Profits from the Monte Carlo casino are helping to spur hotel construction. Some $1.5 million a year of casino earnings are parceled out as subsidies to three hotels—the Lucayan Beach; the King's Inn, built by ship-owner Ludwig; and the 614-room Holiday Inn, Grand Bahama's biggest hotel. These subsidies will continue through 1973.

"We wouldn't have come in without the subsidy," concedes Kemmons Wilson, chairman of Holiday Inns of America, Inc., the Memphis-based motel chain.

Despite Freeport's financial success, Wallace Groves remains deeply bitter over his imprisonment in the U.S. in the 1940s, according to a former aide. "He's never forgotten what he feels was deliberate persecution," says this man. "He believes the SEC used him as an example to the rest of the financial community."

But the ex-associate adds that Mr. Groves unquestionably has come to relish his role on Grand Bahama. "When Groves first came to Grand Bahama, he was strictly interested in making money—and nothing else," says the onetime aide. "But now, with the way Freeport is evolving, Groves sees himself in a different light. He looks on himself as an emperor of a commercial-industrial-resort complex."

Residents say Mr. Groves takes a paternalistic attitude towards the community he has created. He shows up for Boy Scout jamborees and ground-breaking ceremonies, and his Bahama Amusement, Ltd., operator of the gambling casino, recently promised to finance a new Catholic high school.

As befits a monarch, Mr. Groves lives in elegant style in his blue-green palace (the tiles for it were imported from Hong Kong) with his second wife, Georgette, and his five adopted children. All the children's names start with "G"—Gayle, Gene, Gordon, Graham and Gary. Like a monarch, he is inaccessible. Efforts to interview him for this story were unsuccessful; aides said he was vacationing on his private island, Little Whale Cay, south of Grand Bahama, and could not be disturbed.

But Mr. Groves' monarchical style has its shortcomings. "When he does something wrong, there's nobody to tell him," says an American who once worked for him. "People are afraid to criticize him to his face. He's too insulated."

Some residents complain that Mr. Groves' Port Authority acts in mysterious and arbitrary ways. Though the Bahamian government has broad deportation powers and retains control of police, customs and courts, the Hawksbill Creek Act gives the Port Authority the power to "exclude " persons from Freeport "without assigning any reason"— and locally this power is equated with the right to deport. If an employer is dissatisfied with a non-Bahamian employee, it's a simple matter to have the Authority send him packing. A waitress, glancing over her shoulder to make sure she isn't being overheard, tells a visitor: "They deport a lot of people around here. Wham, and you're out."

Rico Heller, formerly manager of the Pub on the Mall, a popular Freeport restaurant, was recently deported to Switzerland. Back in Switzerland, Mr. Heller wrote a letter to the Freeport News, a weekly newspaper that is occasionally critical of Mr. Groves' regime. In his letter Mr. Heller said he had been fired from his restaurant job for failing to produce enough profit. Following his dismissal, he was told at 2 a.m. that he had to pack and leave Freeport by 6 a.m.

"Within the Port Authority," charges Mr. Heller, "there are some little men of power whose favorite expression seems to be, 'I'll have you shipped off the island,' and who create a rather unpleasant and police-state like atmosphere."

The company that owns the Pub on the Mall said Mr. Heller's employment had depended on his good behavior. But certain evidence came to the company's attention last April, and after a full investigation, Mr. Heller was dismissed from his job, the company said. He was then deported.

So far, the Bay Street Boys haven't forced any firm out. The president of one diversified company in Freeport took no chance of alienating Nassau. He sold a substantial interest in his business to a prominent Bay Street merchant. "We decided to get in bed with him," the executive explains.

Over 600 individuals and firms are licensed to do business in Freeport, including, among others, dry cleaners, plumbers, contractors, auto repair men, hair dressers and a soda bottler. One of the major firms to win a license recently was Syntex Corp., the drug producer, which plans to build a plant here. Only two firms have folded, according to a Port Authority official. The Authority's policy

has been to protect infant businesses. "While there's no guarantee of monopoly, we want to create an atmosphere of profit," he says.

The Authority also seeks to keep tight control of Freeport's rate of growth. "If we had laissez-faire here, we'd have chaos," asserts another islander.

Those who know Wallace Groves say his mild appearance is deceptive. "When you talk to him, you get the impression he's a nice old man who knows nothing," says a resident. "But it could be very uncomfortable for somebody to cross him."

The experience of Louis Chesler, the controversial Canadian promoter, shows it doesn't pay to get on the wrong side of Mr. Groves. Mr. Chesler entered into a business venture with Mr. Groves in Freeport five years ago. The two men clashed, and Mr. Chesler, who is known as a forceful character, is no longer on Grand Bahama.

Mr. Chesler has a reputation as a super salesman in the real estate field. A founder of General Development Corp., the Miami Beach land development firm, he pioneered in selling land on the installment plan.

It was Mr. Chesler's real estate experience, coupled with his demonstrated talent for raising funds from investors, that led Mr. Groves to bring him to Freeport in 1961 when Grand Bahama Development was being formed. Mr. Chesler had two assignments. He was to form a syndicate that would raise $12 million for Grand Bahama Development to use to build the Lucayan Beach Hotel. And he was to form a sales organization to sell Freeport land. In return for these services, the Chesler syndicate received nearly 50% of the stock in Grand Bahama Development and Mr. Chesler became president of the company.

Mr. Chesler set up the land sales organization and launched a promotional campaign in the U.S. and Canada to build interest in vacation and retirement homes in Freeport. As Grand Bahama Development's $35 million of land sales indicate, the Chesler promotion was effective.

But on the hotel project Mr. Chesler ran into trouble. The $12 million was raised and the hotel built. Costs ran far over the budget, however, and the rooms ended up costing twice as much as the estimates. Overstaffed and poorly managed, the Lucayan Beach quickly sank into the red after opening in January 1964.

Companies linked to the now bankrupt Atlantic Acceptance Corp. of Toronto fed working capital to the hotel. As collateral, the companies received a minority stock interest in the hotel. The upshot is that Montreal Trust Co., thanks to its role as receiver for the insolvent Atlantic Acceptance and to its acquisition of another interest in the Lucayan Beach from a Canadian group, now controls the hotel.

But Mr. Chesler was already out as president of Grand Bahama Development by the time Montreal Trust took over the Lucayan Beach. He "resigned" in May 1964. The circumstances are cloudy, but it seems evident that the strong personalities of Messrs. Groves and Chesler collided—and that Mr. Chesler was the one to yield.

The two men are very different. One source who knows both says Mr. Groves is a "quiet, secretive man," while the 53 year-old Mr. Chesler is an outgoing, outspoken type. A man who once worked for Grand Bahama Development claims Mr. Chesler was a poor administrator. "He couldn't stand to sit behind a desk and make day-to-day decisions," says this source. "Groves hates inefficiency. So he made it clear to Lou he'd have to go."

Mr. Chesler himself says: "Groves and I didn't see eye to eye. There was a lot of emotion built up. It got to the point that I wanted out." Mr. Chesler is presently selling his Grand Bahama Development stock. At one point he held over 10% of the shares personally. The bulk of the shares are being offered in Europe by a Nassau brokerage firm.

Even though Mr. Chesler may have had enough of Grand Bahama, many less prominent persons who have tasted life on the island have found it to their liking. A variety of reasons have drawn them here.

"A lot of the early ones were running away from something—wives, husbands, tax collectors and the cops," comments a local restaurant manager. Freeports' tax advantages attracted others, "I used to own a business in Florida, but I got fed up," says a middle-aged businessman as he watches gamblers roll dice in the Monte Carlo casino. "Taxes, regulations—I'd had it. Here they let you alone. You keep what you make. It's nice and relaxed." Another businessman resident, and avid golfer, delights in being able to tee off without a wait; despite the small population, there are three golf courses.

For the less affluent, however, Grand Bahama is something less than idyllic. With no tax funds, some social services are lacking. Freeport has no public bus transportation for residents, although the Negro workers who live outside the enclave are brought into Freeport by bus. The Freeport residents use private cars or taxis. Most white residents send their children to private schools and must pay tuition.

But the most dissatisfied islanders are found among the 12,000 who live outside Freeport, most of whom are Negroes. They are housed in shabby settlements along the coast. In the past, some sold land to the Port Authority to supplement the acreage the Authority obtained from the government, and complaints are heard now that the purchase prices were far too low.

The Negroes, many of whom are employed by Freeport hotels, also grumble that they get no benefit from the casino. Maurice Moore, a Negro who lives in a settlement outside Freeport called Pinder's Point, is a candidate of the minority Progressive Liberal Party for the House of Assembly in Nassau. One of his campaign planks is that some of the casino profits should trickle down to help the Negroes.

"Unless we get a greater share of the wealth, it could all go up in smoke—not just a riot but insurrection," he warns dramatically. —*October 19, 1966*

Politics & Business

Contributions by Firm To Illinois GOP Follow Helpful Racing Ruling

Company Run by Phil Levin, Allowed to Operate Tracks, Gives the Party $100,000

Officials Deny a Connection

By STANLEY W. PENN

Philip J. Levin, the short, aggressive president of Madison Square Garden Corp., has a net worth of about $100 million. He has a 106-acre estate near Plainfield, N.J. and maintains an apartment decorated with Monet and Degas paintings in Manhattan's elegant Pierre Hotel.

The 62-year-old industrialist gives generously to liberal causes. He has financially backed the political campaigns of all the Kennedys, as well as former New Jersey governors Richard Hughes and Robert Meyner. In 1964 Mr. Levin was a delegate to the Democratic National Convention. He recently gave $5,000 to the Vietnam Veterans Against the War to help defray transportation costs for the group's antiwar demonstration in Washington last month.

Last summer, the New York-born Mr. Levin ran afoul of the Republican-dominated Illinois Racing Board. The board, at public hearings, challenged Mr. Levin's fitness to conduct horse races at two tracks near Chicago—Arlington and Washington Park—that are owned by a Levin-run company, Chicago Thoroughbred Enterprises. Grave concern was expressed by the racing board over reports from Illinois investigators that Mr. Levin, who had gained control of the tracks in 1969, might have ties with some unsavory characters.

Mr. Levin's harshest critic at the highly publicized hearings was racing board Chairman Alexander MacArthur, an appointee of Republican Gov. Richard Ogilvie. Mr. MacArthur, who showed up at the Chicago hearings in cowboy hat, cowboy boots and a cowboy belt with holster to keep his sunglasses in, gave Mr. Levin a stern lecture about morality in the Midwest. "We like our racing clean in Illinois," Mr. MacArthur said. At another point, the chairman asserted, "A man running a racetrack in Illinois should be like Caesar's wife—he should be above reproach."

The racing board, consisting of four Republicans, two Democrats and one independent, held hearings during June, July and August. In August, racing board Chairman MacArthur gave Mr. Levin a clean bill of health by saying the probe turned up nothing to justify cancellation of Chicago Thoroughbred Enterprises' racing license.

The Wall Street Journal has learned that last Aug. 31 Mr. Levin, through Chicago Thoroughbred Enterprises, made political contributions of $100,000 to Illinois Republicans seeking election to local and state offices last November. Corporate documents show that:

—$50,000 was given to the 1970 Cook County (Chicago) Republican campaign fund.

—$25,000 was given to the Illinois Republican Victory Dinner Fund.

—And the remaining $25,000 was earmarked for the campaign fund of Edmund J. Kucharski, chairman of the Republican Cook County Central Committee, who was defeated by a Democrat in his bid for the post of Illinois State Treasurer. Mr. Kucharski is presently assistant secretary of state, a job he was appointed to by the Republicans.

Mr. Levin, when asked about the matter, acknowledged the contributions were given to Illinois Republicans. He said (correctly) that they were perfectly legal since Illinois law permits corporate donations to local-state political campaigns. Mr. Levin added that the boards of Chicago Thoroughbred and its parent company, Transnation Development Corp., approved the political contributions. But Mr. Levin refused to say why Chicago Thoroughbred felt it necessary to aid the Republican cause in Illinois.

Sources familiar with his thinking say Mr. Levin believed he had been unfairly attacked by the racing board and was fearful that the racing license might be in jeopardy as a result. He is said to have held the belief that he, a liberal Democrat from New Jersey, had to improve his standing in Illinois' Republican circles.

Mr. MacArthur, a cousin of the late Gen. Douglas MacArthur, said he had no knowledge of any political contributions by Chicago Thoroughbred until so informed by his newspaper yesterday. He insists that no pressure from Gov. Ogilvie or anybody else was put on the board to renew Chicago Thoroughbred's license. "The governor is as square as a box," Mr. MacArthur said. "Everything is black and white to him. He is a nonmeddler. The only instructions I ever received were, 'Sail the ship, captain.' Nobody has put pressure on me. I would walk out if anyone tried. There has never been any politics that have come into it."

Gov. Ogilvie, through his press aide, said Mr. MacArthur has his complete trust and confidence "in trying to make Illinois racing regulation clean and above board."

The governor said, "I told MacArthur when he took the job that I wanted a totally straight operation, and that he would get no interference from me—nor would I tolerate it from others—in the performance of his job. I had no conversations whatsoever with MacArthur about the Levin matter last summer and fall, and I have no knowledge of any contributions Levin may have made to anyone."

Efforts to reach Mr. Kucharski by telephone last month and again yesterday weren't successful. However, in response to letters asking whether he had received political contributions from Levin-run Chicago Thoroughbred Enterprises, Mr. Kucharski wrote that "I cannot confirm" the contributions. He said he didn't choose to disclose the source of his campaign funds, indicating he felt this would put him at a disadvantage with respect to other Illinois political figures who don't disclose their contributions.

As for his relationship with Mr. Levin, Mr. Kucharski said: "Suffice to reiterate that I do not know P. Levin, have never met him and do not know any of his associates, nor have I ever met one."

When the funds were passed to the Republicans last August, Chicago Thoroughbred was a 98.5%-owned subsidiary of Transnation Development. Mr. Levin was Transnation's president, chief executive officer and owner of 31% of the stock. On Transnation's board was Charles Bluhdorn, chairman of Gulf & Western Industries, which, with 43% of the stock, was Transnation's largest stockholder.

This past February, Transnation, together with Chicago Thoroughbred, was merged into Madison Square Garden Corp. through a stock swap. Mr. Levin then became the $150,000-a-year president and chief operating officer of Madison Square Garden, owner of the Garden sports palace as well as

professional basketball's Knickerbockers and ice hockey's Rangers. The sports complex also owns 96.5% of the Roosevelt Raceway harness track at Westbury, Long Island. Mr. Levin, with 13% of the stock, is the Garden's second biggest holder, while Gulf & Western Industries is the biggest stockholder with 17%.

The $100,000 given to the Illinois Republicans was in the form of checks from Chicago Thoroughbred Enterprises and two of its subsidiaries—Western Concessions, which operates food-beverage facilities at the Arlington and Washington tracks, and Washington Park Trotters Association, which conducts race meets at the Washington track.

Chicago Thoroughbred was Transnation's chief asset. In 1970, Transnation reported a loss of $967,000 on revenue of $24.6 million. It blamed the red ink on declines at the Arlington and Washington race tracks, coupled with operating losses at the company-owned Arlington Park Towers Hotel, located near the Arlington track.

Mr. Levin got off on the wrong foot in Illinois when he fired the socially prominent Mrs. Marjorie Everett from her $50,000-a-year job as president of Chicago Thoroughbred Enterprise. Mrs. Everett's late father, Ben Lindheimer, was well known in Illinois racing circles. Mrs. Everett had obtained a 10-year contract to head the racetrack company in 1969 when she sold her controlling interest in Chicago Thoroughbred to a company that later became Transnation Development.

Mr. Bluhdorn of Gulf & Western sensed it would be a mistake to fire the Chicago woman. "I personally did not agree with her dismissal," Mr. Bluhdorn told the racing board. "I told him, 'Phil, don't do it.' We had a great moral obligation to her. What it got down to, I pleaded with Mr. Levin without any success at all. I wasn't the only one that did it. But I particularly did it. And he said, 'I like her but I can't live with her.'"

The blunt-spoken Mr. Levin's dismissal of Mrs. Everett was in character. Mr. Levin often bridles at the labyrinthine ways of big companies. He recently told a reporter, "Charlie Bluhdorn says to me, 'Phil, you were never meant to be corporate.'"

The Chicagoan's ouster in March 1970 helped touch off an investigation of Mr. Levin. At the request of the racing board, the Illinois Bureau of Investigation, a state agency, dug into Mr. Levin's background. The sleuths talked with law enforcement officials in this country, Canada and Mexico. One investigator said he posed as a real estate speculator to conceal his identity from

Mr. Levin's acquaintance.

A good part of the Levin past is public record. He made his pile largely by building supermarkets and shopping centers from Maine to Florida. He retained ownership of many of these real estate properties, which he leases to retailers.

Mr. Levin's efforts to win control of Meto-Goldwyn-Mayer Inc. in 1967 were widely publicized. He narrowly lost the proxy battle, but he lost no sleep over it. He sold his MGM stock for a profit of over $21 million to Time Inc. and Edgar Bronfman, a wealthy New York industrialist.

Mr. Levin, an MGM director as well as big stockholder at the time, enjoyed the excitement of show business. He and his wife, Janice, often showed up for MGM premieres. One time a traffic cop wouldn't let the Levins' Rolls Royce park right in front of the theater to discharge the Levins. "He got off a single-space letter to us," a former MGM executive recalls. "He said henceforth the way should be open for him to park directly at the curb and not in the second or third lanes."

After MGM, Mr. Levin bought a 4% stock interest in Gulf & Western Industries. He became a company director, and Chairman Bluhdorn named him to head a newly formed real estate subsidiary. In 1969, that subsidiary became a public company through a partial stock spin-off. Mr. Levin swapped his Gulf & Western stock for 31% of shares in the new firm, which became Transnation, ultimately a unit of Madison Square Garden. Mr. Levin quit as a director of Gulf & Western last fall.

A different part of Mr. Levin's background was uncovered by the Illinois Bureau of Investigation.

Investigators testified that Mr. Levin had business dealings in 1968 with one Moe Morton, a Californian, who was described at the board's hearings as an associate of organized crime figures. Mr. Levin had been a member of a 10-man group that bought a 50% interest in Acapulco Towers, a luxury apartment-hotel in the Mexican resort town, from a partner of Mr. Morton's. The other 50% was owned by Mr. Morton, who managed Acapulco Towers. In 1969, Transnation Development agreed to buy for $1 million Mr. Morton's 50% and the other 50% owned by the group including Mr. Levin.

Investigators said that Meyer Lansky, a leader of organized crime now living in Israel, had hidden at Acapulco Towers to escape police surveillance. Agents also reported they were informed that Mafia chief Sam Giancana, now in exile in Mexico, had visited Moe Morton's yacht in Acapulco harbor.

Mr. Levin said he had no knowledge of Mr. Morton's alleged association when he first bought a 5% interest for $50,000 in Acapulco Towers. He said Sidney Korshak, a member of the buying group and presently attorney for Chicago Thoroughbred Enterprises on labor matters, had encouraged Mr. Levin to buy in and then put the idea in his head to get Transnation to buy out all the partners in the apartment-hotel.

Mr. MacArthur scolded Mr. Levin for not digging into Mr. Morton's background. "You know," he said, "I find this incredible. I buy cattle (Mr. MacArthur is a cattle farmer) and you think I just look at the weight slip and the price? No, I go out and look at the cattle."

The Illinois sleuths reported that 36 phone calls were made from the New Jersey home of Mafioso Angelo (Gyp) DeCarlo to Mr. Levin's home in 1967, and two calls were made from Mr. Levin's home to DeCarlo's home in 1969. DeCarlo is in prison on a federal extortion conviction.

Mr. Levin testified that the phone calls were between DeCarlo's son, Lee, and Mr. Levin's son, Adam, both of whom played in the same dance band and went to the same private school in Plainfield. Mr. Levin said parenthetically that he had bought a New Jersey country club that DeCarlo belonged to. Mr. Levin converted it into an all-Jewish club, and DeCarlo, who's not Jewish, was forced out.

The board's heaviest criticism of Mr. Levin was for his purchase of a 9% interest in Parvin-Dohrmann Co., a Los Angeles-based firm that owns Las Vegas gambling casinos. The commissioners voiced fears that Mr. Levin was a stockholder in casinos where odds are legally set for basketball and hockey games that are played by teams owned by Madison Square Garden Corp. (The plan to merge Mr. Levin's Transnation Development into Madison Square Garden Corp. had already been announced at the time.)

Mr. MacArthur also named some questionable types associated with Parvin-Dohrmann in the past and said to Mr. Levin: "Let me make my point clear as one member of this board. You are coming to Illinois. You are going to take over a very sensitive business in the state, legalized parimutuel wagering. Just putting it in direct language, calling a spade a spade, are you going to bring in the camp followers with you?"

"I don't know what you mean by camp followers," Mr. Levin snapped. "You have to tell me what you mean by camp followers."

MacArthur: "Well, people that just follow

144

along for the action."

Mr. Levin said he tried to interest Transnation Development into buying control of Parvin-Dohrmann. But the Transnation board—led by Mr. Bluhdorn—turned thumbs down on grounds it wanted no part of gambling casinos. Mr. Levin then personally bought his 9% interest. Last November, he sold out his Parvin-Dohrmann stock at a $700,000 loss to satisfy a requirement of the Transnation merger with Madison Square Garden.

Parvin-Dohrmann was familiar to many of the racing commissioners. The Securities and Exchange Commission in a 1969 civil suit charged the company with falsifying stockholders' reports and engaging in stock rigging. Defendants included Delbert Coleman, then chairman, and Mr. Korshak, Mr. Levin's associate at Chicago Thoroughbred Enterprises. They eventually submitted to a consent decree.

Mr. Korshak was reported by the SEC to have played a key role in arranging for Parvin-Dohrmann to hire Nathan Voloshen for $50,000 to intercede with SEC officials in an effort to get a trading ban lifted against Parvin-Dohrmann. The SEC charged that Martin Sweig, a principal aide to then House Speaker John McCormack was involved with Voloshen. Voloshen last year pleaded guilty to a conspiracy charge to peddle his influence; Sweig was convicted on a perjury count.

A new management team now operates Parvin-Dohrmann, which changed its name to Recrion Corp.

—*June 15, 1971*

FROM CHAPTER 6

Smoke Screen?

To Jamaican Coptics, Marijuana Use is a Rite; To Police, It's a Wrong

U.S. Agency Says the Church Is a Cover for Smuggling: Its Leader Denies Charge

Much Ganja but No Ketchup

By STANLEY W. PENN

The 90-minute drive from Kingston ends on a hilltop outside a fenced-in enclosure that bears a sign: "Righteousness endureth forever." A guard unlocks the gate. Inside, four men with beards and long, straggly hair are sitting on the porch of a farmhouse, puffing marijuana from a long-stemmed pipe that they pass around.

This is one of the principal communes of the Ethiopian Zion Coptic Church, which has elevated the smoking of "ganja," or marijuana, to a religious rite and which is suspected of being one of the chief sources of the growing flood of illegal Jamaican marijuana that is pouring into the United States.

Most of the church's followers are poor, black Jamaicans, with a sprinkling of white, middle-class dropouts from the U.S. Nevertheless, the organization is believed to have become one of the largest private landowners in Jamaica. The Coptics also control property in Florida, Iowa, Massachusetts, Georgia and Maine, and in recent years have purchased as much as 7,000 acres of "prime agricultural land" in Colombia, according to the U.S. Drug Enforcement Administration.

The DEA regards the religious aspects of the Coptic creed as a cover for a large-scale marijuana-smuggling ring. "This is a criminal organization that is violating U.S. and Jamaican law," says Peter B. Bensinger, the outgoing head of the drug-enforcement agency. Last month, nine American members of the Coptic church were convicted in a federal court in Miami on charges of conspiracy to smuggle marijuana into the U.S.

Jamaican police also say they keep a close surveillance of the Coptic communes and have raided them 11 times in the past six years seizing "many tons of ganja." In the most recent raid, last February, 20 tons were grabbed, an officer says.

However, Jamaican law makes convictions of marijuana offenders hard to obtain. Prosecutors need proof of possession to nail users and sellers. In one raid, a police officer recalls, "to get in, we had to climb over a (high metal) gate. By the time we got in, nobody was smoking. There was no ganja around."

Another difficulty in getting convictions is the central role that marijuana plays in the Jamaican culture. About half the population smokes it or uses it as tea. Rural families believe that as a medicine, it is particularly efficacious in the treatment of colds, fever and asthma. "It's so commonplace that on the first night after birth, a child may be given it in tea," says one expert on Jamaican culture.

The leader of the Ethiopian Zion Coptic Church is Keith Gordon, a fierce-eyed 40-year-old Jamaican, known to his followers as "Niah" (the Chosen One), "King" and "Brother Keith." Despite his short, slight build, he is an imposing man who speaks in a solemn, oracular manner, embellished with Biblical-style parables. He asserts confidently that the U.S. government, no matter how hard it tries, never can rid the world of marijuana. "God makes ganja," he declares. "Before the U.S. (was founded), there was ganja. After the U.S., there will be ganja."

Mr. Gordon's followers number about 2,000, headed by approximately 100 priests in Jamaica and up to about 30 priests in the U.S., according to Melanie Dreher, a Columbia University anthropology professor who has made a study of the sect. Mr. Gordon's church doesn't have any organizational ties with the Coptic Church, which is the native Christian church of Egypt and Ethiopia. It is considered an offshoot of the Rastafarians, another rapidly growing Jamaican group that, like the Jamaican Coptics, preaches self-reliance and the superiority of blacks.

Unlike the Rastafarians, many of whose members wear their hair in distinctive corn-rolled "dreadlocks," the Jamaican Coptics don't accept the divinity of Haile Selassie, the former emperor of Ethiopia. Instead, the Coptics look to Marcus Garvey as their prophet. Mr. Garvey, a Jamaican who migrated to New York early in this century, was the founder of the Back-to-Africa movement. His writings, combined with ideas from the Old and New Testament, form the Coptic scripture.

To the Coptics, the Christ of the Bible is an African who was brought up by a poor African carpenter named Joseph. They reject the use of wine in the sacrament of Communion as representing the blood of Christ and substitute the smoking of ganja—a natural herb provided by God, as they see it.

All life, in the Jamaican Coptic view, is a constant struggle between good and evil. Beards are obligatory for men. Women, demure looking in granny dresses, must wear scarfs on their heads. Although they are called "queens," they are required to play a subservient role. During the menstrual period, they are segregated in separate quarters and forbidden to prepare food or to smoke ganja.

Liquor, wine, beer and tobacco are regarded as drugs and thus are forbidden. Pork (but no other meat) also is taboo. Holy colors are red, green and gold, the colors of the Ethiopian flag. Children are allowed to smoke ganja at prayer meetings; at other times, a parent will give the child a draw on his "scliff," or ganja cigaret, as a reward for good behavior. At this commune, the elders say, prayer meetings are held for at least six hours daily—at 4 a.m., 3 p.m. and 8 p.m.—in a cone-roofed tabernacle. During the services, the members chant psalms, bang on drums and smoke ganja.

Here, at the St. Thomas Parish commune, developed farmlands stretch as far as the eye can see from the hilltop headquarters. The commune's principal crops are pumpkins, peanuts, ginger and coconuts. Besides its own members, this commune employs as many as 1,200 workers from surrounding villages to till its estimated 3,000 acres of land. With farms like this scattered throughout Jamaica, the Coptics have become one of the nations' largest producers of food for domestic consumption—unlike many of Jamaica's other big farmers who produce tobacco and sugar cane for the export market.

A church elder shows a visitor around. The elder is a white former New Yorker from Manhattan's Upper West Side who quit his publishing job in 1970 and settled in Jamaica.

"When we came here, there was just wilderness," the elder says. He points to a scallion patch, banana trees, a generator for electricity, and a water tank that the religious group has erected. "We don't burden anyone. We don't beg," he says. "We practice self-reliance and self-control. Everything we eat is fresh." He gestures toward the Caribbean, off in the distance. "If we want fish, we drop a line and get fish."

Does the church grow marijuana?

He replies evasively. "Anywhere you drop a seed, it grows. Ganja is a tree that comes out of the earth. Ganja is no crime. We don't break any of God's laws. Ganja is an herb, not a drug."

The elder denies that the church is in the business of selling marijuana or that it has become wealthy from smuggling. "We don't have money stored up. We don't have big bank accounts."

This is sharply disputed by U.S. Law-enforcement officials. Manny Funes, a Tampa-based investigator for the Florida State Police, has been looking into the church's activities for more than three years. He says flatly, "They're the largest exporters of marijuana from Jamaica. They're using everything to smuggle it out—planes, boats, large containers."

Mr. Funes says the Coptics in the 1973-1980 period spent $10 million for real estate in the U.S. and Jamaica and for oceangoing vessels, aircraft, trailer trucks and legal fees against prosecution. In late 1977, one raid on a Coptic "stash house" in Dunnelion, Fla., unearthed an underground storeroom equipped with fibrous glass walls and blowers to store marijuana in a cool, moisture-free environment. Police seized 14.5 tons of marijuana in the raid, according to Mr. Funes.

A Miami Beach mansion, worth $400,000 by some estimates, is headquarters for the Coptics' American branch. And in Jamaica, the sect has extended its enterprises beyond farming to include trucking (Coptic Groups of Cos. Ltd.), automotive parts (Coptic Spares & Sales Corp.), a supermarket and a furniture store. Most of these businesses are in Kingston, the nation's capital.

A 1979 report by U.S. law-enforcement agents to the Royal Canadian Mounted Police asserted that Mr. Gordon has become wealthy from the marijuana trade and his various legitimate enterprises, according to Richard McEnany, a special DEA agent in Miami. Most of Mr. Gordon's money has been squirreled away in Cayman Islands banks according to the report, which estimates the church's marijuana shipments to the U.S. and Canada over a five-year period at 450 tons.

Possession and sale of marijuana in Jamaica are as illegal as they are in the U.S. But enforcement activity on the island has fluctuated wildly. In 1974, The U.S. and the Jamaican governments jointly conducted "Operation Buccaneer," a crackdown on Jamaica's marijuana production. The hills were searched, marijuana bushes were uprooted and the leaves were burned by enforcement agents. This was Jamaica's last big push against ganja.

"Over the past two years," according to a recent U.S. Government report, "Jamaica has been the most rapidly growing supplier of marijuana to the illicit U.S. market."

In fact, Jamaica may have surpassed Mexico as the second-largest supplier to the U.S. (Colombia is still by far the largest). More than 1,000 metric tons (2,200 pounds per ton) is believed to have been sneaked into the U.S. by plane and ship from Jamaica last year, about 10% of the estimated U.S. supply.

Jamaica's desperate poverty offers plenty of incentive for the rise in illegal shipments. "Farmers are getting $30 to $50 per pound for marijuana," an American at the U.S. embassy in Kingston says. "How can you ask these people to go back to some $3-per-pound crop?" In Florida, meanwhile, Jamaican marijuana is wholesaled for more than $200 a pound.

This presents the government of Prime Minister Edward Seaga, who came to power last October, with a devilish problem. On one hand, the island nation can use all the foreign exchange it can get—even from marijuana. On the other hand, the ganja trade is a constant corrupting influence on local police and public authorities.

Even worse, according to Winston Spaulding, Jamaica's minister of national security, "it is leading to problems of security and defense by the proliferation of illegal airstrips which threaten the very sovereignty of this country." Smugglers' aircraft enter and leave Jamaican territory almost with impunity and on occasion have reportedly been carrying weapons for Jamaican militants. More than 30 clandestine landing strips are believed to exist, some of them 5,000 to 7,000 feet long, enough to accommodate a DC6 or DC7.

Mr. Spaulding says his government isn't going to tolerate the situation. (Mr. Seaga declined to be interviewed.) However, a U.S. specialist in the marijuana problem says Jamaica lacks the resources to curb the illegal traffic. "They have no radar to spot (the smuggling) planes," he says. "They only have one or two helicopters working at a given time. They have no spare parts for vehicles. Even if they managed to seize a quantity of marijuana, they might not have a truck in working order to take it to court."

A visitor is driven to the St. Thomas Parish commune, near the village of Four Horses, by Peggy Cooke, a Jamaican Coptic. Mrs. Cooke, 42, a former real-estate saleswoman, is Keith Gordon's personal assistant. Driving her white Honda to the commune, Mrs. Cooke divides her time answering the reporter's questions and giving orders to various aides over the car's private radio hookup. Her code name is "Pentagon."

Among Mrs. Cooke's current activities is merchandising cookies made from Coconuts that grow on Coptic Farms. She is also hoping to develop a commercial use for coconut husks, possibly as a fiber for stuffing mattresses and upholstery in car seats.

She appears to be handsomely compensated. She lives in an attractive section of Kingston, in a spacious, high-ceilinged house with an outdoor swimming pool and two-car garage. At dinner that night in her house, Mrs. Cooke is attired in a navy-colored evening gown, with a scarf on her head. She says the steak dinner she is serving was prepared by a former chef of a top Kingston hotel.

"We eat no artificial seasoning, such as ketchup," Mrs. Cooke says. "We boil our milk. We eat no canned foods." Mrs. Cooke has good things to say about marijuana as a remedy. "It's good for chest colds and fever," she says. "Boil water, put marijuana leaves in and drink it just like green tea." During dinner, Mrs. Cooke does public-relations work by showing her visitor a film on her color-television set of a Coptic prayer meeting in the St. Thomas commune.

Later, a chauffeur drives the visitor to meet with Keith Gordon. His home is in an upper-income district of Kingston called Beverly Hills. Mr. Gordon and his aides are seated in a dimly lit outdoor patio, smoking marijuana from a pipe they share. Questions about revenues from the various Coptic enterprises irritate Mr. Gordon. He says he doesn't keep tabs on such things, nor is he interested.

How large is the Coptics' following?

He replies, "Would you attempt to count all the sand in the sea?"

Mr. Gordon is asked for comment on the U.S. government's belief that his organization smuggles marijuana into the US. "The government is a liar," he says.

One of Mr. Gordon's aides chimes in, "This is the same government that gave us Richard Nixon, Agnew and Watergate. Can you believe anything it says?"

What is Mr. Gordon's background?

"He came from the people," an aide says. Mr. Gordon began as a street vendor, selling peanuts; then he began selling food in a restaurant, the aide adds.

Jamaican police give other details. Mr. Gordon, also known as Edmund Gordon, Rasta and Bredaman, is believed to have gotten started in the marijuana trade in 1953, when he was convicted for possession of marijuana and received a six-month sentence at hard labor, a police agent in Kingston says. In 1969, Mr. Gordon drew a three-year sentence for marijuana possession. In 1975, the officer says, Mr. Gordon was fined $60 for possession. In 1978, police say, they raided on of Mr. Gordon's premises. Some $75,000 (Jamaican) cash was found.

Mr. Gordon, through his Kingston attorney, won't comment on the police assertions. Mr. Gordon was among the Coptics indicted in Miami on marijuana-conspiracy charges. He failed to appear for trial. —*June 17, 1981*

Ill-Starred Venture

Holders' Suit Charges Buckley Misused Funds Of Starr Broadcasting

It Says He, 3 Others Sold To Firm Ailing Theaters They Owned in Texas

A Friend Terms Him Naive

By STANLEY W. PENN

William F. Buckley Jr. has a long list of accomplishments. He is a columnist, author, publisher, lecturer and television talk-show host. But as chairman of a broadcasting company his performance doesn't even rate a gentlemanly "C." In fact, some stockholder critics contend in a federal suit that he and three of his associates have had their hands in the company's till through a "bail out" scheme, a charge the Securities and Exchange Commission is currently investigating.

In 1966, a year after he was an unsuccessful candidate for mayor of New York on the Conservative Party ticket, Mr. Buckley helped to launch Starr Broadcasting Group Inc. It went public in 1969, and by August 1972, the company's shares had reached a high of $31.25. At its peak Starr Broadcasting owned and operated 14 radio and TV stations.

Starr has since fallen on hard times. It is in default on part of its $25 million long-term debt and has had to sell several of its properties to keep going. Losses sustained in the past two fiscal years have totaled $7.2 million.

Some of Starr's problems don't differ much from those of other companies that grew too fast in recent years. In making acquisitions, Starr piled up debt, and then high interest payments contributed to wiping out earnings. But other Starr woes aren't so conventional. The current SEC investigation, together with a stockholders' derivative suit, filed in New Orleans federal district court last year, raise the possibility that the company's assets have been misused to benefit Mr. Buckley and other Starr Broadcasting officials.

Among the questions raised is whether Starr acted against its own interests and bailed out Mr. Buckley and three other Starr officer-directors when the company in 1975 bought a string of ailing drive-in theaters in Texas from entities equally owned by the same officer-directors. Besides serving as chairman of Starr, Mr. Buckley is the company's largest shareholder with 19% of the 1.4 million outstanding shares. The three other officer-directors who were Mr. Buckley's partners in the Texas drive-ins and who last year severed all ties with Starr Broadcasting are Peter Starr, who had been president, his brother, Michael, who had been executive vice president and treasurer, and Gordon Ryan, who had been Starr's general counsel.

Starr's purchase of the 12 drive-in theaters was a disaster. SB Theatres Inc. was formed as a wholly-owned Starr subsidiary to buy the Texas properties. It agreed to pay $8.6 million, of which $900,000 was cash and the rest were obligations. SB Theatres last December filed a Chapter 11 proceeding under the Federal Bankruptcy Act in a Houston bankruptcy court, seeking protection against creditors while attempting to reorganize.

Of the 12 theaters, mortgage holders have taken back nine because SB Theatres was unable to meet debt payments. SB Theatres retains the three remaining properties which are valued at $2.5 million. The company has reopened the three theaters and is counting on theater revenues to service the debt.

Some $2 million of the theaters' debt was guaranteed by Starr Broadcasting. Obligations that SB Theatres took over included $430,000 of bank debt owed by Peter and Michael Starr and Gordon Ryan. Assumption of this debt by SB Theatres was based on a decision of directors to "assist" the three, who were then officer-directors in Starr, in the belief it was a "proper business decision," the company has told the SEC.

A source at Starr Broadcasting who is friendly to Mr. Buckley says it's his belief that Mr. Buckley played a "passive" role in the controversial matter. Mr. Buckley, the source notes, is an unpaid chairman. "The worst you can accuse him of is naivete as to what was going on." Moreover, according to the source, Mr. Buckley has supplied $350,000 of his own funds to help pay some of the debt guaranteed by Starr Broadcasting when it bought the drive-ins.

Another source who is close to Mr. Buckley says the 51-year-old Starr chairman was completely unaware that the SB Theaters subsidiary had taken over the $450,000 bank debt owned by the two Starrs and Mr. Ryan. "His reaction was one of surprise when he found out," according to the source.

Mr. Buckley through his secretary said he was too busy to give an interview.

Starr Broadcasting says that none of the four sellers of the drive-in theaters participated in the vote of the Starr directors to buy the properties. Only "disinterested" directors voted, the company has told the SEC. Among directors participating in the vote, the company says, was an officer of a bank that held "certain business and personal debt of the sellers." Another Starr director who voted was an officer of a Starr subsidiary.

Through Starr's counsel, Mr. Buckley says he didn't play a self-serving role in the theater transaction because as a Starr director he refrained from voting on the matter.

Besides subpoenaing Starr Broadcasting documents in connection with the purchase of the theaters, the SEC has demanded records that deal with company loans to past and present officers, with the issuance of company securities to officers, and with bonus arrangements to officers.

In papers filed with the SEC, Starr Broadcasting reports that Peter and Michael Starr together borrowed from the company—but haven't as yet paid back—about $980,000 to buy 60,000 company shares in the 1970-71 period. In 1973, the directors awarded the Starr brothers a 10-year bonus-employment contract providing bonuses over that period in sufficient amount to wipe out their debt to the company. The Starr brothers had paid an average $15 a share for their 60,000 shares. The shares have since shrunk to slightly over $6 in trading on the Midwest Stock Exchange.

The company says that when the brothers quit their jobs last year the bonus agreements required that the 60,000 shares be returned to Starr Broadcasting within 30 days as collateral for the loans; if the shares were not returned, the loans would become due and payable. The company has been informed that all 60,000 shares "are or were pledged to secure other indebtedness and that the brothers don't have funds available to pay these loans."

In addition, the Starr brothers, after quitting the company, allegedly used company credit cards to run up bills of $3,900, "apparently for personal use," according to the company.

Peter Starr says the credit cards were used for business purposes. Moreover, he says, he is owed by the company $180,000 under the bonus-employment agreement. In addition, he says he and brother Michael didn't actually borrow cash from the company when they bought 60,000 company shares. "We took authorized but unissued shares from the company and gave the company our note in return for the stock," Peter Starr says. He adds he has offered to return his shares for cancellation of the notes but the company won't accept them.

Mr. Starr denies any special treatment when the SB Theatres subsidiary assumed the $450,000 bank debt owed by the Starr brothers and Mr. Ryan. "The money had been borrowed for theater operations, and we didn't make a dime out of the deal."

Peter Starr says his first job when he got out of college was as a salesman for an Omaha radio station controlled by Mr. Buckley. Mr. Starr later became general manager. Under his reins, the 35-year-old Mr. Starr says, the station became profitable after having lost money. Mr. Starr was a co-founder (with Mr. Buckley) of Starr Broadcasting in 1966.

It's Peter Starr's contention that the Texas drive-ins were in relatively good shape when purchased by Starr Broadcasting in June 1975. The chain was earning money "before interest and depreciation charges," he says. The company says it made the acquisition with the idea of eventually selling off the theater land at a profit.

But shareholders Paul and Jacqueline Solomon of Phoenix charge in the New Orleans suit that Starr Broadcasting was in "precarious financial condition" when it bought the Texas properties. Starr's management, according to the suit, had little if any expertise in dealing with Texas real estate. The purchase by Starr Broadcasting represented a "bail out" of the sellers from a "losing business venture." The suit seeks damages on behalf of the company as a result of losses sustained from the purchases. Among the defendants are Mr. Buckley, the Starr brothers and Mr. Ryan.

Starr's directors okayed the purchase of the theaters on June 12 and June 20, 1975. At about that time, Starr Broadcasting was feeling the pressures of heavy interest payments on loans the company had incurred. In addition, according to Peter Starr, the company's FM radio station, WNCN, in New York, was a drain on earnings.

Starr Broadcasting had bought WNCN-FM in 1972 when its programs consisted almost entirely of classical music. Three years later the company said that this programming was unprofitable and announced a switch to a rock-music format. WNCN's listeners were outraged and formed protest groups denouncing the company. Finally, in 1976 Starr sold the station. In the fiscal year ended June 30, 1975, Starr reported a net loss of $2.1 million.

The Texas theaters carried a $7.7 million debt when they were sold to Starr's SB Theatres Subsidiary. Unclear to this day is the exact amount of the obligations that SB Theatres assumed. While Starr says it guaranteed $2 million of the debt, it has told the SEC that it can't get a legal opinion as to whether SB Theatres is obligated on other mortgage liabilities.

The theater properties were appraised at $8.3 million when Starr took an option to buy them from the Buckley-Starr brothers-Ryan group in 1974. (They had purchased the theaters in August 1972 and May 1973.) After Starr had purchased the properties in 1975, a different appraiser retained by the company valued the properties at $5 million—some $3.3 million below the original estimate. Starr Broadcasting says it has been told the reasons for the wide disparity include changing economic conditions and "differences in appraisal judgments."

Peat, Marwick, Mitchell & Co., the accounting firm, was asked by the company to audit the theater properties' balance sheet as of June 30, 1975. But Peat Marwick last December reported that it couldn't perform the audit because it couldn't find various documents it needed for its study. A Starr Broad-

casting source says, "It's difficult to tell where everything went. But I haven't found any illegal payments or any ripping off of the company."

Besides the theater properties, Starr Broadcasting says it agreed to receive from the sellers more than 37,000 shares of Starr Broadcasting stock. Mr. Buckley has given the company his one-quarter portion of the 37,000 shares, but no shares have been received thus far from the other sellers, the company says.

Gordon Ryan, one of the selling group, says he has a debt which has been collateralized with 9,407 Starr Broadcasting shares. When the debt is paid, these shares will be turned over to Starr Broadcasting, he adds. (Efforts to reach Michael Starr, the fourth member of the group, were unsuccessful.)

Bruce F. Johnson, a veteran of the broadcasting industry, came in as company president and chief executive last August. He says things have taken a decided turn for the better. "We're in pretty good shape now," he insists. Earnings in the six months ended last Dec. 31 were $571,000 against a $34,000 loss in the year-earlier period.

Mr. Johnson says that proceeds from the previously reported sale of Starr's Bristol, Va., TV station will reduce company debt by more than $8 million. The transaction was closed on Monday.

Starr Broadcasting then hopes to refinance its senior debt to remove the company from default, Mr. Johnson says.

—*May 4, 1977*

Mob's Legacy

Teamster Local Greets Court Trustee Angrily After He Takes Reins

But Joel Jacobson Tries Hard To Prevail in New Jersey; Getting Rid of a Law Firm

Is Rank and File Intimidated?

By STANLEY W. PENN

Many rank-and-filers at Teamster Local 560 view Joel Jacobson with suspicion. He is the outsider, brought in by the federal government to replace their elected leaders, purge the local of corruption and exorcise the ghost of its imprisoned boss, Anthony "Tony Pro" Provenzano.

"The government wanted to give me FBI protection," the 68-year-old, silver-haired Mr. Jacobson says. "Ridiculous. How can I walk into union meetings with three FBI guys?"

The 7,800-member local, one of the largest in the International Brotherhood of Teamsters, was put under federal trusteeship last June after the Justice Department charged in a civil suit that it had operated under Mafia control for more than a quarter of a century. In a non-jury trial in federal court in Newark, Judge Harold Ackerman upheld the Mafia charges and ousted Local 560's executive board. Mr. Jacobson was installed as trustee for a minimum of 18 months.

The trusteeship is the first imposed on a union under the Racketeer Influenced Corrupt Organization Act, or RICO. The President's Commission on Organized Crime last year linked 36 Teamster locals to Mafia infiltration and warned that trusteeships may be the only effective tool against the mob. In New York City, federal prosecutors are seeking a court order to clamp a trusteeship on Local 6A of the Cement and Concrete Workers union and its district council.

Failure of the Local 560 experiment would cast doubt on the efficacy of trusteeships. Judge Ackerman and Mr. Jacobson have no illusions about the difficulties ahead. Even now, the judge warns, "elements" of the old regime are plotting to regain power. "They're there, I know it," he says. "It's like squeezing dirty water out of a wash rag. There's still a lot of dirty water in that rag."

Local 560 members who oppose the old regime are afraid to do so publicly. "We have nothing to gain," says a veteran truck driver. "There's 20 different ways they can get rid of you. You can have an 'accident,' like getting a pipe in the head. Or they plant stuff in your truck and say you were stealing." What's more, many members doubt the trustee's willingness to stand up to employers as forcefully as the old regime seemed to. "When Jacobson came in," a New Jersey truck company official says, "many of our [Local 560] guys were angry. Their initial reaction was that the government's coming in and the companies will totally have their way."

From 1958 to 1984, Local 560 was bossed by Mr. Provenzano, a reputed member of the Vito Genovese crime gang, and his two brothers, Salvatore and Nunzio Provenzano. The three are currently in federal prison for crimes committed while serving as Local 560 officers. During their reign, two Local 560 dissidents were murdered, union funds were misused, former convicts were put on the payroll, and officers took illegal kickbacks from employers in return for labor peace and "sweetheart contracts" calling for reduced wages.

Even so, Tony Provenzano's hold on the members of Local 560 remains strong. "Tony Pro was a Robin Hood to them," says a dissident in the local. "Because of Tony Pro, there were medical benefits and good wages. Whatever he may have done that the government charges him with," he adds, the union members "remember that he took care of them."

No stranger to unions, Mr. Jacobson was an organizer for the International Ladies Garment Workers Union in the late 1940s. For the next 25 years, he was a leader, successively, of the New Jersey CIO, the AFL-CIO and the United Auto Workers.

He was also among the first to urge Brendan Byrne to make his successful 1974 bid for the New Jersey governorship. After that, Mr. Jacobson headed the state's public utility commission and then its energy department. "Bored silly" as a member of the New Jersey Casino Control Commission, he says, he quit to become Local 560's $71,000-a-year trustee.

His first—and virtually only—priority has

been to win the confidence of the members. With obvious delight, he relates that some rank-and-filers last Christmas invited him to a party at a terminal. "I didn't want to speak, but they dragged me to the mike," he says. "After I spoke, they gave me an ovation."

He says that he typically gets up at 5 a.m. so that he can get to the freight terminals where the men are. "I try to resolve problems," he says. "Ackerman's decision to select a union man—not necessarily me—was a wise choice. If he had put in, say, a former U.S. prosecutor or former attorney general, that would have guaranteed defeat for the trusteeship."

On a recent morning, Mr. Jacobson met with 15 union members at the offices of Brinke Transportation in Jersey City. Stressing that he had no hidden motives, he told the men: "I'm not running for office, and I'm not sponsoring anybody. I look forward to the day when I can play with my two grandchildren."

He also regaled his audience with an account of his response to a firing last year by Conway-Eastern Express in Jersey City. A Teamster, Dominick Romano, was dismissed because of what Mr. Jacobson calls "trumped-up charges" that he had someone else punch his time card for him. The firing cost Mr. Romano his non-paying post as an elected Teamster shop steward at Conway-Eastern.

When the company refused Mr. Jacobson's entreaties to rehire Mr. Romano, the trustee decided to play hardball. He hired Mr. Romano as a salaried business agent in charge of Teamster matters at Conway-Eastern. "The company went wild," Mr. Jacobson says gleefully. "They recanted the allegations and reinstated Mr. Romano." Conway-Eastern declines to comment on the incident.

To show his decisiveness, Mr. Jacobson says he dumped a law firm employed by Local 560 that charged some members "unauthorized administrative fees" for legal services. Moreover, he says, his trusteeship has won pay increases in some new contracts. And he is expanding the availability of dental and vision care.

But his foes are unimpressed. Over drinks in a back room of a Union City tavern, a group of shop stewards vent their feelings. Says Anthony Valdner, employed at TNT Freight: "A trusteeship is a waste of time and money. I want my officers back." James Bartolomeo, of Carolina Freight, says employers are trying to take advantage of what they see as weakness. "Since June 23 [when Mr. Jacobson became trustee] we've got five grievances [against the company]," he says.

"In the three years prior to Jacobson, no grievances."

Nunzio Spano, of Pacific Intermountain Express, scoffs at the notion that rank-and-filers are afraid to speak out. "I've been a shop steward 11 years," he says. "I run every year." Noting that he was reelected in June by a vote of 79 to 29, Mr. Spano adds, "They can vote any way they like." His fellow members at Pacific Intermountain, in Moonachie, N.J., crowd around. "I been in this local 36 years," an angry Ed Taglieri says. If the government thought the local was being intimidated, he adds, "why didn't they ask us, 'Do you want a change?' We weren't asked!"

Shop steward Valdner, who wears a baseball cap inscribed "Free 560," says that when a petition demanding that Judge Ackerman permit immediate Local 560 elections was circulated early last year, "5,300 people signed it. Nobody was intimidated, coerced or threatened." But a dissident, asked about the petition, says: "They shoved it in front of you. They watched to see if you'd sign it."

The shop stewards provide a powerful base of support for the old leadership, says an official of a company employing Local 560 drivers and warehousemen. "The guys know it's not in their interest to antagonize the shop steward," the official says. "If a guy is facing a discharge, a discharge will occur by the steward's lack of support. Or, if a guy is facing disciplinary action, it'll be a lot harsher if he doesn't have the steward's support. It's a big fact of life."

For union dissidents, another fact of life is the local's long history of violence. Tony Provenzano drew a life sentence in 1978 for ordering the 1961 murder of a Local 560 rival, Anthony Castellitto. Mr. Provenzano is to serve that sentence after a 20-year term for taking illegal payoffs from employers.

Walter Glockner, a member, was murdered in 1963, one day after denouncing a Provenzano crony at a membership meeting. No one was indicted for the crime.

In 1983, August Muller, another member, criticized Salvatore Provenzano, then Local 560's president, in the presence of 300-pound Stanley "Stosh" Jaronko, who at that time was a member of the local's executive board. Mr. Jaronko, according to testimony at the 1983 trusteeship trial, then struck Mr. Muller, who was 58 and had a heart condition, and knocked him against a wall. Mr. Jaronko's attorney says that his client merely pushed Mr. Muller and wasn't aware of his illness.

Mr. Muller was exceedingly reluctant to discuss the incident as a government witness at the trusteeship trial. He was "in the grip of extreme fear," Judge Ackerman said in his decision ousting the executive board.

The Provenzanos last faced opponents in local elections in 1962 and 1965, says Raymond Wren, a Labor Department special agent in Newark. Many of those opponents suffered economic retaliation, Mr. Wren says. "They were fired and weren't adequately defended by the union."

Local 560 has contracts with more than 300 employers. Its members include office and factory workers, but drivers and warehousemen predominate, and it is from them that the Provenzanos drew their support.

In 1978, after his murder conviction, Tony Provenzano resigned as secretary-treasurer of Local 560. He was succeeded by Josephine Provenzano, his 23-year-old daughter. Josephine, who had been a Local 560 office worker, was elected—by the unanimous vote of more than 1,000 members—to a job that paid $64,000 a year and included a white Lincoln as a perquisite. Miss Provenzano, in testimony at the trusteeship trial, said she told her father that the standing ovation she received after her election was for him. "Don't think I am dumb enough to think it was for me," she told him.

Tony and Nunzio Provenzano are barred by court order from any future association with Local 560; Nunzio is serving a 10-year term for a 1981 kickback conviction. Salvatore Provenzano, who drew a three-year term in 1984 after conviction in a kickback conspiracy, is prohibited by law from seeking union office until five years after he is freed from prison.

If elections were held today, Michael Sciarra, a member of the ousted executive board, would be the clear favorite to win the presidency. Says a Teamster at Pacific Intermountain Express: "Mikey Sciarra knows my name and knows my family. When there's a problem, Mikey's there."

Conceding Mr. Sciarra's strong following, Mr. Jacobson says: "I've seen Sciarra come into the barn...and members come up and kiss him and hug him."

Mr. Sciarra received the most votes—2,062—of any of the 10 delegates from Local 560 who helped reelect Jackie Presser, the Teamsters national president, at the 1986 union convention. The meeting at which Mr. Sciarra was elected a delegate was "like a circus," a Teamster recalls. "These were full-grown men, stomping their feet, chanting, 'Mikey, Mikey,' over and over."

The 51-year-old Mr. Sciarra makes no secret of his admiration for Tony Provenzano. "I don't know anything bad about the guy," he says. "He was great for labor. He might be a tough guy, but that's what this union is."

Mr. Sciarra was the local's interim president, appointed by the board after the 1984 jailing of Salvatore Provenzano and forced to vacate when Mr. Jacobson became trustee. His role in Local 560 came under sharp scrutiny during the trusteeship trial. In the early 1980s, Mr. Sciarra handled contract and grievance matters for hundreds of Local 560 members, including drivers employed by Canny Trucking Co. in Elizabeth, N.J. Federal prosecutor Thomas Weisenbeck charged in court that during this period, Canny was using nonunion drivers supplied by a New Jersey trucking firm headed by Mr. Sciarra's longtime friend, Fred Furino. The prosecutor called this a violation of Canny's contract with Local 560.

Mr. Sciarra said that he wasn't aware of Canny's actions until Mr. Furino's death in 1982 and that he warned Canny never to use nonunion drivers again. Canny declines to comment.

Some of Mr. Jacobson's supporters fault him for failing to denounce corruption. "He's got to make the guys wake up, show them what's going on," says one. Otherwise, says another, "Mikey Sciarra's a shoo-in. And when he gets back, it'll be the same old story."

Another sore point is Mr. Jacobson's decision to keep Joseph Sheridan, a vice president of the ousted board, on the union payroll. In his decision, Judge Ackerman characterized Mr. Sheridan as "decent, devoted, blind and bought." Arthur L. Fox, a Washington attorney who has represented Teamster dissidents, says that retaining Mr. Sheridan "strikes the wrong message to the rank and file, if you're expecting real leaders to come out of the woodwork to clean up the union."

Mr. Jacobson cites "humanitarian" reasons for keeping Mr. Sheridan, who will be eligible for a union pension in five or six months. As for denouncing corruption, Mr. Jacobson says it would be poor strategy. "You force all the Sciarra loyalists to come to his defense," he says. "The candidate running against Sciarra—that's the guy who should be scoring points, not me."

But so far, no one has come forward to challenge Mr. Sciarra. Will Judge Ackerman permit an election if Mr. Sciarra is the sole candidate? "I'll jump off that bridge when I come to it," he says.

Clyde Summers, a University of Pennsylvania law professor who was a government witness at the trusteeship trial, says that free elections are a pipe dream until dissidents feel so secure that they "are willing to talk to reporters and let their names be used." Rank-and-filers backing Mr. Jacobson say it's ridiculous to believe that free elections can be held by year-end, as planned. "To undo what's been done will take three to four years," says one. "By then, the fear may be gone." *—February 10, 1987*

Nominee to Head SEC Was Sued for Breach Of Securities Laws

Casey Settled Out of Court In 1964; Two Senators Seek To Reopen Hearing on Him

---

By STANLEY PENN and GEORGE NIKOLAIEFF

William J. Casey, President Nixon's choice to head the Securities and Exchange Commission, was once accused of violating the Securities Act of 1933 by helping to sell unregistered stock in a small New York company on the basis of a false information.

The civil action was filed in 1962 in federal district court in New York. Mr. Casey denied the allegations, but in 1964 a pretrial settlement was reached, with Mr. Casey and the small company paying the plaintiff $8,000. In the action, $10,000 had been sought. Mr. Casey yesterday termed the action as a "nuisance" suit, "just a piece of civil litigation."

Informed of the suit, Sen. William Proxmire (D., Wis.) said yesterday that he was requesting that Sen. John Sparkman (D., Ala.), chairman of the Senate Banking Committee, reopen the committee's hearings on the nomination of Mr. Casey. On Wednesday the banking committee cleared the nomination after a brief hearing.

Reached by telephone yesterday, Mr. Casey said he hadn't informed the Nixon administration of the securities suit. "I'd forgotten about it," he said. "I don't think it's relevant." He also added, "If you led an active business life, as I have, people are going to make claims against you."

Indeed, this is the second claim, that has come to light against the 57-year-old New York corporate tax lawyer. He and a publishing company on whose editorial board he sat were named in a $175,000 plagiarism suit in 1959. They were accused of pirating parts of a manuscript and using the material in a publication that Mr. Casey edited. Mr. Casey and the publisher denied the charges, but lost a special verdict following a trial in federal district court in New York. The amount of the settlement was around $15,000, Mr. Casey has indicated. Because of his suit, full Senate action on his nomination to head the SEC has been delayed until committee members can examine the sealed transcript of the trial.

The latest case involves the very security laws that Mr. Casey must uphold as SEC chairman. The action was brought by Roland H. Boggs, who alleged he paid $10,000 for stock in Advancement Devices Inc. Mr. Boggs alleged that Mr. Casey was a director and "controlling person" in the corporation and alleged that the stock later became worthless and the company went into receivership. He asserted that Advancement Devices Inc., which was engaged in electronics development work, made a public offering of stock between Dec. 1, 1961, and May 30, 1962. He said he received from the firm a variety of information that was false and misleading.

Mr. Casey was the only defendant in the suit. He denied he controlled the firm, but in legal papers filed in court he conceded he was chairman of the board, had owned 6.8% of the stock and had advanced the financially strapped company some $100,000 to pave the way for the firm to obtain a $50,000 bank loan. Mr. Casey's New York law firm was counsel for Advancement Devices.

Mr. Casey also responded with a $40,000 counterclaim against Mr. Boggs, but that was dropped as part of the settlement.

The SEC itself did not become involved in the action. Private individuals, such as Mr.

155

Boggs, have the right to bring actions for civil damages charging violation of federal securities laws. The SEC rarely participates in this type of case.

Still, it is the type of action that "involves the whole reason for the SEC's operation, which is to insure full and fair disclosure," Sen. Proxmire said yesterday. "And according to the allegations in this case, Mr. Casey apparently failed to comply with that," he said. Because of the nature of the case, Chairman Sparkman is expected to reopen the hearings into the nomination. "Sen. Sparkman has been around here a long time, and he'll understand the implications of all this," one member of the Banking Committee said late yesterday.

Sen. Proxmire, who had abstained in the committee's endorsement of the Republican nominee, said late yesterday that the new "revelation that Mr. Casey was involved in a civil action involving violation of our securities laws casts new doubt" on the proposed nomination.

"The Senate should not act on the nomination until it has all the facts," he said. "Perhaps there are other cases which would shed additional light on Mr. Casey's nomination. It may be that Mr. Casey has a valid explanation of his alleged violation of the securities laws, but until the matter is fully resolved he should not be confirmed."

Late yesterday, Sen. Harrison Williams (D., N.J.), chairman of the Banking Committee's securities subcommittee, said he was joining Sen. Proxmire in the request to reopen the hearings. Mr. Williams, the third-ranking Democrat on the committee, was absent when the committee endorsed Mr. Casey on Wednesday.

The offering of Advancement Devices stock had not been registered with the Securities and Exchange Commission. Mr. Casey said the offering was considered a private placement and therefore wasn't subject to registration. Mr. Boggs, the plaintiff, contended otherwise. He alleged it was a public, interstate offering and should have been registered; thus, he brought his action under the federal securities law.

Mr. Boggs charged that the company had claimed it had developed and owned diversified components and systems including "the Toroidal Potentiometer, the Integral Calculus Computer, High Speed Clutch and Brake, High Speed Selector Switch, Battery Charger, Fuel Battery System, Aircraft Anticollision System, Infrared Telemeter, Information Correlator and Antenna Feeds."

According to Mr. Boggs, those systems weren't Advancement Devices' property, nor did it develop them or have proprietary rights to them. The representations that Mr. Boggs said were made on behalf of the electronics firm omitted its "precarious" financial condition—that it wasn't operating at a profit and that it was unable to predict with certainty that it would operate profitably for fiscal 1962, among other things.

Mr. Boggs, who lives in New Jersey, sought to convey the impression in court papers that he was an unsophisticated investor who was misled into buying the stock by false claims. He noted he had a high school equivalency diploma. At the time of his lawsuit, he said he was an assistant superintendent in charge of expediting work projects for Western Electric Co.

In a pretrial deposition, Mr. Casey said he had received the impression that Mr. Boggs was a sophisticated investor because Mr. Boggs had bought stock in a company named Kalvar that Mr. Casey knew was involved in highly technical developments.

The board of Advancement Devices had talked over the possibility of a public financing, Mr. Casey said in the deposition. But the plan was abandoned because the company had too many problems and wasn't in shape to register or sell stock to public investors, he said. "It was only suitable for sophisticated investors," he said.

In his deposition, Mr. Casey sought to play down his role in the firm. Asked by Mr. Boggs' lawyer if he was the company's chairman, Mr. Casey said, "They called me chairman of the board of directors, but it didn't mean anything. What constitutes a title? I don't know. I don't know that there was anything in the by-laws or charter that called for a chairman of the board. I acted as secretary and I used to write out the minutes and (the president of the firm) would run the meetings."

Mr. Casey said in the deposition that the company used a stockbroker to raise $100,000 through the sale of shares to a "small group of investors of about 10 people." Those proceeds were used to repay Mr. Casey for the money he had advanced to the company.

In the phone interview, Mr. Casey said he never met Mr. Boggs before the latter bought his stock. After "the company had blown up," Mr. Casey said, Mr. Boggs came to him saying he'd been advised to get his money back and that any lawsuit he started would probably involve Mr. Casey.

Mr. Casey said, "I assumed all the directors would be involved in the action." He said he was surprised when Mr. Boggs sued only him. He said Mr. Boggs had singled him out although Mr. Casey "had not encouraged him to make an investment."

Mr. Casey said he notified the board of the company at the time that Mr. Boggs would have no legal rights against him inasmuch as he "didn't participate in making the sale to him."

"If by some remote stretch of the imagination, if there were liability against me, it would be equal liability against all other directors," Mr. Casey informed the directors.

To dispose of Mr. Boggs' suit, the company agreed to pay $8,000 of the $10,000 back to Mr. Boggs, according to Mr. Casey. The company gave Mr. Boggs notes. Mr. Casey and another company executive endorsed the notes. The company paid off some of the notes, with Mr. Casey and other executive paying the balance, Mr. Casey recalls.

—February 12, 1971

* * *

Casey, SEC Choice, Complains of Bum Rap in Press; Third Suit Against Him Disclosed

By STANLEY PENN and WAYNE GREEN

William J. Casey, President Nixon's choice to head the Securities and Exchange Commission, said in a wide-ranging interview yesterday that his record is clean and complained that he has been getting a bum rap in stories about suits filed against him years ago. Even as he was talking, a third suit against him—and the second involving the securities laws he must uphold as SEC chairman—was coming to light.

"A serious breach of civil liberties could be being perpetrated here," he declared. "Self-serving allegations are being treated like an indictment, and an out-of-court settlement to dispose of the matter is being treated like a confession."

The 58-year-old New York tax lawyer has denied all charges in all suits, though he lost the suit that didn't involve the securities laws and he agreed to an out-of-court settlement in the previously disclosed securities suit. The latest suit, which has been in and out of the courts since 1965 and which still is pending, "consists of self-serving allegations," he said yesterday.

The Wall Street Journal and Business Week magazine simultaneously turned up the latest suit.

In yesterday's interview, which was arranged at the request of friends of the nominee, the gruff and brusque Mr. Casey termed all the suits the kind of normal, meaningless actions that often are filed against active businessmen. He implied that he considers it highly unfair that these suits are being aired now.

Mr. Casey's nomination was cleared unanimously by the Senate Banking Committee earlier this month, but when The Wall Street Journal on Feb. 12 disclosed the first securities suit two Senators moved to reopen the hearings. The committee is scheduled to meet Tuesday in executive session to determine if the hearings should be reopened.

At the time, the White House said it supported reopening the hearings. Yesterday, a high White House source said the administration still supports Mr. Casey and isn't considering withdrawing the nomination.

The latest action to come to light against Mr. Casey involved his role as a director of Kalvar Corp., a New Orleans-based company that makes duplicating machines, paper for office copiers and other products. He and several other officers and directors were charged with violating securities laws by giving misleading information about the terms of Kalvar's acquisition of S.O. Systems Inc., of Burlingame, Calif.

The suit was filed by dissident Kalvar stockholders in federal district court in New Orleans. The dissidents also charged in the suit that the Kalvar management disregarded the stockholders' interests by arranging the purchase for a supposedly unreasonable amount of Kalvar stock.

Kalvar said the suit didn't have any merit, and Harry McCall, a Kalvar lawyer and a defendant, said this week that the two sides once had agreed to a settlement. But at the last minute, some dissidents rejected the settlement, he said. Kalvar then sought to have the suit dismissed on the ground that the plaintiffs had originally agreed to settle, but the request was rejected by the court. The case still is on the docket in New Orleans, and

157

Mr. McCall said yesterday that a pretrial conference is slated for next month.

The suit failed to block the merger. The plaintiffs currently are seeking damages from the defendants on behalf of Kalvar. According to the Kalvar lawyer, the dissidents represented about 600 shares out of 12,000 Kalvar shares then outstanding.

Kalvar originally had intended that the exchange agreement would become effective only after a permit was issued by the Commissioner of Corporations of the state of California. S.O. Systems, a small marketing organization, then was based in California. The dissidents sought to block the merger by requesting a public hearing before the California commission, and at this point, one source says, Kalvar decided against seeking the California permit and decided, instead, to effect the stock exchange in New Orleans. Mr. McCall said Kalvar concluded it wasn't necessary to obtain a clearance in California as the principal S.O. Systems stockholders had moved to New Orleans.

One source told The Wall Street Journal this week that the transaction was moved to New Orleans on the advice of Mr. Casey's law firm.

Yesterday, Mr. Casey said he had a "vague recollection" of a situation in which S.O. Systems shareholders were brought to New Orleans to approve the transaction instead of simply voting in California. He denied it was an attempt to avoid the jurisdiction of the California commission, and he frankly said the move was designed to avoid any further delay in the transaction that might have been fatal to Kalvar, which he said had financial problems at the time.

"It was entirely a matter of this company (Kalvar) being in perilous shape," he said. "A hearing would have been injurious to that company." He said there was nothing improper or unusual in the procedure.

At the time, Mr. Casey was chairman of the Kalvar executive committee as well as a director.

It isn't clear whether the Nixon administration knew about the Kalvar suit, at least until recently. In an earlier interview, Mr. Casey said he hadn't informed the administration of the first securities suit to come to light. "I'd forgotten about it," he said. "I don't think it's relevant."

That suit, a civil action filed in 1962 in federal district court in New York, accused him of violating the Securities Act of 1933 by helping to sell unregistered stock in a small New York company on the basis of false information. The company was called Advancement

Devices Inc., and Mr. Casey was a director, chairman and a major stockholder. He was the only defendant in the suit.

The plaintiff, a stockholder, said he received from the firm a variety of information that was false and misleading. He sought $10,000. To dispose of the suit, the company agreed to pay $8,000 to the plaintiff, according to Mr. Casey. The company gave the plaintiff notes which were endorsed by Mr. Casey and another executive. The company paid off some of the notes, with Mr. Casey and the other executive paying the balance, Mr. Casey said.

Before the securities suit came to light, it was learned that Mr. Casey had been a defendant in a 1959 plagiarism suit seeking $175,000 in damages. He and a publishing company on whose editorial board he sat were accused of pirating parts of a manuscript and using the material in a publication that Mr. Casey edited. Mr. Casey and the publisher denied the charges but lost a special verdict following a trial in federal court in New York. The amount of the settlement was around $15,000, Mr. Casey has indicated.

Mr. Casey's name has also cropped up in connection with an SEC investigation of Occidental Petroleum Corp., a diversified Los Angeles-based concern. His name arises because he was a stockholder in Agro Resources Inc., which owned several thousand acres of farmland in Texas that were purchased and then resold by Occidental. It's understood this is one of several Occidental transactions being looked at by the SEC.

Mr. Casey said that at the request of a friend in California, he joined a group that was purchasing the Texas farmland by investing $70,000. His 5.4% interest in that group, which became Agro Resources was handled entirely by the California friend. Mr. Casey recalled, adding that he was completely "inactive" shareholder. He said his only knowledge of the Occidental transaction came through a report that the Agro Resources president sent to shareholders. "I knew nothing about it—I had no involvement," said Mr. Casey. He said an SEC official informed him of the SEC inquiry as a "courtesy" because, according to the official, about 20 SEC staff officials knew of it. The feeling was the agency was like a "sieve," it was bound to be leaked to someone outside the SEC, and the agency didn't feel it should come as a surprise.

Mr. Casey feels that he has been treated unfairly in the press. Talking of the first securities suit, he said yesterday that "the impression has gotten around that I sold (the plaintiff) stock and that I gave him questionable information. The fact is, as his testimony indicated, he never met me until six months after he made his investment. He made that investment at his own request, after talking to the president of the company."

Mr. Casey says the plaintiff's lawyer has written a letter to Senate Banking Committee chairman John Sparkman (D., Ala.) declaring that "the liability asserted against Mr. Casey was an imputed liability and the evidence disclosed no personal wrongdoing on his part."

Mr. Casey said that another investor in the company has wired Sen. Sparkman that the SEC nominee actually tried to dissuade him from investing in Advancement Devices.

"I never tell anyone to make an investment," Mr. Casey said. "The most I'll ever tell anyone is that I have my own money in it." He added: "There have been a great many other things that I've been involved in, and in all these I have been respected, my participation valued. I am a fellow who tends to step up and take responsibility when needed.... I have lived actively, but my reputation has always been first-class."

—*February 26, 1971*

* * *

A Breach of Duty?

SEC Head to Be Sued For Role as a Director Of Small Firm in '68-'70

Trustee of the Concern Says Casey, Others Mismanaged; Judge: "Inconceivable Acts"

Casey Denies Wrongdoing

By STANLEY PENN

The court-appointed trustee for an obscure farming company that is in bankruptcy proceedings will go to court any day now and file a $1.5 million suit alleging mismanagement by the little company's former directors.

One defendant will be William J. Casey, a founder and former director.

For the past two years, Mr. Casey has been the chairman of the Securities and Exchange Commission, the agency that is charged with upholding the nations' securities laws. At the time of his nomination to the post two years ago, there were revelations that he had been named in two civil actions alleging breach of these securities laws. And now that he is leaving the post—he has been nominated by President Nixon to serve as Under Secretary of State for Economic Affairs—he is about to be accused of wrongdoing again.

The case here directly involves a company known first as Ivanhoe Associates Inc. and later as Multiponics Inc. Tangentially, it involves companies as diverse as the giant and gigantically troubled IOS Ltd., which made a big investment in Multiponics, and a little outfit in Grapevine, Texas, that planned to grow vegetables in a nutrient solution rather than in soil.

From its inception in January 1968 until February 1971, when it voluntarily filed in federal district court here under Chapter 10 of the federal Bankruptcy Act, Multiponics Inc. sustained losses of more than $6 million. One problem, the trustee alleges, was that management misused corporate funds through questionable transactions. Indeed, one transaction was so questionable that the federal judge in charge of the case says, "This may be a matter that should be referred to the Department of Justice."

No one is charging Mr. Casey with any criminal wrongdoings (nor has he ever been cited in a criminal complaint during his various brushes with the securities laws). The main charge that will be leveled against him and other directors in this case is that, in effect, they breached their fiduciary duty to the 100 or so stockholders in Multiponics by not stepping in to question or halt various deals made by the board, of which Mr. Casey was a member from early 1968 until May 1970. Under the law set forth in the securities acts and broadly expanded by court decisions in recent years, a director has a vast responsibility to protect the interests of the stockholders, whom he represents. But at Multiponics, "some of the things the directors did are inconceivable," Federal Judge Herbert Christenberry, who is overseeing the case, said in

159

court.

Mr. Casey denies any wrongdoing in this latest action, just as he did in past securities suits against him. (He settled both of those out of court without admitting any wrong.) He has repeatedly said that any big business-man—which he was before he left his Wall Street law firm to become head of the SEC—faces threats of suits from disgruntled stockholders. He generally refers to such actions as nuisance suits.

Mr. Casey yesterday said that he believes he acted honorably in his dealings at Multiponics, and he said he will defend his actions in court.

If Mr. Casey's action is open to question, so, too, is his agency's, some people charge. The SEC often investigates Chapter 10 bankruptcy cases to help the court untangle the financial mess and to see if corporate funds were wasted through mismanagement; civil and even criminal action against any wrongdoers may result from these SEC investigations. During fiscal 1971, for instance, the SEC entered 19 new Chapter 10 cases and was a party in 114, many of which were instituted in prior years, a source says. Yet the SEC thus far hasn't investigated the Multiponics case, although the commission, by order of the federal court here, has been receiving copies of the proceedings for nearly two years.

Asked why the SEC hasn't looked into the allegations of possible corruption at Multiponics, a commission spokesman says: "Because there's no public investor interest. That's our basic criterion. This case is no different from hundreds of others that we haven't entered. There are a great many Chapter 10 cases filed. We only get involved in a limited number." Asked whether the SEC should have involved itself because of SEC Chairman Casey's involvement in Multiponics, the spokesman says, "We make a decision on the merits of the matter."

A former attorney with the SEC disagrees with the SEC's decision not to intercede, however, "Even though there may be small public stockholder interest, I'd want to bend over backwards to avoid publicity of possible favoritism toward Casey," he says. "There's also the matter of IOS. I'd like to know what induced the IOS fund to make the investment in the company."

Mr. Casey himself says the SEC decision not to investigate Multiponics was made by the staff. And an SEC spokesman says the decision was made a month before Mr. Casey was sworn in as chairman in April 1971.

If the SEC does decide to look into Multi-ponics, it won't have much difficulty tracing the fall of the company. All told, there are 30 volumes of bankruptcy proceedings on file in federal district court here, and they vividly tell the story of the collapse. Among other things, the court documents:

-Raise the possibility of management's misuse of corporate funds.

-Raise the possibility of criminal wrong-doing in at least one instance.

-Disclose several examples of apparent conflicts of interest on the part of some directors and managers (but not directly involving Mr. Casey).

-Show how the company tried, and failed, to go public.

-Disclose how one director negotiated a large personal bank loan that was secured by corporate funds. This transaction, according to court testimony by the former chairman of Multiponics, was drawn up but not participated in by William J. Casey.

The predecessor of Multiponics was formed on Jan. 10, 1968, and Mr. Casey was immediately named to the board, court records show. The company bought or leased 44,000 acres of farm land in Florida, Louisiana, Arkansas and Mississippi. According to Carl Biehl, a former director of Multiponics, the management had hoped to cash in on a world-wide demand for soybeans. "But somebody invented some new type of grain, and that theory got blown up," he says in a deposition on file in federal district court here.

And matters went from bad to worse. In 1968, Multiponics bought a Florida farm from N. Leslie Carpenter, then a Multiponics director. The company paid $2.1 million for the farm including cash, stock and assumption of liabilities, according to court documents. That was about $600,000 higher than an appraisal of the property prior to purchase, Peter Butler, counsel for the trustee of Multiponics, says in a deposition on file here. And it was $1 million more than Multiponics got for the property when it sold it at public auction in 1971; oddly, the buyer at auction was the same N. Leslie Carpenter.

It was this deal that prompted Judge Christenberry to declare that "this may be a matter that should be referred to the Department of Justice."

Alfred Moran, the former chairman of Multiponics, was asked in court if he paid any particular attention to the purchase of the Florida property in light of the fact that Mr. Carpenter, the seller, was on the board of Multiponics, the buyer. "No more or less than we would any transaction," the New Orleans businessman replied.

Corporate lawyers say dealings between an officer or director and the corporation aren't illegal per se, but the parties must be able to show, if challenged, that the arrangements were so-called arms-length transactions in which the officer or director wasn't given favorable treatment because of his position.

The Florida farm, known as Lisbon Development Corp., had never shown a profit, documents on file in court here indicate. Judge Christenberry asked why one ailing company had bought another. Mr. Moran replied that the acquisition was aimed at giving Multiponics greater geographic diversification, thereby perhaps paving the way for a public stock offering.

"In other words," the judge said during the proceeding, "one corporation in distress was not large enough, but you felt that two corporations in distress would give you a better opportunity with a public issue."

Mr. Casey says the price did, in fact, bother him, though he denies the price came anywhere near $3.1 million. "I raised a question about the price." he says, "But the others thought it was all right. It was the collective judgment (of the board) that the price was justified."

Although Multiponics never seemed to be a cash-rich corporation, management apparently felt it could pledge $200,000 of company funds as collateral for a personal bank loan by Lawrence F. Orbe, a Multiponics director at this time in 1968.

Mr. Orbe, a former vice president of Glore Forgan, Wm. R. Staats Inc. (which since has been absorbed into duPont Glore Forgan Inc.), obtained a bank loan in New Orleans to buy 50,000 Multiponics shares at $4 each. Multiponics used the proceeds from the sale of the stock to buy a $200,000 certificate of deposit at the same bank, allowing the certificate to be used as security for Mr. Orbe's loan. If Mr. Orbe had defaulted, the bank could have kept the certificate, according to testimony by former chairman Moran.

The trustee's lawyer has charged that Multiponics failed to disclose this deal in a registration statement that it filed with the SEC in July 1970 when it had hopes of going public. (The registration statement failed to clear the commission.) In court here, Mr. Moran was asked if he felt the use of corporate funds as security for a director's personal bank loan was a "material factor" that should have been put into the registration statement. Mr. Moran replied that he left that matter up to Mr. Casey and his old law firm,

Hall, Casey, Dickler and Howley of New York, which was counsel to Multiponics.

"As a matter of fact," Mr. Moran deposed, "the author of the transaction was William J. Casey."

Mr. Casey, however, says Mr. Moran is mistaken. Mr. Casey insists he wasn't aware that corporate funds had been used to back up the loan to Mr. Orbe.

Mr. Moran also testified that the Casey law firm gave advice that led to another transaction that came in for harsh criticism from Judge Christenberry. In 1968, Multiponics bought 100,000 shares of CBK Agronomics Inc. of Kansas City in exchange for 200,000 Multiponics shares. In late 1969, Multiponics arranged to reverse the deal, paying CBK a $400,000 penalty.

In his deposition, Mr. Moran said the Casey law firm had warned that Multiponics wouldn't be able to get a registration statement through the SEC "unless we unwound."

"Just a minute." Judge Christenberry said. "Do you want the court to understand, and the trustee, and everybody here, that a corporation which is already in financial difficulty would be required to put out $400,000 of short cash under these circumstances so that you could solicit the public?"

"Yes, sir," Mr. Moran replied.

"Does that make any sense to you?" the judge asked.

"It makes sense to the investment banking community, judge," Mr. Moran replied.

(At the time Multiponics okayed paying the $400,000 penalty, Mr. Orbe was both a director of Multiponics and a financial advisor to CBK. Was the Multiponics board aware of this? "Yes," Mr. Moran testified. CBK Agronomics in 1971 was delisted from the American Stock Exchange on the ground it failed to meet earnings and asset requirements.)

Another controversial stock deal involved Multiponics' purchase in early 1970 of a 48% stock interest in American Hydroponic Systems Inc. of Grapevine, Texas, for cash and stock in Multiponics. There was talk of a possible merger.

Though American Hydroponic wasn't in good financial shape, Mr. Moran in his testimony tried to justify Multiponics' purchase of the stock. "They had a know-how, judge. They were at that time the only outstanding authority on hydroponically growing vegetables in the U.S. or the world," he said. (This involves the growing of vegetables in nutrient solution instead of soil.)

Multiponics bought 264,000 Hydroponic shares. Some 29,000 of the shares were bought at $116,000 from J.J. Cirenza Associ-

161

ates of New York. In his deposition, Mr. Moran concedes he and his mother together had a $300,000 interest in Cirenza, an "investment 'go-go' fund." He said the Multiponics board knew it at the time of the stock purchase. But Mr. Biehl, the former Multiponics director, insisted he didn't know. He'd have resigned from the board if he'd known, he said in a deposition.

Mr. Casey says he didn't know any of the details when Multiponics bought the Hydroponic stock in about April of 1970. "I attended my last board meeting in January or February of that year," he says.

It cost Multiponics $805,000 in cash and stock for the 264,000 Hydroponic shares. According to the New Orleans accounting firm of Malcolm M. Dienes & Co., the trustee's attorney said the Hydroponic stock had no value as of June 1971 and "to charge off this investment as worthless." The Dienes firm audited the Multiponics' balance sheet.

Besides these alleged irregularities, Multiponics may have violated an indenture agreement with First National City Bank of New York, trustee for the Multiponics' bond holders. Court documents suggest that Multiponics was prohibited by the indenture agreement from using cash to repurchase its own stock. But in late 1969, Multiponics paid the $400,000 penalty to get back its shares from CBK Agronomics.

William Meyers, a New Orleans lawyer representing First National City Bank, discussed the possible violation in a February 1972 letter to the Multiponics trustee. Mr. Meyers then pointedly suggested an investigation into the "conduct of officers and directors," including Mr. Casey.

Clearly, things at Multiponics haven't worked out so well for Mr. Casey. No matter how the forthcoming suit turns out, he probably took a loss on his investment. It isn't clear how much he put into the little company, but at about the time it filed for bankruptcy proceedings in February 1971 he was listed as owning about 66,000 shares, or nearly 6% of the stock, though Mr. Casey says he sold that stock in December 1970. The Sophia and William Casey Foundation of New York held $50,000 in Multiponics bonds, court records show, and Mr. Casey says he isn't sure if the foundation still has the bonds. In addition, Mr. Casey had an option to buy 10,000 shares of Multiponics at $4 a share in consideration of a $200,000 loan he had made to Multiponics. The company repaid the loan before Mr. Casey moved to the SEC.

Mr. Casey, of course, isn't the only person stuck. Insiders held about 26% of the stock at about the time of the Chapter 10 filing; all told, there were 100 or so stockholders. One of these stockholders was IIT, a Geneva-based mutual fund managed by IOS Ltd., a long-time target of SEC probes. IIT held 105,000 shares, or nearly 10% of Multiponics stock, as well as $1.5 million of bonds. The securities were acquired in late 1968, while Mr. Casey was a Multiponics director and when IOS was controlled by the controversial Bernard Cornfeld.

IOS later came under the domination of financier Robert Vesco. Last November, the SEC brought a civil fraud suit against Mr. Vesco and others, charging that huge sums were diverted from the IOS-managed funds for Mr. Vesco's benefit.

—January 16, 1973

162

Crop Busters

U.S.-Mexican Project For Planes to Wipe Out Drug Crops Is Faltering

Illicit Narcotics Keep Flowing As Problems With Pilots, Aircraft and Parts Pile Up

Many Acres of Dead Poppies

By STANLEY PENN

CULIACAN, Mexico—The five Bell 206 helicopters begin threading their way through narrow 7,500-foot mountain passes. Suddenly, a tell-tale hint of scarlet in the underbrush ahead betrays a target.

One chopper eases in at tree-top level. Pilots have learned to be wary: They sometimes find wire mesh waiting to snare them. And occasionally gunfire. Today there is neither. An empty tin-roofed hut and some hastily abandoned tools, blankets and a ratty cowhide below indicate no one stuck around. The pilot opens fire with a herbicide spray and the airborne armada then whirls back to base.

The kill: a garden-sized plot of flowering poppies.

This is the Sierra Madre, still hiding a treasure that corrupts. Only these days the treasure is the opium-bearing poppy, the raw material of Mexico's burgeoning heroin trade. For peasants tending tiny, secret mountain plots, the showy red flowers are a cash crop. But as far as U.S. policy makers are concerned, they are a primary target in the war against illicit drugs.

Federal strategists some time ago decided that destroying so-called narcotics crops—poppies and marijuana—while they are still in the ground would be more efficient than chasing smugglers. Today, the U.S. backs joint crop-eradication ventures with governments of a dozen drug-supplying countries. This is the biggest.

It is also one of the most troubled. The program is hobbled by mismanagement, red tape, and the whiff of corruption. Finger-pointing between U.S. and Mexican officials over blame strains relations between the countries. Meanwhile, poppy and marijuana growers continue to produce bumper crops. And Mexico continues to be America's chief heroin and marijuana supplier, raising questions about just how workable such foreign eradication programs really are.

At bottom is the question of who is in charge. Most of Mexico's 92 drug-fighting aircraft were purchased with U.S. money. And last year alone, the U.S. spent $14.5 million here for maintenance, parts and pilot training. But Mexico runs the program, on the ground and in the air.

"The whole thing has turned into a shambles," asserts Rep. Lawrence J. Smith, head of the House Foreign Affairs Committee's anti-drug task force. "Cajoling, pleading, begging, diplomatic inquiries—none of them works."

The Reagan administration and the Democratic-controlled Congress both are reluctant to push a key ally like Mexico too hard. The Senate last April voted to sanction Mexico for failing to do enough, but the measure died in the House after Mexico promised to try harder to destroy opium-yielding poppy fields.

Top Mexican officials bristle at that kind of U.S. pressure. "The U.S. attitude is, father knows best. We're not little kids who need tutors," says Mexico Deputy Attorney General Jose Maria Ortega Padilla.

A prickly attitude is somewhat understandable, too. The State Department's drug-eradication agency in Mexico has had seven different bosses in the past seven years. "How do you establish rapport with Mexicans and gain their respect with so much turnover?" asks one American with close ties to Mexican drug fighters.

Under the best conditions, aerial crop destruction is difficult. Expensive modern machines, chemicals and trained pilots are used to find and annihilate obscure plots of plants one at a time. But under conditions existing here, the job is daunting.

U.S. and Mexican officials have squabbled over just about every aspect of the program—right down to the choice of aircraft.

At one point, the U.S. pushed a fixed-wing plane called the Turbo Thrush, used for narcotics-crop eradication elsewhere in Latin America and Asia. The Thrush is fast; a poor target for snipers. It carries 400 gallons of

163

herbicide—six times the payload of a Bell 206 helicopter.

But Mexican authorities complain the Thrush is too fast. "It overshot the poppy fields," and would accidentally spray legitimate crops such as corn, says Deputy Attorney General Ortega. By contrast, they rave about the Bell's maneuverability and even spent nearly $6 million of Mexico's own funds a while ago for a dozen of them. A fatal Thrush crash early last year settled the issue—four remaining ones and their American pilots were withdrawn from service. The Bell helicopter is now the fleet's workhorse.

The plane issue pales, however, next to other problems. A big headache is poor pay for pilots and mechanics, and the low morale and the turnover that causes. Mexican government spray pilots currently earn $800 per month—a better-than-average Mexican wage, but less than what they could make in private industry. American pilots on the State Department's payroll who were flying here until last year say their salaries—including expenses—were $9,500 a month, or more than 10 times what the Mexican pilots made.

"The Mexicans took the same risks as us, but they got paid this cornbread living," observes one U.S. flier. A State Department offer to supplement the Mexicans' pay only irritated Mexican officials. "The pilots cannot have two bosses," declares Deputy Attorney General Ortega.

In the view of one former U.S. adviser, the wage disparity influences the pilots' work habits. Americans took off at daybreak and flew two missions by lunchtime. "The Mexicans," he says, "wouldn't take off till 9. When they got back, that was it for the day." (No one flies in the afternoon, when stiff, hazardous winds rattle through the mountains.)

Mechanics aren't much happier. An investigation of the program's U.S.-funded aircraft maintenance last year showed a mechanics' work slowdown because of poor pay, says Robert Fox, a senior vice president of Evergreen Helicopters Inc., the Portland, Ore., concern hired to do the State Department study. The slowdown was keeping some aircraft grounded unusually long for repairs.

Mexican authorities now claim they are turning the corner with pilots and mechanics. After pilot pay was increased 120% last year to the current $800-a-month, the pilot roster, which had fallen to 100 last autumn from 159 in 1985, rebounded to 141. Mechanics also got 120% more, and officials are promoting some to higher-paying jobs as inspectors to keep them.

But the raises have barely kept up with Mexico's inflation rate. And Mr. Fox says that government mechanics, at least, still can readily double their pay by moving to private industry.

In addition to personnel troubles, shortages of repair parts hamper the program. "A plane would sit for weeks because it couldn't get replacement parts," recalls Marvin Foster, until last January a paid aviation adviser to the State Department's narcotics assistance unit here.

At a big Mexico City hangar where spray planes are maintained, the problem is quite evident. Mechanics have stripped one airworthy helicopter down to its skeleton for parts to fix three others.

Shortages occur even though stockpiles are bulging, because many items on hand are obsolete or nonessential. Overall, inventories in 1986 were about twice the $7 million typical for a fleet this size, according to a recent report by the U.S. General Accounting Office.

Pinpointing the cause is another matter. Rafael Garcia-Delgado, Mexico's director of aviation services, blames poor U.S. workmanship. "Parts are sent to the U.S., but aren't repaired properly, so we have to send them back," he says.

Deputy Attorney General Ortega criticizes E-Systems Inc., the Dallas electronics and defense company that, until recently, advised Mexico on maintenance and parts procurement. "In '86 and '87, I never got spare parts in timely fashion, or I didn't get the right amounts," Mr. Ortega says.

E-Systems doesn't argue, but says it isn't to blame. "On a number of occasions during 1986 and 1987, we stopped procurement of parts because funding wasn't available," a company official says. The State Department, in turn, denies any financing problems. Mexico replaced E-Systems with Bell Helicopter Textron Inc., a Textron Inc. subsidiary, when E-Systems' contract expired May 31.

Parts can even be a problem for ground vehicles. One American recalls seeing inoperable fuel trucks at the base at Culiacan and being told various components had been stolen. "They'd tell us there was no battery, or no generator, or no tire, or it needs spark plugs," he says. Mexican authorities won't discuss such allegations.

Hints of corruption dog the spray program, though proven incidents are scarce. "They wouldn't let us work in certain sectors," says one American formerly employed in drug eradication. "Our pilots would fly over these fields. After they got back, they'd check with the zone coordinator, who said he'd have them sprayed by helicopter. He never did." The American suspects those crops were off-limits, though he hasn't any proof.

Mexico concedes some low-level corruption. In the past year, two Mexican pilots were jailed for accepting payments in return for not destroying drug-crop fields. But Deputy Attorney General Ortega denies that crops are regularly protected. "Pilots have the freedom to fumigate whatever fields they might find. They have an obligation to report fields they might find," he says.

In a war where victories are measured by the quarter-acre, assessing progress is slippery business. Last year, Mexico claimed that the equivalent of 6,200 acres of poppies were destroyed, up from 5,900 acres the previous year. But more than 15,000 acres of poppies remained under cultivation, and Mexico's 1987 opium production actually increased over 1986, according to U.S. estimates.

Mexico reported destroying the equivalent of 9,300 acres of marijuana last year, up from 7,350 acres in 1986. Still, the U.S. estimates that the 1987 crop rose to as high as 7,130 tons from 6,000 tons in 1986.

Mexico verifies crop destruction by flying over sprayed sites; it calls on-ground inspections too risky. But the U.S. is pushing for more thorough, on-ground inspections, using helicopters capable of landing in small clearings.

As a step in that direction, Americans here two years ago asked to borrow a Mexican helicopter. The Mexicans said they couldn't spare one. After a year of U.S. badgering, they relented. There was a catch: The proffered helicopter had to be pried off the side of a mountain where it had crashed. It took a year to rebuild.

The incident still irritates Mexican officials. "We have fixed-wing planes for verification, but, no, the Americans want a helicopter," one snaps. "We gave them a helicopter. Soon they'll want ten helicopters. Then 50."

To refine the guesswork on results, the State Department has talked for more than a year of equipping a Mexican plane with a powerful camera. So far, that's only produced more hassles.

First, the Americans dickered among themselves. "The question was, how sophisticated a camera was needed? Should we spend $50,000, or $100,000?" recalls a State Department official. Then, an East German model was rejected because "we weren't prepared to buy from them," the official says. Finally, last September, the Americans settled on a camera.

It still hasn't been purchased. Mexico hasn't yet produced a plane to carry it. "When that will be is up to the Mexicans," the official says.

—August 3, 1993

Family Rift

An FBI Informant Gives Rare Inside Look At Life With the Mob

Ron Fino Tells of Growing Up As the Son of a Mafia Boss, And 15 Years Undercover

Star Witness Against a Union

By STANLEY PENN

The heat was on, and Ronald M. Fino's precarious double life was about to unravel.

The devoted son of a high-ranking Buffalo mobster, Mr. Fino had for 15 years headed that city's Local 210 of the Laborers International Union of North America. During all those years he had also been an informant for the Federal Bureau of Investigation, feeding the government evidence of the union's ties to organized crime.

Now, by late 1988, the mob had finally turned wary. A Mafia official summoned Mr. Fino to a sit-down in the coffee shop of Buffalo's Veterans Administration hospital. "I'm going to have to frisk you," he told Mr. Fino. "I had known this man a long time," Mr. Fino recalls today. "I said, 'Shame on you.' He said, 'Out of respect for your father, I won't do it.'"

The wire Mr. Fino was wearing that day—in a pack of cigarettes in his pocket—went undetected. Nonetheless, the mobster delivered a warning: "He told me," Mr. Fino says, "that I couldn't be trusted any longer."

Mr. Fino took heed. Soon afterward, he fled Buffalo, assumed a new name and went into hiding, where he remains today. So far, Mr. Fino's information has helped indict three Local 210 officers, and has linked the Mafia to Laborers union locals in other cities, says G. Robert Langford, the FBI's Buffalo chief.

As a prosecution witness, Mr. Fino will figure prominently in the government's attempts to smash the Mafia leadership in Buffalo and clamp a court trusteeship on Local 210 under civil provisions of the Racketeer Influenced and Corrupt Organizations, or RICO, law.

"He was a very big help," says the FBI's Mr. Langford. "He steered us in the right direction in a number of investigations."

In telling his story to The Wall Street Journal, Mr. Fino provides a rare account of a life and career shaped by his Mafia birthright—a legacy that he freely chose to betray. It is a portrait of the informer's dangerous tightrope act: of the duplicity, agility and nerve such a performance demands, and of its aftermath of bitterness and fear.

The government has in recent years come to rely heavily on undercover informants to combat organized crime. The imprisonment of numerous mob bosses under RICO has served to weaken the Mafia's code of silence, long bred of fear and the perception of invincibility. Stiff RICO penalties have further eroded Mafia loyalties, giving mobsters and their associates powerful incentive to cooperate in return for lighter sentences.

As an informant, Mr. Fino is something of an anomaly. He never joined the Mafia; he declined an invitation to become a member, though it came from the same reputed "capo" who earlier had recruited his father. Nor was he coerced to become an informant; he wasn't facing criminal charges when he volunteered his services to the FBI. (Years later, while working undercover, he pleaded guilty to a misdemeanor in a fraud case and received two years' probation.)

Mr. Fino wasn't paid by the FBI during his years undercover. He began receiving payments—now $6,000 a month—from the bureau in March 1989 after agreeing to become a prosecution witness in future trials. FBI agents accompany him on plane trips and during court appearances. "We have heard there is a price on his head, and we consider it a valid threat," says the FBI's Mr. Langford.

Mr. Fino, now 44, never relaxes his guard. When jogging, he says, "if I see somebody who looks like a stranger, somebody looks like he's checking me out, I report it to the FBI."

In Buffalo, Mr. Fino is denounced by Paul Cambria Jr., the attorney for a Local 210 officer whom Mr. Fino has implicated in a crime. For many years, Mr. Cambria contends, the FBI has tried without success to brand Local 210 as mob-controlled. "It looks as if this time they're going to attempt to prove it by using

166

Ron Fino," who, he says, "resigned from Local 210 probably because he was not able to take it over and run it the way he would like to."

Mr. Fino's personal life is in shambles. His wife, Donna, to whom he never disclosed his FBI spying, divorced him last November. His two brothers no longer speak to him. One of them, Patrick Fino, says: "Shame on him because he left his wife and kids." Fear for his own safety kept Ron Fino from attending his mother's funeral in Buffalo last December.

"I try to live a halfway normal life," he says. "But it's difficult. I can't go and come like a normal person. The toughest thing is my children—I don't see them." His son, 19, and daughter, 17, live with their mother.

Life in solitary exile is a far cry from his heady years as a labor leader, when his salary and benefits totaled $85,000 a year. There were union-supplied Cadillacs, trips to Miami and Hawaii, bottles of Montrachet, friends in high places.

"Fino had a generally good reputation," says Dennis Gorski, county executive of Erie County, where Buffalo is situated. "He participated in a wide variety of civic and humanitarian projects."

A frequent fund-raiser for worthy causes, Mr. Fino was honored by the Buffalo chapter of the National Association for the Advancement of Colored People. And under his leadership, Local 210 was part of a group that lent money for downtown redevelopment projects, including construction of Buffalo's Hyatt Regency hotel. "When Ron Fino gave his word, to my knowledge he kept it," says Paul Snyder Sr., managing director of the partnership that owns the Hyatt Regency.

Some people in Buffalo are still puzzled why Mr. Fino would forsake everything for the dubious privilege of exposing Mafia crimes. One explanation is that he never intended to pay so dearly. Another, perhaps, can be traced to deep conflicts about his Mafia upbringing.

"I could never get rid of the feeling that I was one of them," Mr. Fino says. "You have this original sin that never washes away.

"It affected everything. In high school, I'd date a new girl. Next time I called up for a date, her parents wouldn't let her go out with me. They'd read about my father in the paper."

Milwaukee-born Joseph (Ebe) Fino worked as a bookie, taking bets on horses and baseball. A 1963 U.S. Senate report on organized crime traces his rise in the Buffalo Mafia from "hoodlum status to upper-echelon

rank." He was boss of the Buffalo crime family from 1968 to 1972.

For a time, according to the Senate report, Joe Fino served as a Mafia enforcer. Once, his son says, the elder Mr. Fino killed a man—the lover of a mobster's unfaithful wife. "The mob directed that the guy be killed, and my father drew the assignment," Ron Fino says. The murder went unsolved. Ron Fino says he never revealed his father's involvement to outsiders until after Joe Fino died in 1984.

Secrets and subterfuge were part of growing up in a Mafia household. When Ron Fino was five, his mother took him to New York's Attica state prison, where his father was serving time for grand larceny. "She told me Attica was an Army fort, and that we were going to visit my father in the Army," Mr. Fino recalls.

When he was 11, he watched his father pay off two detectives at a restaurant. "I thought they were going to arrest my father," Mr. Fino says. "But all they wanted was their cut."

Only gradually did it dawn on the boy that Joe Fino was a member of the Mafia. Once, young Ron came home from school in a novelty T-shirt inscribed: "World Order of Mafia. Paid-Up Member." His father angrily demanded that he remove it. "I couldn't understand what he was mad about," Mr. Fino says.

By the time he was in high school, however, Ron Fino was working weekends in a Mafia gambling parlor, tending dice tables.

To the family, "my father was a very caring man," Ron Fino says. "He gave me money if I needed it. He never hit me—I never saw him hit anyone."

Through his father's connections, Ron Fino joined Local 210 at age 18, working summers in construction while attending college. He moved up quickly, and was elected Local 210's operating head and business manager in 1973, at age 27.

Just as Ron Fino's star was rising, Joe Fino's began to sink. He was perceived by the mob as ineffective, and in 1972 was removed as Buffalo chief by the Commission, the Mafia's New York-based ruling council. As Mafia leaders looked the other way, he began to lose customers to other bookies.

Two years later, he wound up on the losing side of a factional dispute that had split the Buffalo Mafia. Rumor had it that he was to be killed. Ron Fino went to his father's home and urged him to leave. "He wouldn't budge," Mr. Fino says. "He said to relax. He didn't leave the house for three days. Then it all blew over. Later I was told by Sam Pieri that he saved my father's life."

The late Mr. Pieri, a reputed Mafia "capo" and member of the dominant faction, was an old friend who had recruited Joe Fino into the Mafia. He invited Ron Fino to join as well—three years after Mr. Fino had turned informant. "We were driving back from Cleveland," Mr. Fino says, "when Sam Pieri said it would be easy to introduce me as a 'friend of ours,' which meant, 'Would you like to join?'" Mr. Fino says that neither he nor his father, who didn't want him entangled with the mob, favored the idea. "My father said, 'Let me take care of it.' And I never heard any more about it."

By 1976, Joe Fino was reduced to taking handouts from his son. When his father's four-bedroom suburban house burned down, Ron Fino made the monthly payments on a new house. "All the time he'd been in the mob, my father never had life insurance, or medical insurance, and never provided for the future," Ron Fino says. "Toward the end of his life, I brought him into Local 210. I got him work as a laborer. I said, 'As a union member, you're entitled to a pension.' I explained to him the strength of legitimacy."

Ron Fino rode to election as business manager on a promise of greater responsiveness to the local's 2,000 members. But it soon became clear that his hands were tied. "After two weeks on the job, I was told by the [Mafia] bosses who to put on the union payroll and who would be involved in the benefit funds," he says.

"When deserving people came to me for jobs," Mr. Fino adds, "I couldn't do anything for them." Instead of an equitable hiring hall, he says, "there's a Who's Who list of guys to be taken care of. If you're not on it, you're out of luck." Mr. Fino insists that it was only after he was elected union leader that he realized the full extent of mob influence.

The Washington-based Laborers International Union is aware of FBI allegations that the Buffalo local is mob-controlled, says Robert Connerton, general counsel of the international. "If something is proven, the international is prepared to do something about it," he says. Mr. Connerton adds that as Local 210 leader, Ron Fino "probably did a good job. My feeling was he was very bright, very flaky, some sort of shadowy character, always by himself."

Mr. Fino says that frustration over being a union figurehead in thrall to mob bosses led him, shortly after his election in 1973, to begin assisting the FBI. He was recruited by an acquaintance, an FBI agent to whom he had earlier voiced his contempt for the mob. The FBI urged him to join the Mafia to better penetrate it. He refused, he says, fearing that the mob might order him to kill someone.

Even so, the FBI had a highly useful operative in Mr. Fino. In 1976, he met with Anthony D. Liberatore, then business agent for Cleveland Laborers Local 860. Mr. Liberatore, according to a 1988 U.S. Senate report, is a "capo" in the Cleveland Mafia.

"Liberatore thought I was a member of the Buffalo family, so he spoke freely," Mr. Fino says. "He told me the mob had a leak into the FBI office in Cleveland—someone in the FBI feeding stuff to them. I was concerned. It meant the mob would have access to the FBI computer, which had a list of informants, including me."

Mr. Fino reported the leak to the FBI. In 1978, an FBI file clerk and her husband pleaded guilty in Cleveland to receiving $15,000 from Mr. Liberatore in exchange for confidential FBI files, including a list of informants. (Mr. Fino's name apparently wasn't on the list.) The couple received five-year prison sentences. Mr. Liberatore, convicted in 1982 of racketeering and for his role in bribing the FBI clerk, was recently released from prison.

Mr. Fino and his FBI contact met secretly, often at night, behind the Buffalo Bills' football stadium. "I told my wife it was business," Mr. Fino says. "She accepted it."

Once, a Mafioso spotted him sitting in an FBI agent's car in broad daylight in downtown Buffalo. Mr. Fino was hauled before Sam Frangiamore, who at the time was Buffalo's Mafia chief, according to the FBI. "I told Frangiamore I was coming out of the union hall when an FBI agent told me to get into his car," Mr. Fino says. "I said I thought I was under arrest, and that I told the FBI to go talk to my attorney. Frangiamore accepted my explanation."

Another time, the Mafia obtained FBI documents outlining the bureau's surveillance of mob figures in Buffalo. The documents, snatched from an FBI agent's unlocked car, were brought to Local 210. Tipped by Mr. Fino, federal lawmen barged into Local 210 and retrieved the papers.

To deflect suspicion from himself, Mr. Fino told Mafia leaders that the FBI knew of the documents' whereabouts because they had bugged the union office. Knowing that the mob would sweep his office, Mr. Fino bought a Radio Shack transmitter and installed it in his office ceiling. The fake bug was duly uncovered.

The close calls took their toll, and by February 1988 Ron Fino was burned out. He wanted to resume a normal life. He told the FBI he would no longer serve as an informant and resigned his job at Local 210. "The crime family urged me to stay in my job," Mr. Fino says. "I had this good public image. They were afraid they'd have problems without me."

The Mafia might never have discovered he was an informant were it not for the 1988 indictment of Joseph Rosato, a Local 210 shop steward. Mr. Rosato, who denies wrongdoing, is set to stand trial in September on charges that he accepted payments from a construction employer for work not performed, a so-called no-show job scam.

"The mob asked me to testify as a defense witness that Rosato didn't violate any law," Mr. Fino says. This put him in a bind, because he had implicated Mr. Rosato. "So I kept ducking them," Mr. Fino says. "I was evasive. Then the mob decided something was wrong."

After his ominous encounter at the VA Hospital coffee shop, he asked to meet with Joseph Todaro Jr., the reputed boss of the Buffalo organized crime family and a former Local 210 business agent. "He refused to see me," Mr. Fino says. "Then I got word from a relative of someone in the 'family' that I had a 'problem,' and I should get out of town."

Mr. Fino fled Buffalo in a rented black Thunderbird on the morning of Jan. 13, 1989, accompanied by a woman with whom he was then romantically involved. A few weeks later, the Buffalo News reported that he had been an FBI informant.

He left behind a dying waste-removal company, which he had founded after leaving Local 210. James A. Ryding, a former president of the company now being liquidated by a federal bankruptcy judge, blames its demise on Mr. Fino, who was its chief executive officer. "He was a bad administrator," Mr. Ryding says. "He just ignored things. And he couldn't say no to people." Mr. Fino blames the mob, which he says forced him to pad his payroll with unnecessary employees and controlled which contracts he could bid on. The FBI is investigating his charges.

Mr. Fino's public exposure has been a boon for federal prosecutors: Now he is available to testify in open court about Mafia influence in the 500,000 member Laborers union.

This September, Mr. Fino will make his first appearance in his home town as a prosecution witness, to testify against Mr. Rosato, the former Local 210 shop steward. Other Local 210 officers implicated by Mr. Fino are John Catanzaro, a former shop steward, and Leonard Falzone, the local's pension fund administrator.

Last November, after pleading guilty in a no-show job scam, Mr. Catanzaro received a 27-month prison sentence. Mr. Falzone was indicted last August in federal court in Buffalo on loan-sharking charges. His attorney denies the charges and the allegations in an FBI affidavit that his client is a member of the Todaro crime family. No date has been set for his trial.

So far, Mr. Fino's courtroom record is good. His initial appearance as a prosecution witness was last March in Binghamton, N.Y. He testified that Anthony F. (Guv) Guarnieri, a reputed "capo" in Pennsylvania's Bufalino crime family, exerted improper influence over Binghamton Laborers Local 7. Mr. Guarnieri was convicted on RICO conspiracy and racketeering charges.

Mr. Fino also testified in the recent racketeering trial of John M. Riggi, the reputed Mafia boss of New Jersey. Mr. Riggi, a former business agent for Laborers Local 394 in Elizabeth, N.J., was charged in Newark's federal court with shaking down contractors.

Mr. Fino stated that Buffalo Mafia leaders—including his own father—had told him that Mr. Riggi is a Mafioso. He also told the court that a third of his annual $72,000 FBI fee goes to his ex wife, and that his current income doesn't match his previous union compensation. "I lost my family," he testified. "I lost my home, my way of life."

Mr. Riggi was convicted on seven counts of extortion and labor bribery on July 20.

Mr. Fino's work as a prosecution witness has just begun. "Before this is all over," he says, "I expect to testify in 50 criminal cases."

He eventually hopes to resettle in Europe, but worries that he may be murdered before he gets there. "The fear never goes away," he says. He considered plastic surgery, but says, "Doctors tell me that they can't change my features enough to make me unrecognizable."

Meanwhile, he tries to maintain the semblance of normality. He takes a college course, works out in a gym and avoids fatty foods. But close relationships are out of the question. When a date asks him what he does for a living, "I say I'm a consultant to the Labor Department."

His life in hiding leaves him time for reflection. "Would I do it again? No. The price is too expensive," he says. "Look at the pain it's cost my children. They have to defend me to their friends."

As always in his world, firm moral bearings are elusive. One night, he says, as he listened to his daughter weep recriminations into the phone, "I began to feel I was the evil one."

—July 31, 1990